DIRECT
TO THE POOR

DIRECT TO THE POOR

GRASSROOTS DEVELOPMENT IN LATIN AMERICA

edited by
SHELDON ANNIS and PETER HAKIM

LYNNE RIENNER PUBLISHERS • BOULDER & LONDON

The chapters in this book first appeared in slightly modified form in the Inter-American Foundation journal, *Grassroots Development,* except for "Wandering the Boundaries of Development," by Ariel Dorfman, which first appeared in the *Massachusetts Review,* Fall-Winter 1986, XXVII, 3-4; and "Can Small-Scale Development Be a Large-Scale Policy?" by Sheldon Annis, which appeared in *World Development,* 15, Autumn 1987. The editors gratefully thank the Inter-American Foundation, the *Massachusetts Review,* and *World Development* for permission to publish.

Published in the United States of America in 1988 by
Lynne Rienner Publishers, Inc.
948 North Street, Boulder, Colorado 80302

and in the United Kingdom by
Lynne Rienner Publishers, Inc.
3 Henrietta Street, Covent Garden, London WC2E 8LU

Library of Congress Cataloging-in-Publication Data
    Direct to the poor: grassroots development in Latin America/edited by
    Sheldon Annis and Peter Hakim.
       p.   cm.
    Bibliography: p.
    ISBN 1-55587-118-6 (lib. bdg.) ISBN 1-55587-120-8
    (pbk.)
    1. Transfer payments—Latin America. 2. Economic assistance,
Domestic—Latin America. 3. Poor—Latin America. I. Annis,
Sheldon, 1944-   . II. Hakim, Peter.
HC130.P63D57 1988
362.5'83'098—dc19   87-36936
                                                      CIP

British Library Cataloguing in Publication Data
    A Cataloguing in Publication record for this book
    is available from the British Library.

Printed and bound in the United States of America

The paper used in this publication meets
the requirements of the American National
Standard for Permanence of Paper for
Printed Library Materials Z39.48-1984. ∞

Contents

What Is Grassroots Development?

SHELDON ANNIS AND PETER HAKIM

This book explores an approach to economic and social development that may be appealing if for no other reason than its simplicity: namely, the best way to help poor people is to give money to the organizations that they themselves create and control. That approach— or rather, its result among the poor—is what the authors of this volume call "grassroots development." This very uncomplicated idea is based on a belief that, despite their poverty, poor people possess substantial resources: knowledge and understanding of their circumstances, the will and persistence to make things better, and a capacity to organize and mount collective action. Direct financial assistance allows them to "capitalize"—put into production—their noneconomic resources. In small but important ways, it helps them to gain better control over their local environments, allowing them to build upward and outward from there. This kind of assistance is not a substitute for broader social change or just, competent governments. Direct assistance is intended to strengthen the poor economically in the short run so that they can mobilize through organized collective action and confront the fundamental causes of their poverty in the long run.

The title of this book, *Direct to the Poor*, suggests an ideal—resource transfer with no strings, no baggage, no politics, no diversion, no waste. Most development agencies, of course, do not give aid "direct to the poor." Indeed, they have not been very effective at giving *any* benefits, direct or indirect. The nongovernmental, antibureaucratic approach is born of frustration. It argues that public agencies are more likely to absorb than distribute resources. If so, why not circumvent the system by investing directly in institutions that the poor create for themselves?

That, in a nutshell, is the theory and intent of grassroots development. But how well does it work in practice? With hard resources in hand, what do the poor do? In what do they invest? Are the poor more honest, farseeing, competent, and effective than public sector bureaucrats? If they are sometimes—but not other times—why? And in the long run, does it make any real difference at all?

Such problems are the subject of this book, a collection of articles that evolved from studies conducted over several years by the Inter-American Foundation, a U.S. government agency that supports grassroots development in Latin America and the Caribbean. By sharing these eighteen authors' experiences and insights, readers will be able to explore for themselves the mechanics, limitations, contradictions, and promise of grassroots development.

The volume begins with an essay by the distinguished development economist, Albert O. Hirschman, who sets forth a concept that may appear more humanistic than economic. Hirschman asks the fundamental question of grassroots development: where does the "energy" for collective action come from? How is it generated and captured and then put to work? How is the seemingly limitless good of social energy turned into economic growth and political power?

In a sense, the rest of the book is an exploration of Hirschman's questions. The first part looks at individuals—rare individuals, admittedly—who seem to embody social energy, *campesino* leaders like Ramon Aybar and the members of the Jamaica Society for the Blind. Other parts delve into organizations—all kinds of organizations—that serve and mobilize poor people and give them the power they could not obtain alone. Many nuts-and-bolts problems are examined—for example, those of worker-managed business enterprises in Peru and Chile, of agricultural cooperatives in Bolivia, and of community-run consumer stores in Colombia. Novelists Patrick Breslin and Ariel Dorfman approach development from another point of view. To what extent is culture itself a basis for investment in development? And finally, the book asks, can small-scale achievements be replicated on a large scale? What is the relationship between grassroots and public policy?

The book is ultimately ambiguous in its answer to the basic question: Does it work? Certainly, grassroots development is not presented here as a magic solution to the problem of poverty. The book does not conclude that self-help is a substitute for just and competent governments or efficient, effective, and equitable macroeconomic policies. Self-help cannot by itself replace large-scale development projects and programs. And it does not always succeed, or at least not readily.

Yet it does work, sometimes. It has made a difference, for some people and some communities. It does start larger processes in motion, if not inexorably. This is a book about small victories.

PART 1

The Idea of Social Energy

The whole venture of grassroots development has arisen in good measure from a revulsion against the worship of the "gross national product" and of the "rate of growth" as unique arbiters of economic and human progress. Grassroots development refuses to be judged by these standards. The workers in this vineyard look at their activity as valuable in itself without regard to its "overall" impact and they do quite well without being reassured at every step by optimistic reports on the macroeconomic consequences of their work.

—Albert O. Hirschman

The Principle of Conservation and Mutation of Social Energy

ALBERT O. HIRSCHMAN

"The desire of bettering our condition," Adam Smith noted in *The Wealth of Nations*, "comes with us from the womb and never leaves us till we go into the grave." He issued this statement as a self-evident axiom and proceeded to make it account for people's urge to save. The very term "bettering our condition," like the more contemporary expressions "getting ahead" or "making it," seems to point to individual effort. But other patterns of action serving the same goal must also be considered: they involve collective initiatives such as formation of interest groups or cooperatives, protests against new taxes or higher prices, or even the joint occupation of some privately or publicly owned idle lands near a city by a group of people without adequate housing. These are also actions people take to "better their condition," and a fair number of such actions with a collective dimension took place in Adam Smith's own time (for example, the Wilkes riots), but in *The Wealth of Nations* they are either ignored or—in the case of combinations of businessmen—castigated as "conspiracies against the public." There is in fact a continuum of actions—from the wholly private to the most outspokenly public, with many intermediate and hybrid varieties in between—that come under Smith's rubric; they are all conceived and intended by the participants as means to the end of "bettering their condition."

Inspired by that objective, groups of poor people in Latin America have undertaken a large number of collective efforts in recent years. An interest in the origin and performance of these groups made me return to the region in 1983, when my wife and I spent four months traveling in the Dominican Republic, Colombia, Peru, Chile, Argentina, and Uruguay to visit grassroots development projects.

The conditions under which action for economic advance (or against economic decline) is undertaken as a group activity have not been closely studied. To bring some order into this diffuse field, I shall make a basic distinction: in many cases collective action is provoked by some common, usually adverse, experience to which a group of people is subjected; in others, cooperative action emerges without any such prior shock from the outside.

People can be aggressed either by the hostile forces of nature or by some, often even more hostile, forces of state and society. We came across a large number of such aggressions that led to the development of solidarity and, eventually, to joint or cooperative action. While it is worthwhile to look at the varieties of such reactive cooperation in some detail, it is no great mystery why people who are jointly and newly oppressed by acts either of nature or of their "fellow men" should develop a solidarity spirit which leads to cooperative reform efforts. After all, they are only conforming, if in collective form, to the French adage: *Cet animal est très méchant / Quand on l'attaque il se défend.* (This animal is very mean / When it's attacked it will hit back.)

The more difficult problem is, therefore, to understand collective efforts at grassroots development when no immediate antecedent aggression is present. It is probably not possible to account exhaustively for these more complex situations. Nevertheless, a large number of them shared one striking characteristic: when we looked into the life histories of the people principally involved, we found that most of them had participated previously in other, generally more "radical," experiences of collective action. It is as though their earlier aspiration for social change, their bent for collective action, had not really left them, even though the movements in which they had participated may have aborted, petered out—or perhaps ended successfully. Later on, this "social energy" becomes active again but likely in some very different form. It may therefore be quite difficult to notice that we are in the presence of a special kind of sequence, that is, a renewal of energy rather than a wholly new outbreak. For the sake of brevity, I shall refer to this phenomenon as the Principle of Conservation and Mutation of Social Energy.

I am of course aware that the principle does not necessarily hold at all times or in all places; it may even be strictly tied to the particular time and place of my formulation. Here I am reminded—half in contrast and half in parallel—of the last verse of an old song celebrating the failed German peasant war of the sixteenth century: *Geschlagen ziehen wir nach haus / Unsere Enkel fechten's besser aus.* (Vanquished we are returning home / Our grandchildren will take up our fight with better luck.) The difference of our principle from this text is, first of all, that the present Latin American generation is not waiting for their grandchildren: they seem prefectly able to resume a fight (that is, to join in some collective movement) several times in the same lifetime. In part this may be due to what has been called the acceleration of history. But it has perhaps more to do with the second and more important difference between the Latin American and the German situation: the Latin Americans are not taking up the same fight again; the next time around, they involve themselves in a very different cause.

SOME COLOMBIAN EXAMPLES

The most massive evidence for the principle comes from Colombia, and perhaps the best illustrative story is of the fishermen's cooperative at the small settlement of Cristo Rey on the country's Caribbean Coast. From Montería, the hot interior capital of the Department of Córdoba, we drove along rich and sparsely cultivated haciendas to the coast. There we met with fishermen in a round, well-ventilated open shed with a thatched roof. Being of European background, we took for granted that we were dealing with a people who had been fishermen for generations. But we soon learned that, like the rest of the villagers, the coop members had grown up as agriculturalists, each tending their own small plots and working on nearby haciendas as day-laborers.

How did they become fishermen? It turned out to be a remarkable story: In 1975, a group of peasants from the village invaded a piece of land that had been idle for a long time, with the idea of working it collectively. They undertook this action toward the end of a period of fairly widespread peasant unrest and land invasions, particularly in the flatlands near Colombia's Atlantic coast. This period of peasant activism in the late 1960s followed the more vigorous application of the land reform law of 1961 under President Carlos Lleras Restrepo, and the simultaneous establishment of a peasant union—Asociación Nacional de Usuarios Campesinos (ANUC)—that was conceived by Lleras as a way for peasants to participate more actively in the reform. Soon enough this union became independent from government tutelage and developed considerable momentum and following. By 1975, however, the political situation had changed substantially: the agrarian reform had been brought to a halt, and ANUC had lost strength as a result of internal divisions. Not surprisingly, therefore, the Cristo Rey peasants were ejected by police from the land they had sought to cultivate.

But this is not the end of the story. For the next few years, the peasants wondered what they might do together next. At some point, looking out onto the Caribbean and noticing some fishing boats in the distance, they thought: "As long as we cannot take the land, why not take the sea?" So the twenty-two peasants who were closest to each other as a result of the joint action (and no doubt other ties) decided to build two boats and set out to sea. Then they mobilized various kinds of assistance: from courses in cooperativism given at Montería by Acción Unida (an evangelical social action group), to credit from the Caja Agraria (the agricultural credit bank), and accounting courses from SENA (the wealthy and always helpful national vocational training agency). A major step forward was the acquisition of outboard motors that permitted the crews to venture much farther out to sea and significantly increase production.

The coop has been a financial success. After some time it was able to expand its activities by setting up a consumer store which also housed freezers for the catch. The coop recently bought a sizable piece of land close to the sea where their meeting hall, offices, consumer store, and other activities will be concentrated. (A fish restaurant and small hotel are in the planning stage.) Another project, currently under consideration, is to expand their present "fleet" from one to eight boats. It is moving to learn that the coop members, true to their original vocation as agriculturalists, now think of renting some land from a nearby landowner and cultivating it collectively. As a cooperative with a *personería jurídica* (legal status) and some pledgeable assets, they will be treated with the respect that is usually denied the single, virtually landless farmer. Thus the dream they were pursuing in 1975 may yet come true—after a long detour and "with different means!"

The story is edifying. But could it have happened without that first step, the failed attempt to seize the land? The coop members certainly perceived a connection between their first collective action and its failure, on the one hand, and the fishing cooperative and its success, on the other.

The link between these two so dissimilar parts of the story can be interpreted at different levels. From one perspective, one may argue that the takeover of land is a daring act with revolutionary potential, whereas, in comparison, the "taking" of the sea through cooperatively operated fishing boats seems a tame entrepreneurial initiative. From this point of view, the taking of the land looms as far more arduous and demanding than the taking of (or to) the sea. One might then interpret the sequence from attempted land takeover to fishing cooperative as a renunciation of former goals, an acceptance of the existing order, and a settling down within it.

Yet, a good argument can be made for the opposite conclusion. The most obvious, simple, elementary collective action for *minifundista* peasants surrounded by partially idle *latifundios* is to seize as a group some of the idle land by a one-time act. The formation of a fishing cooperative requires, in comparison, a complex process of working out rules and procedures and of acquiring new knowledge and collaborative habits. From this perspective the takeover of land seems rather simplistic, while setting out to sea looks far more complex, and in its own way, more hazardous.

There is some truth in both conceptions, and both help explain what happened. Once the historic moment when land reform was a real possibility in northern Colombia had passed, people obviously resigned themselves and looked in other, less daunting directions. But the experience of the attempted land takeover was a real steppingstone to the fishing cooperative in the usual sense of stepping up rather than down. Having cooperated in the takeover of land, the Cristo Rey peasants had practiced cooperation at the most rudimentary level. Having thus dispelled original mutual distrust, forged a community, and—perhaps most important—created a vision of change, they were now ready for joint endeavors that required much greater sophistication and persistence.

This sort of dynamic can account for the numerous other cases where early participation in public action of one kind leads later to involvements in collective endeavors of a very different nature. In Colombia's Cauca Valley, we had long sessions with two groups of peasant leaders that organize cooperatives and other kinds of community efforts throughout the valley. They are known as *Líderes de Tuluá* (leaders from Tuluá) and *Muchachos de Buga* (the Buga boys).

The Líderes de Tuluá are men in their fifties and sixties who are now primarily concerned—when they don't work their own farms—with building up a network of consumer and producer cooperatives. These cooperatives now have a central warehouse in Tuluá, the geographical center of the valley. Seeing the gleaming warehouse and its offices full of shiny furniture, one would never suspect it is run by poor peasants who have been actively involved with the successive experiments in social change and reform in Colombia during the past twenty-five years. They all started with the *Acción Comunal* (community action programs) which mobilized people in the smaller towns and villages for cooperative construction of urgent public works in the early 1960s, and later participated in efforts at more active implementation of land reform in the late 1960s and early 1970s.

The story of the Muchachos de Buga is a bit different. This group of about ten younger men—now in their early thirties—were selected in their late teens to attend an experimental educational program at Buga (Department of Valle) which was called the Academia Mayor Campesina. The program's founder and director was a strong-minded Jesuit priest who set out to form peasant leaders able to help improve the communities to which they were expected to return upon graduation. The Muchachos were so fired by their educational experience and the then-favorable prospects for substantial changes in Colombia's agrarian structure that they decided to stay together as a group and to work actively for change, not only in their own communities, but wherever they might be helpful. They participated, during the early 1970s, in a few land invasions that were largely unsuccessful.

By the end of the decade, the group had changed; now, they looked out for other kinds of opportunities to "better the condition" of the people in Colombia's villages. They became, in fact, a private group of extension agents. There was, however, a difference: they imparted not only improved agricultural techniques, but also advice on how to form cooperatives and other community organizations, how to lobby for needed public improvements, how to use the courts, and so on. They were hired by various local groups doing "social promotion" but have maintained their own organization. In this endeavor, they were aided by a grant that enabled them to acquire a dairy farm near Buga that will be an income-producing asset for the group. For the time being, however, the farm functions mainly as a temporary haven for any Muchacho who is out of work. The possibility of staying at the farm for a limited period strengthens the independence of any individual Muchacho working as an "extension agent": he knows that he does not need to fear unduly the consequences of speaking out (of using "voice") in his job, since quitting or being fired (deciding or having to "exit") is an eventuality of last resort that is not too costly.[1]

The consistency with which our Principle of Conservation and Mutation of Social Energy could be observed in Colombia is impressive. How could I expect to find it in operation once again when visiting a hammock-weavers' cooperative in Morroa, in the Atlantic coast Department of Sucre? The cooperative was composed almost entirely of women weavers who had set up their enterprise with some guidance from the Bogotá-based *Museo de Artes y Tradiciones Populares* (Museum of Popular Arts and Traditions). The museum is a remarkably effective organization that is providing various types of assistance to the practitioners of traditional handicrafts in the country without forcing artisans into mass production. On the contrary, the organization is attempting to revitalize the genuine traditions of individual workmanship. We visited the almost-completed locale of the cooperative on the much-travelled Medellín-Cartagena highway. In part a gift of the Inter-American Foundation, this locale was soon to house the cooperative's offices as well as a sales outlet. There we were introduced to many members of the coop, and all of its leaders were waiting for us. All were women and active weavers except for the president, a highly verbal man in his early forties who was—somewhat incongruously—the chief person to speak for the group. It was explained to us that a man was needed to deal with the authorities and banks in this somewhat backward Colombian department (perhaps also he owed his position to the fact that many of these women weavers had recently been swindled by one of their own companions who had talked them into a fraudulent "cooperative" arrangement).

However that may be, I was curious about the motivation of this man. I engaged him in conversation as we walked from the highway to the village where we were to view the handsome looms of some of the coop members. Within the first three minutes of our conversation, he told me that in the early 1970s he had actively participated in some of the land seizures in the department and that, ever since that heady, if largely unsuccessful, experience, he had wanted to involve himself again in "doing something for the community"!

EXTENSIONS OF THE PRINCIPLE

There is not much point in multiplying the illustrations. Other instances of our principle-in-operation could be cited: from the leadership of the *pueblo joven* (El Rescate) in Lima, to the recent revival of some agricultural cooperatives in the Llanquihue province of southern Chile. But perhaps it is of greater interest to connect the principle briefly with some other aspects of social change.

First of all, I must refer it to an old point of mine: I have often complained about the excessive and (I have come to think) highly damaging tendency of Latin Americans to categorize most of their experiences in social and political reform—or for that matter in economic development—as utter failures. This failure complex, or *fracasomania*, may itself lead to real failures, or so it has seemed to me. Not surprisingly, the Principle of Conservation and Mutation of Social Energy fits right into my campaign against the failure complex. As long as the operation of the principle is not perceived, it will seem as though a social movement that has not achieved its preordained objective, such as the movement for agrarian reform in Colombia, is an unqualified failure. But this judgment must be altered, at least in part, once it is realized that the social energies that were aroused in the course of that movement did not pass from the scene even though the movement itself did. These energies remained, as it were, in storage for a while, but were available to fuel later, perhaps very different, movements. In a real sense, the original movement must therefore be credited with whatever advances or successes were achieved by those subsequent movements: no longer can it be considered a total failure.

The fishing cooperative of Cristo Rey could only come into being through the sense of comradeship and community, the dispelling of isolation and mutual distrust (almost in the sense of original sin), that resulted from the common action taken many years before. An interesting parallel situation came to our attention later on, in Bogotá, when we were talking with the director of an organization that is supplying financial assistance to worker-managed enterprises. Among them are some firms, primarily in clothing and footwear, that are staffed and managed predominantly or exclusively by women. These firms invariably originate, so we were told, in some other common activity where the women have gotten to know and like each other. Most frequently, the women met in courses given by SENA, the vocational training agency of the Colombian government. Upon graduating from the course they decided to try to create an enterprise of their own rather than look for work as employees of existing firms.

The sequence involved here is not too dissimilar from the ones discussed earlier. The common experience of the land invasion at Cristo Rey, which led to other, more complex forms of cooperation, is replaced here by the common experience of taking a course together and getting to know and trust each other. Obviously the ties formed in this fashion are likely to be less strong than in the Cristo Rey case, but the experience apparently can fulfill the basic function of bringing like-minded people together in a joint endeavor. As an economist I had expected that the need to mobilize a minimal amount of capital would be at the root of at least some of the cooperative, worker-managed enterprises. It turned out that a more fundamental need is, once again, some experience dispelling isolation and mutual distrust.

NOTE

1. I am referring to my book *Exit, Voice, and Loyalty* (Cambridge: Harvard University Press, 1970).

PART 2

Social Energy and Uncommon Individuals

Leadership is one of the rarest of human resources. Strong leadership often means effective organization; the absence of leadership often means social chaos or futility. However, campesino associations and cooperatives often suffer from too much reliance on a single strong and charismatic leader, and Ramon's strength and effectiveness may also be his associations' weakness. Too much direction and decisionmaking come from one person. Many worry about the federation's future after Ramon steps down. Only time will tell, but it is perhaps significant that there are other associations which actively collaborate with the federation without being members. These groups want their own autonomy and independence, suggesting an awareness of the costs of too dominant a leader.

—Stephen Vetter

2

Portrait of a Peasant Leader: Ramon Aybar

STEPHEN VETTER

The dream came to me frequently as a child: men and women were dwarfed by tall blades of green grass. Anxiously, people went about their business, moving quickly to find a way through the dense maze of fronds. The dim shapes of unknown animals crouched among the foliage, and the air felt hot and dangerous. Men would stop at times, scar the trunks of grass with long, sharp knives to drink a sweet, clear substance, and then move on. But the floor of the forest was a knotted tangle of vines and roots, and people frequently tripped. Flies, rats, and snakes were everywhere. The edges of the grass were razor sharp and human sweat mixed with blood and dirt, covering everything with a wet grime.

Living in the midwestern part of the United States, I used to think the dream was tied to the vast corn fields that surrounded my home town. It wasn't until many years later, when I first saw vast stretches of Caribbean sugar cane, that I knew the source of my nightmare . . .

White, sweet, granular . . . sugar is synonymous with pleasure. Yet each teaspoon for the morning coffee—when you consider the life of the cane cutter who produces it and the land that grows it—should leave a bitter taste.

To see and understand sugar, take the road that leads from the capital city, Santo Domingo, to Rivera de Payabo, a small village in the central part of the Dominican Republic. First, you pass through the village of Yamasa. There, you find the high energy of a Dominican plaza: the many kinds of vegetables, fruits, and grains that are being muled in for sale in the market, the busy vendors, and shoeshine boys. Echoes of music and games seem to be everywhere. The walls of four different political party headquarters are covered with vividly painted

17

posters and graffiti creating an almost psychedelic effect. Yamasa is diverse, active, alive.

Along the first mile of road leaving Yamasa, you see peasant *finquitas* (farmettes) with mules, chickens, pigs, children, and *conucos* (family gardens). The tidy houses of thatch and mud are colorfully painted. Women, drawing easily on *puros* (small cigars), walk proudly down the lanes or stoop to hang their laundry on low bushes. It is like a Rousseau painting: deep greens blossom; men, women, animals, and plants intertwine.

The cornucopia thins out quickly as the first outcroppings of the tall, green stalks of sugar cane appear. To make planting and harvesting easier, all other crops and vegetation have been removed. The land has been leveled leaving the cane to propagate itself by extending its small, clawlike roots. Fifteen minutes from Yamasa and your eye is lost in a vast, monotonous sea of cane.

Following the road, you encounter the first *bateyes*—grim, grey barracks that house the cane workers. The low buildings stretch out parallel to the road. Some are made of block and appear newer and more comfortable, but most are old, wooden buildings with smudged, black interiors. Stooped, dark people sit on the steps in idle boredom. For three years I have driven this road. Rarely have I seen anyone working in the fields.

From the seventeenth through the early part of the twentieth centuries, sugar was called "white gold." And sugar has done to many nations what gold did to small towns in the western United States: left them economically abandoned and broken. The Dominican Republic, like most Caribbean countries, has too much acreage in cane. Only the best lands—where juice content is highest—are harvested, leaving the marginal lands uncut because world sugar prices are low. Over the past three years, even the "best" lands have not been good enough: sugar has sold from 9 to 11 cents a pound although costing approximately 16 cents a pound to produce.

I was surprised to find one of the more colorful and creative approaches to community development emerging here. But there it was—an island in the sea of cane—the Federation of Associations of Neighbors of Rivera Payabo.

The federation is an organization of ten associations of small rice producers, three women's clubs, and one youth club. Most of the approximately 500 members are part-time employees of a large sugar estate managed by the government. These people live in the crowded bateyes and grow rice on lands too marshy for regular sugar production. Members organized the federation seven years ago to improve their income and to develop local job opportunities for their children who were migrating to the cities.

What's in a name? Associations of *campesinos* are found throughout the Dominican Republic. But you will probably not find another "association of *vecinos*"—neighbors. The members of this particular group decided to call themselves "vecinos" rather than "campesinos" after considerable deliberation. To them, campesino suggests "a person with everything": a small, simple house; a conuco to feed a family; and a rich choice of crops, trees, and animals to make a living. Campesinos are like the people who live in Yamasa.

The members of the Federation of Neighbors were once campesinos. Then, in 1953, the dictator Rafael Trujillo seized their lands for sugar production. The landscape was radically and rapidly reorganized: small farms were burned and bulldozed into one large plantation. Those who had lived on the land had to choose between migrating to the capital city or remaining to work the estate. By law, all lands were to be devoted exclusively to the production of sugar cane; no other crop could be planted—not even a family garden—without the permission of the estate manager.

It was an abrupt and startling change, one that threw lives into chaos. The physical landscape was transformed; people were crowded into bateyes; children who were to know no other life were born. The people who stayed found that their days as campesinos were over. What was left for them was a more modest possibility: to be just neighbors.

Education: from the Latin educere, to lead out

The president and founder of the federation is Ramon Aybar. A retired primary schoolteacher and a poet, Ramon was raised in the area; he remembers well the time before sugar cane. Like many rural schoolteachers, his intelligence and training make him a natural community leader.

I first learned of Ramon from *El Buen Vecino*, a newspaper published by the federation. Usually such "peasant newspapers" have a political party, a labor union, or a student organization behind them. But this was no ordinary newspaper: no other organization was in the wings. The paper published some of Ramon's poems and articles about his neighbors; in simple and direct terms, it admonished local readers to lead a good, moral life; and it offered suggestions for constructing latrines and community centers and for improving family diets. Intrigued, I wrote Ramon to discover more about the federation, and through an exchange of letters, we arranged our first meeting.

We set a day and agreed to meet at my hotel in Santo Domingo at 8:00 A.M. By 10:00 A.M. he had not arrived. Finally, the doorman informed me that an older man was waiting outside. When I went to look for him, I found a seemingly typical campesino. All deference and humility, Ramon apologized for his lateness. He had been waiting here for two hours, he said, since perhaps a man should not enter a hotel unless he was going to stay there. After I assured him that there was no problem, he removed his thin, rolled-rim hat and entered.

We walked past the swimming pool, which was surrounded by partially-clad, pink-burned bodies lying on cots. Ramon quickly surveyed the scene, shook his head in dismay, and with a large smile asked why I was staying at a hospital. Why were grown men and women lying around during working hours in the hot sun? Surely, they were ill. I tried to explain to him the concept of vacation as a reward for hard work. He could understand holidays, where people came together to celebrate; and he could understand school recess, when children and teachers returned home to work in the fields; but the thought of idle strangers coming together to lie in isolated silence around a sterilized pool brought a sparkle of amusement and disbelief to his alert eyes. This was as intriguing to him as the Federation of Neighbors was to me.

We sat and talked. Ramon's voice was animated, cadenced, poetic. Ideas flowed from metaphors in the clipped, hyphenated accent of the campo. We soon agreed that I would visit him in Rivera de Payabo the next week. This would be simple, he insisted: I would take a bus or drive to the capital city of Sabana Grande de Boy where anyone could direct me to Rivera de Payabo. Ramon's conviction that he could be located so easily in the countryside was as assuring as his remoteness from the larger world was disconcerting.

To come to know Ramon Aybar is to come to know a place and a people. They are tied to him like skin to his body. Born there, and the father of fifteen children, he can never describe himself without first explaining where and how he has lived and what has occurred in the region of Rivera de Payabo.

> I was born close to the village of Boyá. Not Sabana Grande de Boyá, but Boyá where the last Indians came to die. When I was young my father, Nuno, and my compadre placed me in school. You see, I wanted to learn to read and write. There I learned the basics—the written forms for Table, Mother loves me, Mule, things like that. But after three years—when I was fifteen, around the year 1938—my father brought me home to work in the mountains and hills around here because he was illiterate and didn't appreciate education. And he taught me to cut down trees. At that time, all of

this area was a forest filled with animals. Some old people around here still remember the land the way it was in those years, people who still carry on their faces the battles with the authorities who brought the sugar plantations, people who are ignored by those who were born after the great evictions of 1953.

The campesinos of this area were called "monteros." They were skilled and agile men who raised cattle and kept pigs and chickens. Many wild boars lived in the forest, so each montero also kept dogs to hunt with. Just dogs and a knife or machete. There were many famous men in the trade: Mio, Profundo, Checo, Leopoldo, Frederico, and others. My father moved here because he wanted to hear his dogs bark, the partridges sing. He wanted to unravel the riddles spun by the parakeet, the crow, and the parrot. There were so many birds and animals that the noise left you deaf!

In a short time, we had a ranch with a conuco. I spent my days taking care of the corn field. . . . The Ará River, which is over there, which is the source of water for Payabo, passed by our conuco. Just imagine the fish and crabs and shrimps! The water was so alive that people were scared. My brother and I would fish and no one went hungry. It was a good life, and we lived in innocence. Like the Indian.

Every house would have fresh sweets made from honey, and the mountains were like beehives. It wasn't worth one single cent since there was so much of it, but we made our sweets and had wax for the candles that lit our homes at night.

The people who lived in this region worked hard. The place was so wild we all had to be great fence makers to keep the animals out of our conucos and homes. Because we had so much wood, we made strong fences: nothing unwanted could enter. And when we made these fences, we would organize work parties, which we called convites, among the men. And while we worked we sang.

We had our own folklore and culture. The drummers of the region were some of the best. On holiday nights, we would go from house to house, serenading and dancing.

This all changed when the dictator Trujillo decided to plant this land in sugar cane. It was horrible what he did, and we could never understand it. In 1953, his henchmen came, and they destroyed my father's house. My father lost everything, and ever since then, I have continued thinking about all that we lost. Everytime I see someone, I remember where they lived and the name of their village. And I try to point out where they lived, but all you see now is sugar.

So one day, the day of Saint Ramon, I was dreaming during the early morning: I was talking with a friend. "Yesterday, over there in the village of Don Juan," I said, "See, over there. . . . not there, but much further over." But my friend didn't know what I was talking about. He had forgotten what the land was like before the sugar. And in the dream, there was a big meeting, with a lot of people, and they were talking about how we should organize ourselves. When I awoke, I decided to do something and called a meeting as the school.

We decided to start our first association, and we called it Amantes del Progreso (Lovers of Progress). Later, in Alto San Pedro, 49 members came together and formed Amigos del Bien (Friends of Well-Being). After that, I was invited to Cabeza de Toro, but it was so far away by mule that I told them I could not return. I assisted other communities to organize, and eventually we had seven. That is when we decided to organize the Federación de Asociaciónes de Vecinos de Rivera Payabo.

What can people do to help themselves when their land has been stolen? When they are forced to work on an estate regimented around a single task? When they have only limited mobility and income? When Ramon talks about organizing, he says that the first problem he encountered was lack of imagination. A dream had ignited his vision. But his neighbors (initially, at least) could see only the sugar cane that surrounded them. His job was to ignite their vision, showing them the possibilities they could not see.

Driving the sugar estate lands around Rivera Payabo makes one more sympathetic toward the problem of stunted imagination. Cane has a way of erasing everything—trees, houses, roads, and hills—covering everything with a soft, rolling blanket of green.

Development: from the Latin de (dis-, apart) and the French voloper (to wrap) i.e., to unwrap or uncover

Ramon looks out over the vast sugar lands, and his vision continually "uncovers" solutions, possibilities. Where a stranger might see a small, useless bog, he has seen a place to grow rice and catch crayfish. Ramon's vision is a steady search for the positive, the good. Outsiders will see deprivation in the bateyes; but he finds there the opportunity to develop communalism and neighborly ties. Ever alert for the gray clouds' silver lining, he now argues that while true campesinos may have animals and crops, they—unlike the neighbors of Rivera Payabo—suffer from the loneliness of living and working separated from many people.

The neighbors of Rivera Payabo, however, are isolated from national development agencies. They have little access to training, credit, or public assistance.

What we need here, says Ramon, is something no less than a "perpetual motion machine" for social purposes. According to Ramon, a perpetual motion machine is something that scientists have long tried to build. Such a machine has never been built, but the attempt inspires, and sometimes, as scientists work, they develop other useful machines along the way. Over the years, Ramon and his neighbors have been tinkering away at their perpetual social motion machine. The first problem that Ramon convinced his neighbors to tackle was one that doesn't get a high priority among development planners—providing a decent funeral. As they say in the countryside, "*Morirse en el campo es más problema que estar vivo.*" ("To die in the countryside is even more of a problem than to live in it.") Living on approximately $700 a year, peasants rarely have the $50 to $200 available to cover funeral costs that can include providing food and drink to the mourners at a wake as well as purchasing a coffin and a grave.

It may seem ironic that a preoccupation with burial and death invigorated a community organization, but when one has little or nothing, dignity begins in being able to be buried properly. Thus, one of the federation's first activities was to start a funeral society. The simplicity was remarkable. Each participating member pays in $35 over time. When an adult dies in the home, the family is given $50 to cover the expenses; when an adult dies away from home and is buried in another part of the country, the family is given only $35 because the wake is less expensive. Children usually die in the home and the family receives $35.

The society has 391 members; 45 members have been buried. A total of $1,333 has been disbursed to cover the cost of the funerals. There are no mortuary tables, projections, or records of how many die in or out of the house, but there never has been a deficit in the association fund. A first step was taken: the federation showed that something could be done.

The momentum of the social motion machine was maintained using *convites*—the tradition of pooling voluntary labor—to build communal centers, repair roads, cultivate fields, and build drying-sheds for rice.

As the federation grew, it began to tackle more complex problems. For instance, most members supplement their diets and incomes by cultivating the swamp lands throughout the estate. These lands are available because they cannot be used for cane production. But once their families are fed, members have problems selling their crop at prices that represent a reasonable return on their labor, since intermediaries and local merchants buy at the lowest and sell at the highest possible price.

Ramon worked out a simple scheme whereby the federation would offer members mill and warehouse services for a low fee. Having taken the time to search out and visit other agricultural associations, he had seen a number of programs in action. The income from fees would go into a marketing fund which, as it grew, would allow the federation to provide advances for production costs such as seeds, fertilizer, and cultivation.

The federation tried to finance this program through loans and donations but was unsuccessful. Private banks were uninterested, and the agrarian bank made loans only for production, not marketing. In 1980, the Inter-American Foundation provided a grant of $44,960 to purchase a rice mill, a small truck, and the materials to construct the warehouse and seven cement drying-areas for the rice. The federation covered part of the cost of the materials and contributed the voluntary labor to implement the project. Using convites, association members met on weekends and holidays and constructed the central warehouse in record time. Next, they built the drying-areas.

The marketing plan was simple in design and straightforward in execution, and Ramon thought he had found his perpetual motion machine. But flaws developed, one of which was almost fatal.

The marketing of rice in the Dominican Republic is strictly controlled through a national marketing board. By law, all rice must be sold through the state agency. Those who do not are punished by fine and imprisonment. The marketing board, however, does not always have money to pay for the rice it buys, and must issue promissory notes. As a result, many producers sell in the black market to secure funds to cover their immediate costs. When the federation found that it would not receive cash for its rice, it attempted to sell at the local market. Ramon was jailed for two days, and the federation almost lost its truck.

As an alternative, the federation now cleans and dehulls rice but returns it to members who sell individually. The federation earns less, and members generally receive a lower price since they can no longer negotiate higher prices for larger sales.

Although this marketing setback diminished the federation's return, income was generated, and Ramon channeled it into another project. The federation was trying to reestablish a population of hogs after the previous stock was destroyed by the African swine fever epidemic of 1979. Eating household wastes, demanding little attention, and serving as an emergency savings account, hogs represent a relatively easy way to improve the lives of rural families.

Ramon had seen a number of projects organized by other associations and the Secretary of Agriculture. For its program, the federation combined its earnings with member contributions to buy eight sows and one boar. Using voluntary labor, the federation built a large pigpen behind the mill (which provides, as a by-product, rice hulls for feed) and has agreed to pay medical costs, such as vaccinations, for the swine. Sows usually give birth to seven to fourteen piglets. Depending on the number born, the majority of the sows will be distributed to members who can demonstrate their capacity to feed and house adequately the pigs. Members, in turn, agree to return to the federation two females from the first litter. These females will be bred, and their offspring will be distributed to other members. The federation retains and fattens the boars for eventual sale to help underwrite the project. Each participating member is left with five to twelve pigs to eat, slaughter for market, or trade for other goods. If disease is controlled, larceny held in check, the amorous interests of the boar kept high, and administration well managed, a *huracán de cerditos* should result.

In 1982, with earnings from the rice and the early returns on the hogs, the federation established a savings program. There are no banks in the area, so the cooperative plays an important role by offering members a line of credit. In addition, a small store was built next to the mill to offer basic agricultural commodities.

Refining his idea of a perpetual social motion machine, Ramon has inspired many of these programs to improve income and nutrition. But he has also played a vital role in representing his neighbors on noneconomic issues of collective concern.

In 1966, before the federation was organized, crop dusters hired by the estate sprayed herbicides over the cane fields and poisoned much of the water in the area. Seven people died, and many became ill. Ramon was just beginning his poetry career at that time, and he thought if word of what happened reached the right people, the spraying would stop. So he headed for a church-run radio station and brought national attention to the plight of his people by reading over the radio:

> Toy crop duster
> spitting out
> poisons that cover
> our food. Now
> people are asking
> who wants to live
> in Sabana de Boyá.
> Neighbors just pick up
> and abandon this land.

Nonetheless, spraying accidents continued. The chemicals were wrong or were inadequately diluted; water systems were contaminated; and the subsistence gardens and rice plots that were planted in the estate swamplands were ruined. Since prior warnings were not given, people in the fields often were doused along with the cane.

Prob. if crop dust'g

Words preserved the past, protested against the present, but did not stop the poisoning of the land. That chronic futility, as much as anything else, accounts for Ramon's dream of an association of neighbors.

After the federation was organized, Ramon repeatedly set up meetings with officials to discuss the aerial spraying. Inevitably, the authorities would agree to reconsider the use of planes and administer the pesticides by hand. But every time a new administrator was appointed, the crop dusters took off, and the federation would have to confront the authorities once more. These confrontations took on new force as the federation began to acquire information from estate employees who knew when the planes were going to fly. Members of the federation would gather and, armed with machetes, would hurry to block the runway of the depot.

Eventually, the estate officials were forced to deal with the federation's concern. The federation was not able to entirely prevent the aerial spraying, but the planes flew less frequently. The more dangerous chemicals were banned, and use of handsprayers was increased. No violence ever occurred in the confrontations over spraying, but the federation was able to display—to the authorities and to its members—considerable determination and group solidarity. The organization was successful not only in challenging the authorities on their management of the estate, but in establishing limits on what was tolerable. As a result, many members now point with pride to this defense of their interests as an important victory for the federation.

Those who know Ramon often refer to him as a natural leader. Often, he and I talk of leadership. A leader, Ramon says, is someone who has the gift to inspire others.

Inspire: from the Latin inspirare, to breathe in

Ramon tries to breathe into his neighbors a sense of expectation about themselves and their possibilities. A leader helps restore significance to the mundane.

While Ramon espouses a vision of pure community collaboration, his interaction with members often is surprising. A strict disciplinarian, he organizes and runs every formal meeting. On one occasion, I watched members wearing their machetes walk into the federation's meeting room; Ramon quickly reprimanded them for their poor manners, made them leave and hang their machetes outside. Some who have observed this behavior have characterized Ramon as a *patrón*; others have pointed out that in the social life of the bateyes, a strong personality is needed for the basic order that is a precondition to accomplishing anything.

The leaders of the ten associations, the youth club, and the women's clubs recognize Ramon's importance. Leadership is one of the rarest of human resources. Strong leadership often means effective organization; the absence of leadership often means social chaos or futility. However, campesino associations and cooperatives often suffer from too much reliance on a single strong and charismatic leader, and Ramon's strength and effectiveness may also be his associations' weakness. Too much direction and decisionmaking come from one person. Many worry about the federation's future after Ramon steps down.

When this is brought to his attention, Ramon points to the president of each of the ten associations and the presidents of the women's and youth clubs as the real leaders. Only time will tell, but it is perhaps significant that there are other associations which actively collaborate with the federation without being members. These groups want their own autonomy and independence, suggesting an awareness of the costs of too dominant a leader.

Whatever its drawbacks, Ramon's leadership cannot be divorced from his unique status in his community. As a teacher, he commands a respect that allows him easier access to estate and local political leaders. That access should not be confused with servility. Ramon has been willing to take risks in representing the members of the federation that others could not afford. Other leaders in the federation applaud his willingness to go to jail over the marketing plan and to speak out in opposition to spraying chemicals, implying that a leader protects his followers by staying out front.

And finally, Ramon's leadership depends not on his ability to command respect, but on the quality of his vision. In his writing and drawing, he captures a feeling and an understanding of Rivera Payabo that is unique. He inspires, breathes imagination into his neighbors. And they do not underestimate how rare and important this is. One member pointed out that he "brings us enthusiasm and excitement about the future."

Enthusiasm: from the Greek en (within) and teos (god or god force)

The Greeks may have been right when they identified those citizens who carried a special spirit as having some direct tie to their gods. I find it hard to begrudge the federation for having relied so heavily on Ramon, and I find it no surprise that he would turn to poetry, that pure extract of intense feeling, to help him express himself to his neighbors.

Considering the despoliation of the land, it is surprising that Ramon's poetry, dealing mainly with the flora and fauna of the area, does not dwell on that ravaging. In a very simple, straightforward way, he has written poems about a tree, a flower, a fruit, the roots of plants, a horse, his neighbors.

Through his reading, Ramon has learned a great deal about poetic structure, harmony, and rhythm. But above all, his poetry is the work of a folk artist in love with his people and land. And just as folk art seems to be that stuff without shadow, so Ramon's poetry and oral history hold no abiding anger. His oral history of the Rivera Payabo recounts the burning of farms, the murder of people, and the slaughter of animals—all in the name of that sweet white gold, sugar. But that history is a folk epic: there is no conspiracy theory, no anger or outrage, no environmental manifesto, only the whims of fate.

When I listened to Ramon recount the tragedies that have befallen his home, I asked him why he didn't leave like many of the others. Why has Ramon, why have his neighbors, tried to do anything at all? Ramon returns the question: "If I leave, who will stay here to protect the land and my neighbors?"

The Spanish word *querencia* has no single-word equivalent in English. The word connotes a profound and abiding feeling for a place and its people. Querencia explains much of Ramon Aybar's impossible, fatalistic optimism.

Recently, I tried to cheer him up by telling him what was happening to sugar in the world outside his home. Pepsi-Cola had just signed a multimillion-dollar contract to buy a new synthetic sweetener, and Coca-Cola had agreed to a high-fructose corn syrup that many experts feel will replace cane sugar within the decade. Two years ago, the U.S. ambassador to the Dominican Republic had informed the Dominican Chamber of Commerce that sugar soon would no longer be an export crop and that Dominicans should consider farming other crops as quickly as possible. I told Ramon how ironic it would be if the world economy forced a return to diversified agriculture. Ramon smiled, but shrugged his shoulders. Such a dream would never occur in his lifetime.

Later, I remembered one of Ramon's sayings: "Whoever is not called upon to struggle is forgotten by God."

3

Blindness and Vision in Jamaica

SHELDON ANNIS

Judy McGraw was born blind into a working class family in Brooklyn, New York. Her father died when she was nine, and her mother single-handedly raised four daughters.

"Being blind and being from a poor family made me want to succeed," she says. "I always wanted that badly. I don't think I have exceptional ability, but I do have exceptional drive. When I was very young, I set my mind on going to Harvard, and I did."

McGraw went through Harvard on scholarship, and then, Stanford graduate school. Today she is a Congressional liaison for a U.S. government agency. Because of recent technological innovations that assist the blind—and because she can afford them—she makes surprisingly few concessions to her disability.

She generally carries with her a ten-pound VersaBraille wordprocessor-microcomputer. With it, she can enter the equivalent of four hundred pages of braille information on a single C-60 cassette. She can easily organize, file, recall, edit, and index her material. Through a standard serial connector and telephone lines, she can readily plug into a variety of computer terminals, hardcopy printers, braille embossers, and external data banks.

At home and in her office, Ms. McGraw reads with an Optacan, a four pound scanner that is about the size of a small purse. Through advanced electronics, the Optacan converts printed-letter images into enlarged, vibrating, tactile shapes that can be read with one finger. She has access to virtually anything printed—including foreign languages and mathematical symbols—without its having previously been converted to braille. She reads the daily newspaper, technical articles, Spanish novels, and office memoranda. She can cook with recipes from the back of soup cans, look up numbers in the telephone book, review her monthly bank statement, and even read computer screens.

At her office, she works with a powerful computer system that is connected to her high-speed braille printer. She can call up any information that is in her office data bank—and anything that can be brought to her terminal through a telephone modem. The reports and letters that she writes are printed out simultaneously in braille for her records and in typescript for her colleagues.

And finally, she is mobile. She owns a stocky black Labrador seeing-eye dog who leads and protects her. She uses cabs and public transportation easily, coming and going as she pleases.

Much of the electronic technology that Judy McGraw uses has become available only in the last year or two. Her total investment, including the seeing-eye dog, is about $30,000. Fortunately, her employer has shared some costs.

She is still blind, certainly; yet advanced technology—coupled with her own drive—have enabled her to put her Harvard and Stanford training to practical use. As a result, she is more than economically independent; she is highly competitive in a job market that requires person-to-person interaction and sophisticated skills in information processing.

Doubtlessly, blindness often causes her to feel isolation and despair. Yet she also feels independence. "On a day-to-day basis," she says, "I can operate in the world of the sighted even though I'm blind."

* * *

By world standards, Jamaica is not a very poor country. Jamaicans do not suffer from the kinds of preventable blindness that are endemic elsewhere. There is no trachoma, for example, a disease that afflicts millions of people in the Middle East, South Asia, and parts of North and sub-Saharan Africa. One does not find villages stricken with onchocerciasis—river blindness—as in Malawi, where fully a third of adult men may be blind and disabled.

Nevertheless, measured against a standard of VersaBrailles and Optacans, the situation of the blind in Jamaica is grim indeed. First, modern medical technologies which can alleviate or arrest blindness are not generally available. Glaucoma, a buildup of pressure inside the eye that eventually destroys the optic nerve, is responsible for nearly 40 percent of adult blindness in Jamaica. It is neither preventable nor reversible, but with drug treatment, it can be controlled. The drug (usually imported) can cost about $40 per month for full treatment, placing it well beyond the means of nearly all blind Jamaicans. Ministry of Health supplies are erratic, especially in rural areas. Thus, every day glaucoma worsens among people who cannot afford, cannot obtain, or are not properly instructed in the use of a drug that might control it.

Cataracts, which account for about a third of adult Jamaican blindness, often can be removed in a fifteen-minute operation. Depending on severity, partial sight can often be recovered through glasses or more sophisticated cornea transplants. For those who cannot afford commercial medical rates—again, virtually all of the blind—there is a two- to three-year waiting list for cataract removal and scant possibility for sight-restorative, post-cataract surgery. Many cataract sufferers do not realize that their blindness is potentially reversible.

Second, there is scant institutional infrastructure for assisting the blind or integrating them into society. Vision problems are rarely detected before they become severe; thus untreated child blindness leads to adult blindness, and poor childhood vision leads to lost learning. Opportunities for using braille are severely restricted. The School for the Blind has only a few hundred students. Even among those who know braille, there is little braille material, so few concrete employment opportunities open up as a result.

Not surprisingly, only about a dozen or so blind people—less than one-tenth of one percent of the 14,000 blind in Jamaica—have studied in a university. So there are few people in professional or advocacy positions who can articulate the needs and interests of the blind.

Lacking education or training, the blind are poorly equipped to compete for jobs in a society with nearly 30 percent unemployment among the able-bodied. Ninety-eight percent of the blind do not have regular jobs. Of the two percent who are employed, 90 percent of those earn less than the Jamaican minimum wage.

To have a white cane—and to know how to use it well—is to be among the privileged blind. Those people who have heard of such marvels as the Optacan tend to judge its cost against the number of blind people who could be taught to use a white cane. Even the technology of seeing-eye dogs is considered culturally and economically impractical. Wilbert Williams, a physical therapist who studied at the Royal National Institute for the Blind, brought a seeing-eye dog home from England. He relates, "First, the buses wouldn't allow it. They are too crowded, the aisles are too narrow, and passengers were afraid. The dog was trained for English sidewalks at least four feet wide. He couldn't adjust to the street vendors and the crowds. And the expense and problems of keeping the dog healthy—three-fourths of a pound of meat a day, eggs, milk, vitamins, and booster shots. It didn't work out."

In short: whereas advanced technology has helped to equalize opportunity for Judy McGraw, in Jamaica blindness translates into limited mobility, illiteracy, social isolation, and joblessness. If Optacans and seeing-eye dogs are not immediate answers for Jamaica, what then? Are there supports—human, institutional, and technological—that can reduce inequality? And if technology and institutions do not now serve the blind, how can the blind serve themselves?

* * *

Bunny McGregor is forty-one years old. Many years ago, when he still had one good eye, he used to be a sign painter. But in 1974 he contracted glaucoma, and his sight deteriorated. "Now I just catch a glimpse," he says.

Like most blind adults in Kingston, Bunny McGregor lives in a rented room. He is alone, at the end of a long, dark, L-shaped corridor.

"Careful of the hole in the floor," he says, walking forward down the hall.

"I can't see it," I answer, feeling a little foolish.

His room contains a narrow bed, a weathered armoire, and a straight-backed wooden chair. At one end of the bed is a neat pile of clean clothes; at the other is a messy pile of dirty clothes. His cane leans next to the door; his glaucoma medicine and toothbrush are within reach on a narrow shelf.

In one corner is a small portable kerosene stove with a pot, plate, and utensils resting on it. In the other is a small stack of braille books, mostly portions of the New Testament. A frayed, socketless electric cord dangles from the ceiling. Just below the ceiling, open slats allow air and sunlight to enter. Bunny, of course, does not see the cheesecake magazine clippings and ribald cartoons that a previous tenant left glued to the wall.

Since 1979 Bunny has earned money by making belts and pillows in this room. He also buys soap and peanuts wholesale, repackages them, and sells them on the street. "The belts would sell, but now the cord is too expensive. For a ball, it costs $22. I can't get the buckles anymore (since they are imported), so there is no money in that."

Last year Bunny borrowed $168 (about US $100) from a revolving loan fund of the Jamaican Society for the Blind. The fund was set up with a $15,000 grant. His loan went to buy materials to make pillows. He had three payments to make, of which he was able to make two, repaying about $100. But in early January, business dropped off. "I owed other money: for my food, for my clothes, for the soap I was selling. People were rushing me for the money, and nobody was buying anything.

"My little girl—she twelve years old—she been starting to keep bad company. She want to join the Girl Guides. She need her uniforms, you know, and other things. So what to do? I need to keep her off the street. I give her the money, so she could become a Girl Guide."

But now—though it is only about $60—he is in default on his loan to the society. The society is not unsympathetic, but he will probably not qualify for another loan. Hundreds of people are on the waiting list who have not had access to even $168 of capital.

Bunny McGregor feels he cannot work, beg, or sell; and it seems to him, he owes money to everyone. "Mon," he says, "I have run out."

* * *

"They call me Traveler," says Warren Johnson. "I know every corner of the city; I never get lost. I go to parties, to church, to buy and sell. Sometimes I just move around; I'm the kind of person that got to be active."

Warren is tall—about six feet two inches. As he taps forward—edging through a crush of pedestrians, darting children, vehicles, and street vendors—he occasionally jostles people or hits his head on an overhang.

"Sometimes I bump someone selling on this sidewalk, and they react, 'Why don't you stay home? Someone should carry you where you go!'

"I have to stop and tell them. I say, 'Hey, will you come and clothe me? Will you feed me? Will you shelter me? I have to go my way too. I can't stay home just so I be out of your way.'"

The problem with blind people, he says, is not that they can't get around but "they're scared."

"Scared," I ask, "that they'll get lost or hurt?"

"No, mon, they scared how they look. You feel embarrassed, scared by what people will say.

"You see, I step off a curb and into a puddle of water. I can feel the dirty water soaking into my shoes. I'm standing there, feeling people are looking at me, thinking I look like a big fool. It's terrible. But I say, 'So what, it's not my problem what they think,' and I go on my way."

Warren Johnson is twenty-three. He is bright and painfully restless. It is easier to imagine him like Judy McGraw—in college, studying with his classmates—than spending hours, as he actually does, in front of a family television set that he cannot see.

"Last year I was sitting at home, and I have an idea in my head. I can't get no work, but I have the idea that I can raise chickens. I talk to Mr. Logan at the society and he liked it, so I got a loan."

Warren's brother-in-law helped build the cages. First, Warren bought a feeder, then the 250 chicks which he raised and sold in about seven weeks. Then he bought a second batch.

"One morning my sister came in and told me, 'Your chickens, they all dead.'

"I couldn't believe it! I went out and feel inside the cage, and I find each chicken dead. The rats had gotten in. I just couldn't believe it.

"The lights—the utility—it went out that night. So the rats got bold and chew through the mesh. I took the chickens, dug a hole, and bury them with my hands. So I'm losing.

"Now the landlord come and he tells me not to do that more. The neighbors say the chickens smell bad and attracting flies. Their word against mine."

"What are you going to do?" I ask.

"Maybe I sell biscuits or cigarettes, or things for kids in front of the house. I went to a training center and learned a little woodwork. But I was only there for eight months, so I didn't reach far enough to go on my own. Maybe I'll learn a craft, like making baskets."

"Isn't there a way to get rid of the flies and control the odor from the chickens," I suggest.

"Yes, I think so. I will have to go and find out. This only happened two weeks ago. Yes, I will have to go and solve this thing."

* * *

Dennis Haynes was a blind child with three sighted brothers and sisters. His parents, rural people near Mandeville, believed he would be a lifelong burden and were only too willing to send him to Kingston to the Salvation Army School for the Blind.

Today, at thirty-four, Dennis Haynes is fired up, successful. He produces gospel tapes and records under his own imprint, Insight Gospel. He is founder and leader of a singing group, and he owns a record stand, Narrow Way Gospel Line. To finance his small business, he qualified for two commercial bank loans and then a third, low-interest loan from the Society for the Blind. Gospel, he says, is a steady business, even during a recession. Though always pressed, he has managed to meet his total monthly payments of $240, month after month.

"My goal in life is to meet and interview Stevie [Wonder]," he says. "He's been my inspiration. He takes on challenges, and he comes out winning. His music is good; he is popular; he's got an organization. What I like about him is that he is in business as well as singing. That's my desire, too, to do it total: live it, play it, earn from it."

Dennis' talk is of the future: hopes for tours, recordings, concerts, business expansion. He is enthusiastic about a forthcoming tour to California. "We will play churches, schools, concert halls. We should make enough money to buy our own equipment," he predicts.

I am surprised. "You mean you don't already own your own equipment?"

"No, mon, we don't have any. It all got stolen. We've been renting equipment for three years, saving our money to replace what got stolen."

"Someone here stole your equipment?"

"But not here, in Canada. We were doing a TV thing in Toronto. They said we could leave our equipment in a van while we were there. When we came out, only my sax and our piano was left."

He raises and waves a hand to say: Poof! . . . gone.

"The police recovered one piece, but we couldn't stay to go to court and work it out. No money, no time to do that. That was a total loss: $9,000—everything we had."

But Haynes is a survivor. "I look back at what happened in Canada, and I just have to say: I can't let it happen again. We've learned if you play for other people, they earn. Now we set up our own concerts. We find a location, pay for it, print announcements, advertise, rent a hall. You've always got to be thinking, finding a way to do a little better."

If you let it, he says, blindness becomes a psychological rather than a physical problem. "We are at the lowest scale of the ladder. People don't accept you. They expect you to be dependent. You have to show them that that's not so. I need a wealth of knowledge—about games, about football—to mix with people. My message is: I'm normal, you don't have to take care of me.

"I eat, sleep, and wear music. I'm not as good in my music as I could be. I can't practice as I should. But I'm sure of my path; I'm achieving. I've been able to do what I didn't think I could."

He speaks with satisfaction of a two-day-a-week job at a private preparatory school teaching sighted children to read and write music.

"I keep them close to me, around my desk. I can hear when one is making a mistake, who is fidgeting or not paying attention. 'Wake up,' I tell them. 'Pay attention.'"

"'How you know? How you know?' they say."

He chuckles. "I can just tell."

"I didn't go to college; I didn't study teaching. I was afraid of this; I didn't know that I can do it. But I can."

* * *

Gloria Davis tells a different kind of success story.

Miss Davis is now forty-eight years old. She was born in St. Mary, Mark's district, and came to Kingston when she was very young. Although she learned to read a little, she never developed a special job skill. She never married and has no children. For most of her adult life, she worked as a domestic.

In 1974, she realized she was going blind.

"And then one morning I got up and I couldn't see. 'Oh, Lord,' I said, 'Why me, What did I do?'"

"It's not pretty. I weep day; I weep night. My sight went altogether; I couldn't see not a thing. I couldn't work; I had to be led around."

At the time of her blindness, Miss Davis rented a small room in the house of one of her "church sisters," Phyllis McCouthy (Sister Mac). "It was Sister Mac that helped me make it through."

"We sit together, we pray together," recalls Sister Mac. "She was so discouraged. I felt so sorry for her. We helped her. And the church helped her. We tried to tell her that life is worth living, that there is a tomorrow."

Gloria Davis was buttressed, but she did not immediately become independent. Unlike Warren Johnson, she was afraid to travel alone on buses and to get jostled in the public markets. When she had to shop or visit the doctor, she traveled with someone, usually one of the younger children of the family. She helped around the house as best she could, but she could not assume major responsibility for cooking and housekeeping. To earn spending money she set up a stand—a kind of wire-mesh stall with shelves on it—in front of the house. There, she began selling soap, peanuts, dried milk, and matches. Still, she is five months behind on her $10 a month rent, and her sales alone are insufficient to sustain her.

Through the Society for the Blind, Miss Davis was put on a waiting list for cataract removal. The prospect of an operation terrified her, but she and Sister Mac prayed and fasted, and she went through with it. It was successful; and now, with thick glasses, her sight is partially restored. After a nine-year ordeal with total blindness, she says. "I know true joy."

Her story was gladdening, yet it bothered me. Thinking of the expense and years of caring as I walked out, I asked Sister Mac, "But why did you do all that? Isn't it hard enough to take care of your own family?"

"Why?" she said, looking at me, not fully comprehending the question. "Because I love her. I just do it because I love her. That's all."

* * *

Albert Johnson lives in a harsher world than do Sisters Gloria and Mac. Downtown Kingston, by everyone's account, is rough, on the edge, violent.

To ask for the "blind mon, Mister Johnson," is to be asked a lot of questions: "What you want to see him for?"

I am answering for the satisfaction of Edward Dawson, a burly man whose address is the same as the blind man's but who is noncommittal regarding his whereabouts.

"I'm pure Bandoolu," he says.

"Bandoolu?" I say politely.

"It means I'm a pirate, mon. I rob; I cheat; I hustle. Mess with me, I'll kill you. See this scar"—he pulls at the neck of his t-shirt—"this is where my lady throw acid on me while I sleep."

I smile . . . a little—not very much—for as we speak, I realize that Dawson keeps one eye on me and an eye on a man in the street who is waving a knife and shouting at us.

Finally Dawson produces Albert Johnson and tells this story for him:

When he was nineteen, Johnson got in a fight and was scarred and blinded. Now he scrapes by, a little of this, a little of that.

A few months ago, the society helped him with a loan to set up a chicken coop. He raised the chickens and took them to market for sale. And what luck—someone offered him U.S. dollars, about a thousand dollars.

Johnson sold the chickens; the dollars turned out to be counterfeit.

"When it happen, it really tore me up what they do to that blind mon. We give him a place. Maybe we help him out, you know?"

Dawson has a very short fuse. Interview over. I suspect that someone else in Kingston—someone with a supply of counterfeit U.S. dollars—is also thinking about Edward Dawson.

* * *

Russell Morgan is a "bus preacher." That means his congregation is the bus-riding public. He gets on, say, a Number 2 at Tilda's Crossing, and shouts the gospel until the end of the line.

Cupping his hand like a megaphone, he shouts over the din of the motor. His hoarse voice rises and falls. A few passengers say "amen," a few look irritated, and most ignore him. Many passengers take the tracts that he passes out at the last stop; a very few, occasionally, make offerings.

With help from Dennis Haynes, a small loan from the Society for the Blind, support from his church, and in collaboration with his wife Beverly, Brother Morgan recently produced a musical record album, *First Trumpet*. Once or twice a week, he sells the album from door to door or takes it to gospel record shops around town. He has about twenty-eight albums left from his most recent pressing of one hundred albums.

It is not much of a living. Yet he has almost paid off his loan, and when he does, he will almost certainly try a new loan and a new album.

Brother Morgan is an articulate man, passionate in his belief. He answers questions clearly and patiently; though obviously, he is far more interested in my spiritual well-being than his economic history.

He is serious, engaged. His is a life of service.

* * *

Arvel Grant, executive director of the Jamaican Society for the Blind, is one of the dozen or so college-educated blind people in Jamaica. Amiable and quick-witted, he moves about with seeming effortlessness. He laughs easily and often, yet his manner leaves no doubt . . . he is the kind of man who, if punched, will punch back.

"In the last election I waited in line a half hour to vote. I took someone with me. When I got to the front of the line, the lady said, 'You must vote alone. That's the law.'

"I said, 'I wish to take this person behind the screen to help me. I'll sign a paper that it's OK. I need her help so that I can vote.'

"But she said, 'No, the law says one person at a time in the voting booth. No one can go in with you.'

"I raised a fuss. 'Look,' I said, 'I need to vote, and I'll fight about it! You'll have to drag me away from here. I have a right to vote!' Finally, rather than go through all that, they let me in."

That, in a nutshell, is the distinction between being blind and what

Grant calls the "problem of blindness." To be blind, to not see, is bad enough. But it is another matter altogether to lose rights that have—or should have—nothing to do with seeing: the right to vote, to move about, to have jobs, to have sexual and family life, to become educated.

"A sighted child in our schools needs pencil and paper. But a blind child—to have the same opportunity—needs more. He may need a Perkins brailler and audio aids. If that's what it takes to give him equal opportunity, then that's what we try to get. If we need special provisions to vote, then let's get them. The aim of the society is to do *anything* that will strengthen the capacity of the blind to gain equal opportunity and to be independent."

The Jamaica Society for the Blind—originally, the royal Commonwealth Society for the Blind—has been in existence for about thirty years. It was founded as a benevolent organization in the British welfare tradition. "It was run like a country club," says Arvel Grant, in his blunt way. "The lords and ladies got together as a social event and sent Christmas trees once a year. It was well-intentioned, but it did not begin to address the problem of blindness—that people were spending thirty years in the back of the house without ever coming out."

In the early 1970s, a group of young blind people—many of them, like Grant, graduates of the Salvation Army School for the Blind—began meeting together and agitating for a voice in the organization. Such were the times that the statutes of the society stipulated specifically that not more than one of the fourteen board members could be blind.

Says Derrick Palmer, one of the original activists, "We said, look, these are upper class people. They want nothing to do with us. We were aggressive, and we wanted change. So in 1975 we set up our own organization the Progressive Blind Association.

"We got the blind together and drew up a national plan for the government. We put on dances, parties. We had monthly meetings— anything to get people to associate, to integrate.

"Then we said, look, we don't even have a permanent place to meet. We don't have any money. Why set up a new association? So we started to participate in the society again.

"Night after night we met—about thirty or forty people. For the blind it was something new and exciting. Every meeting was packed. We wrote articles and brought our cause into the media. Even if people didn't want to know, we told them.

"Finally, we got a third of our people on the board. Our advantage was that we *always* attended meetings. We always showed up. Many of the old board members resigned in frustration or protest;

and then, in 1978, I was elected the first blind chairman.

"We had been talking to Steve Vetter [then Inter-American Foundation (IAF) representative for Jamaica] for a couple of years. When we established ourselves in control, IAF came through with its grant for $15,000. And then all of a sudden we weren't just agitators—which is all we really knew how to do—we were administrators."

What are the society's activities today? "Anything," says Arvel Grant, "that will enable people to take greater control of their own lives." In various stages of evolution and success, that *anything* now includes four kinds of activities: those dealing with sight (an eye rehabilitation program, an opthamology clinic, a national blind registration program, drug distribution for glaucoma, eye testing in the schools); those dealing with adjustment to blindness (white cane training, a national braille literacy program, a braille and audio library, a reading club, job counseling, training in typing, the revolving loan fund, a craft cooperative, a food and welfare program); those dealing with the sighted (family counseling, weekly educational radio programs, lobbying and pressuring for services); and recreational and social activities (hikes, beach outings, camping trips, a musical program, Saturday morning debates). Through these activities members are encouraged to get to know and rely on each other.

With never more than two or three full-time paid staff members, the society would appear to be stretched thin. But Grant and Palmer do not agree. The strength of the organization, as they see it, is a reservoir of people with time and extraordinary commitment to a cause. "We understand each other's needs," says Grant, "and we don't get tired of each other's company. There is an unlimited willingness among the blind to give and to help each other."

"Yet if we tell you that we have *begun* to address a significant portion of the blind," says Derrick Palmer, "we would be lying. Look, we may be able to help distribute glaucoma medicine to 2-3,000 people. But are we dealing with them in a meaningful way? No. There are maybe a thousand people we deal with here—a fourteenth of the blind population.   We are not scratching the surface of their need or their potential."

* * *

The blind people who I talked to may be an elite group. They are not only members of the Society for the Blind, but they are people who have concretely benefited from its revolving loan fund. Perhaps they are not very representative of the 13,000 or so blind people who have had no contact with the society. Most of those people, I suppose, are homebound and do not find themselves talking to strangers. Most cannot read braille, even if they could afford or obtain braille books. Unlike Bunny McGregor, most haven't received any loan. Probably they don't have the restless youthful energy of Warren Johnson; or the musical ability and business acumen of Dennis Haynes. Possibly they don't have the religious faith of Russell Morgan, or the loving adopted family of Gloria Evans, or a bandoolu friend like Albert Johnson. I am certain that very few will threaten fist fights at voting booths, as did Arvel Grant. Yet, I wondered, probably each has his own story; and each, within, has his or her own kind of strength and resources to survive.

In truth, the revolving loan fund established by a $15,000 IAF grant can hardly be said to have rewritten the script for anyone's life. So far, the revolving fund has assisted about nineteen projects, twenty-seven people. The loans have helped, but they have not made twenty-seven people economically self-sufficient. Several loans were made with the intention of buying and reselling goods that were scarce in the early eighties but then became either abundant or unaffordable. Many of the society's loans may have been unrealistically small; perhaps larger loans to fewer people would have made more economic sense in the long run. With $160, Bunny McGregor could not really have started a small business; he was only able to get slightly deeper in debt. All things considered, he was probably right in choosing to invest his last capital in a Girl Guide uniform for his twelve-year-old daughter.

People like Arvel Grant and Derrick Palmer understand numbers and the logic of investing in Girl Guide uniforms. They see people in terms of their value rather than their cost. They are aware but unimpressed that the hardware to make one person, Judy McGraw, economically independent in the United States costs twice the entire IAF grant to the society. To that, Grant smiles and responds dryly, "Then I suppose we should have asked for more."

In the meantime, he seems more concerned by the immediate problem of Warren Johnson and his neighbors' objections to flies and chicken odor. "On Monday we will pick him up and see about this thing with the neighbors," he says. "We will talk to them; we will talk to the landlord. We'll change all that."

PART 3

Processes of Collective Action

What does the abstract notion of "community participation" mean when it is put into practice? Concretely, what does a community *do* when it is "participating?"

—Stephen Cox and Sheldon Annis

PART 3

Processes of
Collective Action

4

Lake Titicaca's Campesino-Controlled Tourism

KEVIN HEALY AND ELAYNE ZORN

The island of Taquile, a remote speck on Lake Titicaca, is a land of stone walkways, thatched huts, mountain vistas, vivid color, and ancient custom. Its life had changed little over centuries until it was recently discovered by a new breed of tourists, rugged young travelers who are looking for the "unspoiled."

But Taquile has become no ordinary tourist paradise. Unlike virtually any other Third World community that attracts visitors, the Taquilenos have managed to develop their own facilities to exploit tourism. Until now, they have controlled the tourist trade, and they have reaped its economic benefits. Yet success—even the relatively limited success of Taquile—is not without cost and risk.

* * *

Taquile is an improbable place for tourism. In the 1930s, it was briefly famous as a site for political prisoners, including deposed president Sanchez Cerro; otherwise the island passed centuries in obscurity.

The inhabitants of Taquile are Quechua-speaking Indians. They are subsistence farmers who for countless generations have grown potatoes, barley, and broadbeans in private plots on terraced mountainsides.

Traditionally, the island was divided into six *suyos* (sections). Each suyo contained a single crop that was rotated through a six-year cycle. Taquile's farms produced small surpluses, and the island's modest stores stocked few goods. Unlike other Andean communities, the islanders owned few animals for insurance against crop failures.

The poorest Taquilenos eked out a living by fishing from reed boats on the deep waters of the lake. For cash, the men worked seasonally on coastal farms, in the southern copper mines, and at odd jobs in nearby cities.

To reach the port city of Puno, islanders traveled eight to twelve hours in wooden sailboats. Each boat was owned by ten to twelve families whose members took turns navigating. Although other lakeside communities began changing to motorized boats in the mid-1960s, the Taquilenos were too poor to upgrade their sailboats. Timid, speaking poor Spanish, and wearing baggy Western clothing over their traditional costumes when they came to town, the Taquilenos were emblematic of Peru's rural backwaters.

Yet despite its acute poverty, Taquile was not without resources. The Peruvian anthropologist José Matos Mar has documented how the community ingeniously began to mobilize savings during the 1930s to purchase the island over the next two decades from its *hacendados* (landowners).

Moreover, the superb quality of Taquile handweaving was equalled by only a handful of communities. Everyone—men, women, and children—knew how to weave. The men knitted elegant *ch'ullos* (stocking hats), while the women used horizontal ground looms to weave *chumpis* (belts), *ch'uspas* (bags), *lliqllas* and *unkhunas* (shawls), ponchos, and scarves. Men and boys also wove cloth for tailoring into shirts, vests, skirts, and pants. Weavers bartered for alpaca and sheep's wool from the herdsmen around Lake Titicaca. Trained since they were children, Taquilenos spun ceaselessly—in between other tasks, everywhere on the island.

Taquile was one of the few lakeside communities where both women and men wore—as well as wove—traditional clothing. Their red, white, and black costumes were brilliant against the dry and rocky landscape. Their dress and weaving technique linked the faraway styles of medieval Spain to their Andean heritage.

Although Taquilenos occasionally sold textiles to travelers in Puno, they had little experience with organized textile sales. In 1968, with the assistance of co-author Healy, then a U.S. Peace Corps volunteer, the islanders created a cooperative to market weavings based on the structure of traditional leadership. *Jilakatas* (elders who are the island's traditional and legal authority figures) collected new and used weavings for trial sale in Cuzco, a day's trip by train or bus from Puno. These articles were sold on consignment in a Peace Corps-sponsored store that was set up to sell goods from southern Peru's many artisan cooperatives. When the trial sales produced $150, a commercial boom began. Gradually, islanders began commuting regularly to

Cuzco on community-authorized sales trips.

Since the Peace Corps store charged only a modest administrative overhead and the remaining profits went directly to the artisans, the islanders learned the market value of their work. The sales demonstrated that their everyday weavings were attractive to outsiders, especially tourists, and could produce regular cash income.

Unfortunately, three years later the Cuzco retail outlet collapsed. A local manager had embezzled funds, and the Taquile artisans suffered a big loss when many weavings held on consignment vanished as the store closed. Yet not everything was lost. The islanders had discovered Cuzco's rapidly expanding tourist market, and they knew that their weavings were among the best in southern Peru. Taquilenos who formerly only delivered products to the cooperative store began to use their market knowledge to sell weavings directly to tourists on the streets of Cuzco. They also found buyers and export distributors in the southern city of Arequipa and in Lima. By the mid-1970s, foreign buyers and Lima exporters were selling the red chumpis and ch'uspas of Taquile to sophisticated crafts consumers in Western Europe and the United States.

THE ADVENT OF TOURISM

In 1976, the widely read *South American Handbook* described an out-of-the-way, unspoiled island on Lake Titicaca. It was a short blurb; but for the campesinos of Taquile—largely invisible even to residents of the nearby port of Puno—life would never be the same again.

Despite its beauty, Taquile was outside the tourist circuit and was overshadowed by the area's main attraction: floating reed islands that were populated by a dwindling Indian population and located within a twenty-minute boatride of Puno. The only way to reach Taquile was aboard one of the collectively-owned wooden sailboats. Only the most adventurous travelers were willing to get off the afternoon train from Cuzco and then spend an entire night sailing a cold, windswept, and often rainy lake. After the handbook was published, however, foreign tourists—alone and in groups—began arriving on the dock at Puno trying to book passage to Taquile. Several private Puno boat owners soon added the island to their tourist run on the lake.

By 1977, the Taquilenos had pooled their savings and bought second-hand truck engines to power their sailboats. Travel time between Puno and the island dropped from twelve to three-and-one-half hours, and the tourist traffic increased. In early 1978, new sailboat cooperatives formed with groups of thirty to forty families ordering vessels from local boatwrights. Although still rustic, the new boats had cabins and were safer, more attractive, and larger. They could comfortably carry as many as twenty tourists. A grant from the Inter-American Foundation (IAF) enabled the Taquilenos to purchase spare parts and boat motors for six additional groups. The Peruvian Coast Guard and the Ministry of Tourism licensed the Taquilenos to carry travelers and issued regulations and tariffs to regulate fares.

The islanders proved to be competitive with the private boat owners at Puno. Eventually the islanders displaced the Puno boat owners and obtained an officially sanctioned monopoly. By 1982, the number of cooperative transport groups had expanded to thirteen.

In November 1982, the round-trip fare between Taquile and Puno, which is set by the Peruvian Coast Guard and the Ministry of Tourism, was approximately $4.00. Since the costs of spare parts, fuel, maintenance, and the replacement of motors and wooden boats are high, the boats have operated at a narrow margin between slight profit and slight loss. Yet local control of boat traffic produces benefits other than cash income: it also subsidizes the cost of transport for Taquilenos who travel to and from Puno. In 1982, 435 people (with virtually every family represented) shared ownership and management responsibilities for one of the thirteen boats. Now every family has access to cheap transportation. Taquile's trade and communications with the mainland are substantially improved. Traditionally, Taquilenos slept in their boats at the Puno dock; but recently, they used their earnings to purchase land in Puno to construct an overnight community house for cooking and sleeping.

The increased boat traffic has also provided new personal income and on-the-job learning. The three members of the crew on each Puno round trip now receive regular payment for their work. New boats meant more hulls and fittings to be produced by the island's boat builders. Over the last five years, crew members have acquired valuable skill in engine repair and maintenance—sometimes at the tourists' expense by solving mechanical breakdowns in the middle of the lake.

TOURISM TAQUILE STYLE

Taquile is an environment hospitable for only hardy travelers. There are virtually none of the standard tourist services: excursions, shops, medical facilities, or motor vehicles. In fact, there is no electricity, potable water system, or plumbing. There are few beds on the island—nothing even approaching a third-class hotel. Most visitors are backpackers in their twenties and early thirties. They wear down jackets, alpaca sweaters, and hiking boots. Invariably, they travel on a limited budget. For most, the absence of pre-paid, whirlwind holiday tours is an attraction; but they soon learn that "rustic" on Taquile can mean rugged.

The island is 13,000 feet above sea level, an altitude to which few visitors are accustomed. To reach the island, travelers make a three-and-a-half-hour boat trip. After arriving, they make a 45-minute climb up the side of a mountain along a winding stone stairway. At the pinnacle, a campesino reception committee greets the new arrivals and registers them by age, duration of stay, and nationality. The committee describes the physical layout of the island, its principal attractions—for instance, some archeologically interesting burial towers—and assigns accommodations with a local family in an adobe hut. The owner of the guest hut then brings the tourist to the family's home. Like Taquilenos, the tourists sleep on *tortora* mats on earthen floors.

In 1978, sixty-eight families were authorized by local authorities to take in overnight foreign guests. By August of 1982, the number had risen to 207 families—in effect, every family on the island. Tourists come from North and South America, Australia, New Zealand, Japan, Israel, and especially Western Europe. Community records show that 5,300 tourists visited Taquile between January and August of 1982, an average of more than 750 per month. Most visitors stay for two to three days. In August 1982, a record 1,800 people visited the island. Though the growth has been steady, weeks pass during the slack season with few and irregular visitors.

Taquilenos manage tourism through an array of committees—for example, housing, weaving, food, and transportation. Special tasks such as construction or public maintenance are handled by volunteer work groups set up by the committees. Over the past six years, the islanders have established rules and prices that they and the tourists are expected to respect.

During the first tourist season, two privately-owned restaurants were opened by Taquilenos who had returned from many years in Lima. Seven restaurants currently operate on the island. Each is owned and managed by groups or families and is located in the "urbanizing" village square. Restaurant fare is slightly more varied than the food in peasant households—omelettes, pancakes, and fish in addition to soup, potatoes, and herbal teas. Traditionally, most islanders have not been active fishermen, but the tourists' demand for fish has stimulated the formation of two fishing cooperatives, consisting of twenty-one and fifty members. Fish is also purchased from fishermen in nearby lakeside communities.

Potential and actual tourist income has encouraged household improvements, which are inspected and approved by another island commission. The improvements may include extra rooms, tables, benches, tablecloths, kerosene lanterns, wash basins, and such simple bedding gear as reed mats and woolen blankets. Nearby stores furnish toilet paper and beer. These products are novel to Taquile and are generally considered to be the maximum in allowable creature comforts consistent with an "authentic Andean experience." Each approved household directly receives the tourist income from lodging and in most cases, from meals. An overnight stay in November 1982 cost 60¢; a fish dinner cost 70¢.

TOURISM AND TEXTILE SALES

When Taquile's tourism began in earnest in 1976, textile marketing also changed. Most local crafts had been sold by Taquile's middlemen in Cuzco, Arequipa, and Lima; now, goods could be sold on the island. Taquile's weavers eventually formed a community-run artisan store, where they could sell their diverse and increasingly numerous products. With middlemen eliminated, craftsmen received higher relative incomes.

An elected committee administers the store while the island's men take turns working as unpaid sales clerks. The crafts committee meets each Tuesday to set prices based on the quality of workmanship and the amount of labor. The labor force is the same as the pre-market Taquile of the 1960s. Every man, woman, teenager, and child over eight earns money by producing crafts.

By the early 1980s, store sales averaged roughly $2,500 per month, rising as high as $5,700 during the peak tourist months of July and August. In addition, the island held widely publicized crafts fairs at which tourists visiting the island for only a few hours bought several thousand dollars worth of weavings.

The community store has helped artisans avoid undercutting each other's prices, and the official island policy is to sell weavings only through the store. In practice, however, this rule is difficult to enforce and is violated frequently. Sales in the privacy of one's home are easy, and the craftsman can avoid the long wait it usually takes for the community store to sell the item on consignment. In addition, middlemen from Taquile continue to market textiles in Lima, Cuzco, Puno, and Arequipa during the slack tourist season. Thus, the actual total value of Taquile sales is difficult to calculate.

CHANGES IN TEXTILE PRODUCTION

Nearly two decades of experience with markets and tourists have affected what is produced in Taquile. Responding to demand, the Taquilenos have created new products which have evolved from their traditional clothing styles. Presently, the community store stocks numerous shirts, vests, and pants of homespun cloth in natural colors and in a variety of weaves. "Peasant" shirts are particularly popular among the island's youthful tourist visitors. Male weavers have adapted the techniques and designs used in stocking caps to produce a new *chaleco musico* (vest). The vest, with its rows of bright, multi-colored, fanciful patterns, was highly successful, but when Taquilenos tried to use the same knitted fabric for ties and sweaters, the new products sold poorly and were discontinued. Women continue to weave extraordinarily fine bags and belts of varying widths, colors, and motifs. One tourist-related innovation in bags and belts is more extensive use of natural colors.

Despite rates of return that are normally much less than a dollar a day, weaving output in Taquile and nearby communities has mushroomed in recent years. One reason is that weaving, despite its low rate of return, can be done during spare hours when there are no other cash-making alternatives. Many Taquilenos stay up all night to weave by kerosene lamps.

Apart from raising prices, weavers can improve their incomes only by increasing output or lowering the cost of materials. One way to raise income is by switching to commercially spun yarn. Although this yarn is more expensive, the cost is offset since time once devoted to spinning now can be used for weaving. Several years ago, Taquilenos also began to farm out some tasks. Their shirts, for example, are now partially manufactured by campesinos in the Aymara towns near Chiquito, just south of Puno on the lakeshore. Similarly, more than half of the knitted hats sold in the cooperative store come from Amantani, a nearby island, and some natural-colored bags come from the peninsula of Capachica. Some weavings that are produced by outside craftsmen are of lesser quality, leaving many visitors with the impression that local weaving standards may have deteriorated.

Although the quality of some textiles woven in Taquile has undeniably declined since marketing began in earnest, the drop is less than might be expected from the experiences of other communities. True, the widespread use of commercially spun and dyed yarn lowers the quality of materials. Similarly, men now knit *ch'ullus* (stocking hats) with less detail than in the past; their designs are larger, with more empty space. But the knitters rely far less on repetitive motifs than they once did, and they incorporate a wider range of themes drawn from local culture and daily life. Moreover, the stocking hats retain their soft texture, their rich color combinations, and their beauty. The women have adopted similar measures to reduce production time for belts and bags, but they still weave superbly despite inferior yarn quality.

The steady flow of tourist traffic encourages Taquilenos to advertise their weavings by wearing them. While tourism encourages cutting corners, it also reinforces local pride in dress, workmanship, and native traditions. Taquilenos still save their finest weavings for their own wear and use in festivals. All in all, the quality of both tourist and traditional weavings is probably still among the highest in Peru.

With the assistance of an outside weaver-anthropologist, Taquilenos recently organized a community museum to preserve and display their older, better textiles. In order to help keep weavings in the community, a fund was established to purchase fine, old pieces owned by Taquile families.   The rustic museum has become a popular tourist attraction. Perhaps more important, it helps protect the common cultural legacy. Nevertheless, many tourists privately offer high prices for old textiles, and invaluable pieces continue to disappear.

In addition to operating their own museum, Taquilenos have organized exhibits in the departmental capital of Puno and are recognized as one of the region's foremost and best-organized craft communities. Puno officials now request help from Taquile in organizing public craft shows.

Taquile's tourism has affected the neighboring Peruvian island of Amantani. During the 1960s, there was very little visible textile activity among the 5,000 residents of Amantani. Taquile's community-controlled tourism and the prospect of cash sales have spurred a renewal of Amantani's weaving tradition. Hats are being knitted; belts, bags, and scarves are being woven. Older traditional crafts such as stonework, basketry, and fur-work with alpaca hides are also produced for sale to tourists. Several years ago, when weaving revived, the Amantani   craftsmen marketed their goods through Taquile on unfavorable terms. Now, Amantani has its own steady stream of tourists and its own community store. As the Amantanenos copy Taquile's indigenous tourism example, they suffer similar problems. Tourists are buying and carting off the island's inheritance of old weavings.

THE IMPACT AND FUTURE OF TAQUILE TOURISM

Taquile's style of tourism stands in sharp contrast to the experiences of other Third World communities where benefits are trickle-down at best and are offset by the outside control, erosion of cultural integrity, and disruption of traditional lifeways. More often than not, tourist communities are in the grip of outsiders—foreign firms, government bureaucracies, private tourist agencies, and artisan middlemen—who may have little concern for the residents' welfare, much less for their participation in decisionmaking. Taquile's six years of tourism departs from the conventional pattern and shows that a community can set the terms for tourist development and capture the lion's share of the benefits.

From the outset of the community's attempt to manage its own tourism, the Taquilenos had certain advantages—a spectacular landscape, an unforced friendliness, colorful and highly visible folk practices, and a thriving crafts tradition. The island's greatest previous handicap—its isolation—became a dual advantage. First, Taquile's remoteness attracted tourists who enjoyed a challenging trip and savored the island's "unspoiled" authenticity. But perhaps more important, Taquile's isolation allowed the islanders to keep outside entrepreneurs at arm's length while the community developed facilities and management skills.

The Taquilenos have been fortunate. In several important ways, tourism has reinforced rather than undercut traditional lifestyles. Weaving, for example, has flourished. The islanders are adept at and enjoy making and selling a product that also symbolizes traditional culture and values. This craft can be practiced between other tasks throughout the day, thereby raising the value of otherwise marginal time. Rigorous childhood training in weaving continues, and the integrity of and local esteem for quality textile production is intact.

Boats in Taquile have always been owned cooperatively rather than individually. Tourism has built upon this tradition and produced diverse benefits. First, control of the motorboat traffic allows the community to regulate the flow of tourists, most important for equitable distribution to individual homes. Second, the newer and larger vessels give Taquilenos more comfortable, reliable, and frequent access to the mainland. Third, management of boats has taught the islanders much about business administration and the operation and maintenance of machinery. Finally, boat building has evolved into a mini-industry. Local artisans now design and build all the large motorboats, and they have trained new and younger boat builders. Many neighboring lake communities now order their boats from Taquile.

On the other hand, women have not reaped a fair share of benefits from the tourist boom nor has their relative status on the island improved. The new decisionmaking committees that manage the island's various enterprises exclude women. Most of the popular and more profitable artisan products are made by men, and significant female labor has been displaced as the market shifts from products made by women to those made by men.

Agriculture on Taquile's rugged terrain has always been difficult. With the growth in tourism, agricultural production has been boosted, and more cash is available for agricultural intensification. Taquileno farmers offer produce directly to consumers, earning income that normally goes to middlemen. Moreover, money from tourism provides a safety net against the risks from periodic drought, hailstorms, and frost. This cushion enables the farmer to weather seasons of heavy crop loss, such as the severe drought that has afflicted the *altiplano* during the mid-1980s.

Yet the productive capacity of traditional agriculture on an arid and over-used landscape may be nearing its limits. Not only are there more tourists, there are also more Taquilenos. Since 1968 the population has increased by nearly a half, from 850 to 1,250. Increasing economic opportunity also has encouraged a reverse urban-to-rural emigration. Many Taquilenos are returning to their native island from the city, bringing city-learned skills and consumer tastes. If local food production cannot keep pace with new demands from islanders and tourists, traditional agricultural self-sufficiency may well give way to dependency on imports.

The egalitarian character of Taquileno society emerged, in part, from shared poverty. To buy the island from the hacendados in the 1940s and 1950s, the islanders had to pool capital and act collectively. Similarly, twenty years ago no individual commanded the necessary capital and labor to operate a sailboat. So families joined together and formalized rules to protect individual rights within groups.

Tourism has reinforced this communal tradition (through boat cooperatives, for example) and at the same time, has undermined it. With new kinds of economic opportunity, social stratification—previously based on land ownership—has increased. Restaurant and store owners, textile middlemen, and some individual boat owners have developed specialized services. As they prosper, their needs and opportunities tend to diverge from those of the rest of the community. So far, however, the rules of social behavior have acted to regulate competition and Taquile continues to distribute economic benefits with remarkable equity. Everyone—young and old, male and female, the poorest and the better off—have benefited some from tourism. Without question, there is a widening gap between ideal and actual behavior, but despite the gap, Taquilenos continue to attach great importance to their concept of the common good.

Today's Taquilenos walk a narrow path between holding to tradition and accepting change. Tourism is a powerful force that pushes in both directions. So far, there is a kind of balance; yet the flow of tourists has been relatively modest. That the community has managed to accommodate a moderate number of tourists for several years is no guarantee that its adaptability is unlimited.

No one knows what the limits are. Foreigners are now practically a part of the landscape. In the evening they gather to play musical instruments and to drink in the restaurants, a scene reminiscent of a European pub or coffeehouse. Tourists with clicking cameras congregate at all the major rituals and religious festivals. Community life continues, seemingly stronger than ever—but at what point do the rituals and fiestas become simply spectacles for tourists? When does the community become merely a stage?

The intimacy of contact affects the perceptions of both tourists and Taquilenos. For the young foreigner, the Taquileno is not simply a colorful object seen from a passing bus. There is intense and sustained social interaction. The tourist gains an unvarnished look at the poverty and mechanics of Peruvian village life and sees a different set of values and traditions. In turn, he provides an educational experience for the island-bound campesino. Despite language and social barriers, fast friendships do occur. Taquilenos have gained knowledge about peoples and customs in otherwise unknowable lands. Frequently they receive books, photographs, and letters from their new friends in faraway places. The long-term effects on the hosts of this nonformal education are yet to be felt and seen.

Life goes on as it has . . . yet differently. Fifteen years ago, locked doors were unknown, and strong controls were exercised over social drinking. The past six years have witnessed incidents of tourist-related theft and drunkenness, as well as trampled crops, nude bathing, and drug use. There is a growing garbage disposal problem related to more people, more consumption, and more waste. There is increasing acquisition of consumer goods—wristwatches, record players, radios, cassette players, and binoculars. At the same time, the problems in health and nutrition remain as critical as ever. Maternal death in childbirth is high and so is infant mortality. Children continue to suffer from undernourishment, gastroenteritis, and diarrhea.

Services that are created for the tourists do not always carry over to the community. The town's seven restaurants recently collaborated with local officials to install the island's first potable water system, but so far service has not extended beyond the restaurants. Similarly, there are   no latrines beyond those in the restaurants and in a few homes.   When asked recently about the island's lack of electricity, one leader responded, "An electric generator would make too much noise and therefore spoil the tranquility the tourist seeks."

The people are poor and the temptations are great.   "How to please the tourist" has become a major preoccupation. After a few hours with a Taquile family, foreign tourists regularly receive requests of *compadrazgo* (godparenthood) in an opportunistic attempt to hitch up a family to affluent "gringos." Old pottery and rare weavings are sold occasionally in private deals, despite the presence of the museum and explicit rules to the contrary.

Looking to the future, the community must confront two challenges.   First, can the community continue to adjust to and benefit from tourism without being swallowed up by it? Can a strong culture continue to build on its strengths, and will that future community continue to be proud of itself?

The second challenge may be even greater. As tourism becomes a regional and international phenomenon, it is capturing the attention of more outsiders.   Tourism, whether for better or worse, is now controlled by the community, but as the stakes rise, that control cannot be taken for granted indefinitely. Predictably, there will be overtures from government ministries and private and public tourist agencies that will try to gain a foothold in the growing tourist economy.

Such writing is already appearing on the wall. Mounting pressure threatens to undermine community control over boat transport. Taquile suffered its first accident in six years in 1982, which cost the life of a Spanish tourist and three islanders. Official agencies recently stated that all boats carrying tourists must be yacht-size and equipped with the more expensive diesel motors. The issue is one of both safety and travel time; yet this regulation could effectively return control of boat traffic to the private, Puno-based companies. Higher tariffs to insure profitability for larger boats already have been authorized, and Puno agencies are starting to book tourists to Taquile and charging three to four times the islanders' fare. Not only does this represent loss of transport business, but the larger and faster boats permit visitors to make day trips. Day tourists, in turn, buy textiles but do not generate the room and board income that makes up a major portion of the islanders' earnings.

Tourism development plans are greatly influenced by private groups—in this case, by the Puno-based tourism agencies. Yet the government realizes that not only Taquile—but Taquilenos—are a force to contend with in regional tourism. Only a few years ago the islanders were considered too backward to participate in development programs. Now they are viewed differently. They have scored impressive successes and gained valuable skills in administration, communal organization, and lobbying. Tourism has provided an education in how to deal with the outside world.

Currently, the Taquilenos are seeking to reassert their control of transportation. In accordance with the recent regional development plan, they have built a large yacht that has been used in coordination with the smaller motorboats to handle the tourist traffic. With the islanders of nearby Amantani, they are actively soliciting the government to establish a restricted tourism zone in which island enterprises would be protected from encroachment by private, outside entities.

In the meantime, the tourists arrive and leave—more each year. The Taquilenos have shown that tourism, at least on a small scale, need not be managed by outsiders and culturally destructive. Though the islanders' future is far from certain, they continue to build a community industry based on popular participation and equitable distribution of benefits.

5

Indian Colonization
in Paraguay:
What Is Success?

ROBERT J. SMITH, MARIA REHNFELDT,
AND WILLIAM M. BARBIERI

Four centuries after the Spanish entered their forests, the Paraguayan
Indians who have survived are dispersed and isolated in small groups.
Most have no land of their own, and virtually all are excluded from
participation in the modern economy of Paraguay.

The Asociación de Parcialidades Indígenas (API) was created in
1975 to protect the remnants of Indian society and reduce their
dependency on the Hispanic population. The founders of API were
young Paraguayan anthropologists who visualized the emergence of a
pan-Indian organization independent of government that would enable
Indians to speak and act for themselves. API would defend Indian
interests, increase Indian self-esteem, and gain respect for Indians in
Hispanic society. It would also seek directly to improve living
conditions by helping Indians to acquire land and by promoting
agricultural development.

API drew together representatives from nearly every Indian group
in the country. An Indian Council of thirty members, elected by their
communities, was to direct policies and oversee the work of API's staff.
The association was legally registered with the government in 1976,
and the following year it received an Inter-American Foundation (IAF)
grant for its administrative needs and for a land purchase and
settlement program.

The first of two major activities the project supported was the
continued building of a network of Indian organizations. Meetings
were held locally and nationally to unite communities into an
independent, Indian-managed organization. A second activity was the
establishment of seven colonies for previously landless groups. API
was to help purchase land, provide farming materials, establish a credit

fund for marketing and production, and pay the salaries of resident agronomists.

API technicians worked hard to develop the colonization projects, yet the settlements did not evolve according to their plans. In fact, to API's consternation, what was supposed to happen rarely did. The settlements seemed to follow their own haphazard paths, and no one was entirely certain whether they took hold because of or in spite of API's efforts.

API had assumed that successful Indian settlements, like those of other small farmers, would require extensive technical assistance from agricultural experts and that the communities ought to engage in both cash cropping and subsistence farming. In some cases API's strategy worked; in others, technical assistance and cash cropping turned out to be culturally inappropriate. The simple provision of land was all that was wanted or needed.

The story of two groups of API settlers, the Chamacoco Indians from the upper Paraguay River in the Chaco region and Mbya Indians of eastern Paraguay, illustrates the unpredictability of project results, the dangers of drawing conclusions too quickly, and the difficulty of knowing the right amount of financial and technical assistance that is required.

THE CHAMACOCO SETTLEMENT OF BUENA VISTA: PART ONE

The approximately 1,000 Chamacoco Indians in Paraguay had been scattered for many years. Some lived near Fuerte Olimpo with Catholic missionaries, while others lived about 100 kilometers upstream in Puerto Diana with Protestant missionaries and the army. At a meeting of API's national assembly in Asunción, leaders of both groups agreed that they wanted a settlement where all Chamacocos could live together, independent of either religious or military supervision.

When API received funding for its settlement projects, it organized meetings in Fuerte Olimpo and Puerto Diana, and both groups elected representatives to help API's agronomist find suitable land. Finally, it was decided to purchase a cattle ranch about thirty miles inland from Fuerte Olimpo, along with sixty head of cattle and some goats. Twenty men, who were heads of families from the Puerto Diana group, were selected to go ahead to clear the land and plant at Buena Vista. To assist them, API technicians prepared an economic plan that included farming for family consumption, raising cattle and goats, and cutting palm trees for a cash crop. A cooperative was set up to distribute basic goods according to the amount of work each person contributed to the settlement. The agronomist trained one Chamacoco to run the cooperative. A large communal garden was planted with squash, corn, watermelon, and other vegetables. Some of the produce would be for the settlers' own use; the rest was to be sold.

The men worked well together, and the initial planting was a success. After several months their families joined them, and the settlement soon was firmly established. The gardens were abundant, the workers had used only a small part of their available provisions, and API was satisfied that it had a model project in Buena Vista.

THE MBYA SETTLEMENT OF MARCELINO MONTANIA: PART ONE

Whereas everything went right with the Chamacoco settlement, with the Mbya everything appeared to go wrong. A Mbya group had belonged to API for several years. As a member of the organization's Indian Council, their leader, Marcelino Montania, had continually pressed for land for his people. Unfortunately, just as his request was about to be granted and a project to begin, Montania died.

In January 1978, API was still exhilarated by its success in Buena Vista, and despite Montania's death, a project for the Mbya was approved. Without involving the Mbya, an API agronomist found and bought 1,250 hectares in the Department of Canendiyu, far from where they had ever lived. At a meeting to announce the purchase, the agronomist advised the group to select twenty-five families who would go there as the first settlers. It is not clear how he was chosen, but API recognized Marcelino Montania's brother as the group's leader.

In contrast to the meticulous preparations for Buena Vista, the Mbya settlement, called Marcelino Montania, was hardly planned at all. Eager to get the project underway, the agronomist loaded the colonists and their belongings onto the back of a truck and sent them off to the new land. Arriving in the middle of the night, the driver unloaded them and left. On their own, they lay down beside the road and went to sleep.

The next day the settlers found that their property was a long narrow strip of land, with a river running along one of its ends. The settlers built houses near the water, each choosing the best piece of land he could find. The agronomist visited often and tried to promote projects such as hog raising and carpentry. The settlers, however, were uninterested.

Soon the settlers began to take jobs as day laborers for Paraguayan farmers and neglected the development of the colony. When the men did work in the settlement, they worked on their private gardens and left the communal plot untended. Moreover, the Mbya drank most of what they earned outside the settlement. When the agronomist threatened to withhold all aid if the drinking continued, the Mbya countered with a threat to leave.

Three months later a group of API evaluators arrived and pronounced the settlement a disaster. The Mbya had no coherent plan for developing their colony and did not want one. The settlement was unorganized and in seeming disarray. The leadership was weak and lacked legitimacy among the colonists. The income producing projects promoted by API were in dissolution, and the men were once again working for others as day laborers. They continued to be exploited and dependent. Drunkenness, in the view of the evaluators, was rampant and reflected the larger state of social disintegration.

THE CHAMACOCO SETTLEMENT OF BUENA VISTA: PART TWO

The Chamacoco prospered through the summer, but by March people found less and less to do. The planting season was several months away, and one or two men could handle the cattle. Complaints began. First, the API agronomist was accused of rationing the provisions without consulting the settlers. He was unable to convince them that money and supplies were scarce and had to be used efficiently. None of the agronomist's procedures to control cooperative transactions were followed. Indeed, the cooperative functioned only when the agronomist was in the settlement. When he was gone, supplies would be given away and the storehouse left empty.

The settlers subsequently accused the manager of the cooperative of stealing. He and several successors were fired. Fights erupted, and one manager pulled out a pistol and shot at his accusers. He left without paying his debts, taking several families with him.

Others began complaining that Buena Vista was too far inland, that there was no place to go and nothing to do. Men began returning to Fuerte Olimpo to look for day labor.

The Chamacoco also didn't know how to run their cattle ranch, even though they had worked on ranches as hired hands. They over-used and exhausted the animals. The agronomist accused them of neglecting their equipment. The settlers, in turn, accused the agronomist of acting like a *patron*.

The communal garden caused problems when it was time to distribute the harvest. Those who had worked most in the garden wanted its produce. Others disagreed. The disputes became so bitter that the communal garden was disbanded, and each family received its own plot.

API sought to resolve the problems of the settlement by establishing a local governing council. Neither the council members nor other colonists understood what the council was supposed to do. It ended up with no authority. Its members often complained, "Everybody does whatever they want, and no one listens." There were continual resignations. Traditional Chamacoco leaders were replaced by others who were close to powerful figures in the area—missionaries, ranchers, and military officers—but they too were ignored. Meanwhile one family after another left: first those of Puerto Diana and then those of Fuerte Olimpo. The handful that remained was grateful to have their own land, but they were disorganized and demoralized.

THE MBYA SETTLEMENT OF MARCELINO MONTANIO: PART TWO

The abrupt settling of the Mbya had been declared a failure by API. Two years later an evaluator revisited the project to document what had happened. To his surprise, he found a thriving settlement.

Several of the families had moved alongside the main road. They had found abundant water, and their fields were flourishing with manioc and sweet potatoes. The previous harvest had produced such abundance of food that when the Paraguay River flooded, the Mbya colonists sent a goodwill shipment of sweet potatoes to Buena Vista. Now, the men were cutting fenceposts to sell—carefully winnowing so as not to damage the forest. With the income, the community was purchasing materials to construct a schoolhouse. The settlement's population had not grown, but there was space and food for many more people. The colony's leaders said that soon the rest of their group, those living near Tobati, would arrive to join the colony.

The settlement's problems had not all been solved. Medical supplies had run out. The nearby government doctor was accused of hoarding medicine and charging for visits. The schoolteacher had not been paid in more than four months. Fencing wire promised by API had not arrived. The men still drank and accepted work as day laborers. Nevertheless, on balance, the community had achieved independence. It was making its own way on its own terms.

* * *

Why did a project that was carefully planned and executed fail and an unplanned, haphazard effort succeed? There is no simple explanation; however, one factor was that the Chamacoco and the Mbya were different peoples with different needs.

The Chamacoco have lost much of their traditional culture and are seeking greater accommodation with the mainstream of Paraguayan society. But in Buena Vista, they were unable either to adapt to API's project model or to create their own alternative. More technical assistance might have made a difference, but as it happened, the Chamacoco were unable to adjust to what they and API wished to create.

The Mbya, on the other hand, seldom mix with Paraguayans except to earn money. Their traditional social organization and religion are still vigorously intact. They frequently move to new lands, so when they were abandoned on the road they were in a situation that was normal and familiar. The only intrusion was the agronomist, whose forceful opinions on what should and should not be done were a constant annoyance. It was not until API declared the project a failure that the Mbya finally got what they wanted: land, and to be left alone.

EPILOGUE

The anthropologists who founded API worked hard to create an organization that would enable Indians to speak for themselves. Nevertheless, the anthropologists' continuous presence and better understanding of the white world effectively excluded the Indians from participation in the organization's decision making. In fact, the elected executive council did little more than interpret for the communities the day-to-day decisions made by the professional staff.

Yet just as the Mbya needed time and land to establish their settlement, API, as an institution, needed time to build a truly Indian organization. In December 1979, a new and more effective executive council was elected. Although the four Indian members represented different language groups, they were able to communicate among themselves in Guaraní. Meanwhile, funds to pay professional salaries were exhausted. So, in 1980, API's executive council found itself alone, and for the first time it began to make independent decisions.

The operational difference was evident almost immediately as a new sense of solidarity developed within the council and among the tribes. Indian communities began to identify with API not only as a source of land, credit, and medicine, but also as a resource for solving common problems.

By 1981, the four person executive council was all that remained of the original thirty member staff. In order to secure funds to keep operating, council members accepted a temporary assignment from the United Nations to conduct an Indian census. This work enabled council members to visit even the most remote villages. While doing so, they promoted API and broadened their own understanding of problems confronting isolated communities.

In December 1981, a law was passed which provided *personería jurídica* (legal status) to Indian communities and guaranteed their legal right to own land. The law was a milestone for Paraguayan Indians, who did not understand the notion of private ownership. Traditional values emphasized free access to land and water. Under the new law, the community was guaranteed the right to own and control the land on which it lived and worked.

Also in 1981, the executive council was reelected by a general assembly of Indian representatives. Under its leadership, API applied for and received a small second grant from the Inter-American Foundation. This grant allowed council members to continue community visits to explain the new law, to help communities obtain personería juridica, and to help those who had rights to land to receive legal title for it.

Testimony to API's emergence as a respected voice of the nation's indigenous communities appears in a recent edition of *ABC*, Paraguay's principal newspaper. An entire page is devoted to two of API's achievements: the defense of exploited workers in the Chaco Central and the successful negotiations with Itaipu International for land for the Ava Chiripa Indians.

In the first case, API's president learned that Indians working as farm hands were being paid illegally with vouchers redeemable only in a local store. He initially met with the Indians' employers and then with the Indian ministry and finally told the story to the newspapers. The abuses were not only stopped, but perhaps more important, they were publicly repudiated.

In the second case, construction of the massive Itaipu dam involved the flooding of land inhabited by the Ava Chiripa. Although this was their traditional homeland, the Indians had no legal title to it. API's executive council and lawyer negotiated indemnification for the tribe that allowed them to obtain 4,000 hectares of new land.

Neither case in itself reflects a fundamental change in the position of Indians in Paraguayan society. Nevertheless, some progress has been made. API is now Indian-led and Indian-managed. It is demonstrating the capacity of Indians to articulate and defend their interests. Paraguayans are only gradually realizing that Indian interests *are* an issue—and that there is an organization to defend them.

6

Community Participation in Rural Water Supply

STEPHEN COX AND SHELDON ANNIS

Water and sanitation projects can be effective vehicles for promoting local participation in community development. There are several reasons:

- Villagers usually assign a high priority to the introduction of potable water.
- The benefits of potable water are immediate and tangible.
- Water projects can be designed so that their benefits are equitably distributed.
- Everyone in the community can play an active role in the planning, construction, and maintenance of water and sanitation systems.

Yet most rural water agencies are not particularly interested in community participation. Their interest is in the installation of water systems, as many and as quickly as possible. They normally view the extension of water service as an engineering problem—an investment in infrastructure which can be measured by kilometers of pipe laid and number of taps installed. From their point of view, the key question is not whether water projects can promote community involvement, but whether community involvement leads to more and better water systems.

Agua del Pueblo is a Guatemalan rural water and sanitation program that has made community participation its guiding principle. It believes that local involvement in development is a goal worth pursuing for its own sake, that this involvement is an essential condition for building democratic and self-reliant communities. But it also believes that local participation is ultimately a more efficient way to install rural water systems.

What does the abstract notion of "community participation" mean when it is put into practice? Concretely, what does a community *do* when it is "participating"? The case of the village of Pacul, Guatemala, illustrates how community participation in rural water supply can work.

From the outset, the people of Pacul took the initiative. They knew they needed water. After discussing the matter among themselves, they appointed a delegation to seek technical assistance outside the community. When a technician from Agua del Pueblo arrived in Pacul, the town joined him at the spring to measure the flow rate and the quality of the water and to assess the feasibility of building a gravity-flow system. After his study established that the project was technically possible, every household head put his or her signature or thumbprint on an agreement which specified the obligations of both the community and the agency.

Community members were selected at a town meeting to serve as the water committee. The committee met with the program technician to discuss the work to be done. They placed pictograms on a cloth chart to indicate the proper sequence of activities and to assign individual responsibilities. A project schedule was drawn up to coincide with the return of Pacul's men from the coast, where they find seasonal wage labor on the large plantations. The committee conducted a census and prepared a detailed map with color-coded symbols so that committee members who could not read could monitor the efforts of households under their supervision.

Simple pit latrines are a safe and inexpensive means of disposing of human waste. The committee arranged to show a film on sanitary education, learned how to dig latrines, distributed construction materials, and helped their neighbors with installation. Mothers and children attended discussions and demonstrations on personal and domestic hygiene; the technician worked with the schoolteacher to plan games dealing with hygiene and latrine use. The older children learned reforestation techniques and helped the water committee plant seedlings around the spring site to prevent soil erosion that could cause the spring to shift or dry up.

As the project took shape, a meeting was held to decide what portion of the costs the community would pay. A loan was arranged through Agua del Pueblo. The water committee treasurer visited the agency's office to learn bookkeeping and to discuss the collection of monthly maintenance fees and the terms of repayment by the users.

Actual construction of the system did not begin until the design was completed, the budget agreed upon, and the household latrines installed. The tasks of surveying, calculating pipe diameters, and designing the hydraulic system were handled by the technician, though committee members were often on hand to watch and help. Two villagers were elected to work side by side with the construction foreman and to be responsible for operating and maintaining the system.

The committee held a long meeting with the technician and the construction foreman to draw up a work schedule; select a storage site for materials and equipment; and assign each family its responsibility for contributing labor and for collecting rocks, sand, gravel, and lumber.

Construction began on April 11, 1978. The men of Pacul dug 1,760 meters of ditches, helped build storage and distribution tanks, laid pipe, and helped install twenty household connections. On May 19, the project was completed. A community meeting was held to sum up the total costs, collect signatures on the final loan agreement, and plan a festive inauguration.

A little over a year and a half later, an Agua del Pueblo visitor found the *acueducto* to be in excellent working condition. He also found a second piping network that had been subsequently installed. Several months after completion of the potable water system, the water committee had met to discuss taking out a loan for small-scale irrigation. They had located another spring and had sent a delegation to Guatemala City to discuss their plans with the National Agricultural Development Bank. Eventually, their loan was approved, and the irrigation system was installed.

With the irrigation system in place, the farmers of Pacul grew more vegetables for domestic consumption and also began to produce strawberries, a cash crop that brought good prices in nearby Tecpán. The first yields looked promising, and the committee was hopeful that the extra income would permit both water loans to be paid off ahead of schedule.

* * *

The story of Pacul illustrates how participation in rural water supply can be more than just the contribution of manual labor. Rather, it means direct involvement in every step of the process: planning, implementation, and operation. But *why* do it this way?

There are three reasons: first, to ensure that the health benefits that are possible through water and sanitation investments actually materialize; second, to guarantee that the system will keep operating after the technician has departed; and third, because it is less expensive.

HEALTH BENEFITS

The World Health Organization maintains that ". . . in most small towns and villages in rural areas, more health benefits can be gained from money spent on a water supply program than in any other way." Yet money spent does not necessarily produce the health benefits that are promised.

Why? Primarily because most water programs fail to consider the complex behavioral changes that are required if the transmission cycles of water-related diseases are to be broken.

Traditionally, water programs in Guatemala have concentrated on improving the quality of water by substituting the use of a protected source for a polluted one. Yet even if the family is drinking clean water, the fecal-oral pathogens that cause many water-borne diseases may still be ingested if hands are not washed and dishes are not clean. In part, this is simply a function of quantity. If water is abundant, people will use more of it for personal hygiene; but if it is scarce, distant, or expensive, people will use it only for drinking.

The use of water for improved hygiene also depends on information, and this is where community participation can be critically important. In most villages, children and women are the primary victims of water-related disease. The children suffer from diarrhea and parasites; the women must care for them. When women and children have been closely involved in the water project—by choosing the location of taps, for example, and taking part in health education exercises—they learn how water should be used. The process of participation can also be the process of health education.

Similarly, sanitary facilities must not only be installed, they must be correctly used if potential health benefits are to materialize. Even when their commitment to building a new water system is great, villages are rarely convinced of the need for improved excreta disposal practices. As Elmendorf and Buckles pointed out in a World Bank case study, "Behavioral changes in excreta disposal practices came about as a result of gaining the commitment of important committee members who were willing to persistently address the issue on a daily basis within the community in a practical and persuasive manner." Members of the village water committee can serve that role. They not only provide information and advocacy, but more important, they set visible examples by the installation of latrines in their own homes.

A MORE RELIABLE WATER SUPPLY

As many as one-third of the village water systems in the Third World are estimated to be out of commission on any given day. Reinfection with fecal-oral pathogens can take place literally overnight. One recent study found that breakdowns that force people to use contaminated water for only two percent of the time risk undoing the health benefits of drinking clean water during the rest of the year. Providing villages with clean water and changing hygienic practices are of limited value if the water system works only intermittently.

Rural water and sanitation programs that serve many dispersed communities respond slowly to system failures. Sometimes it takes days to hear about a breakdown in a remote village, and additional days, weeks, or even months for a repair team to be dispatched to the site. Yet many rural water institutions continue to use fees from client villages to finance expensive, centrally-based maintenance teams.

Transferring the skills and responsibilities for repair to the community is an effective alternative. A 1979 study of thirty-four Guatemalan village water projects built over the previous fifteen years found that village involvement in operating and maintaining systems was essential for keeping them working. Where villagers had received practical training in operation and maintenance, there were fewer system failures and fewer days per year without clean water due to breakdowns.

To handle this responsibility, a local water committee needs to assign periodic upkeep responsibilities to community members, collect regular fees from beneficiary families, and purchase new tools and spare parts as needed. Direct community control over the fund establishes an incentive for regular, preventive care of the system. In Agua del Pueblo projects, the community is encouraged to invest part of its fund in other community improvements when the balance exceeds anticipated maintenance needs. Controlling the fund allows the community leaders to pay for outside technical assistance as needed, but it does not force them to subsidize either a centralized program or the repairs of other communities that devote less attention to preventive maintenance.

Villagers selected at the outset of the project to work closely with water program personnel can be taught skills for periodic maintenance tasks and most emergency repairs. In the simple gravity-flow water systems most common in highland Guatemala, the tasks are straightforward: periodically cleaning valves and tanks, routinely repairing broken pipes, and replacing worn-out washers or faucets. For these purposes, an adequate supply of simple tools, lengths of pipe, washers, cement, and spare faucet assemblies should be left in the hands of the water committee when the system is completed. Although more sophisticated technologies may require more extensive training programs, the principle of user-maintenance remains valid for nearly all village water system technologies.

In Pacul, a seasonal flash flood destroyed the supports that carried the pipeline over a stream that runs through the village. The next day, villagers who had participated in the construction of the system used their supply of materials to repair the supports and the broken pipeline. Clean water was available again in a matter of hours.

COST SAVINGS

Community participation can help to trim costs in a variety of ways. First, contributions of local materials and voluntary labor may account for significant savings in project costs. Using prevailing market rates, a recent analysis of Agua del Pueblo's projects shows that these inputs accounted for nearly 40 percent of all project costs. Second, a well-organized committee that can deliver these contributions to the project site when they are needed enables the paid technical staff to go about its work rather than wait for supplies or helpers to materialize. Third, community involvement in operation and maintenance saves money by reducing the number of expensive, post-construction site visits by outside maintenance personnel.

Finally, the most significant economic contribution can be the community's sharing of the system's capital costs. The potential for mobilizing local resources for rural water projects can be quite substantial. Agua del Pueblo uses subsidized loans to cover an average of 80 percent of the costs of purchased materials, the transportation of those materials, and the hiring of the construction foremen. The loans carry an interest rate of five percent and are amortized at $1 per family per month.

If the community is to assume a major share of the construction costs by taking out a loan, then the water committee must be legally authorized to collect payments and be trained in bookkeeping and accounting. The community must be satisfied with the system and willing to take on the obligation of loan repayment. The committee must be able to monitor each household's payments in order to avoid communal delinquency.

Agua del Pueblo's requirement that a substantial capital investment come from the community is unusual among water programs, which normally limit the community's contribution to the provision of labor and locally available materials. To date, fifteen of the sixteen loans in the program's portfolio are up-to-date—testimony that communities will pay for services they value and helped to create.

INSTITUTIONALIZING COMMUNITY PARTICIPATION

Can community participation be "institutionalized"? Can an activity that works well in a small private program be equally effective as part of a nationwide water campaign? Do participatory methods rule out the economies of scale that national bureaucracies seek to achieve?

One difficulty is that water systems installed with extensive community participation may take longer to complete. The organization and training of a village water committee, health and hygiene education, and the instruction of local maintenance personnel all require time and effort from program personnel. This time investment may be large, but it is not time lost. A local water committee can free days of a technician's time by locating alternative springs and collecting census information. A committee can guarantee that contributions of local materials and voluntary labor are available when needed so construction can proceed rapidly. Local responsibility for operation and maintenance reduces demands for institutional attention when breakdowns occur.

Another difficulty with institutionalizing participation is that most water agencies do not employ personnel who are able to invest the kind of time that is required. If the water agency is to use participatory methods to build reliable water systems and to motivate the complex behavioral changes required for health improvements, it must employ someone who can communicate effectively with village clientele. This person must be trained to make technical decisions (what size pipe) and also resolve social conflict (where to put the pipe). Someone must explain principles of hygiene and sanitation. Maintenance and repair skills must be taught. If loans are to be provided, a workable mechanism for repayment must be established.

Traditionally, water programs have employed the relatively expensive services of university-educated civil engineers and other specialized technicians for the performance of most on-site tasks. Typically, these technicians are young, urban professionals who have not had extensive rural experience. In some respects, these individuals are both under- and over-qualified for the job at hand.

The solution of Agua del Pueblo is to train multi-skilled field personnel, similar to the health workers who are now common in many primary health care programs. In Agua del Pueblo's program, high school graduates from rural backgrounds receive six months of instruction in surveying, basic hydraulic engineering, system design and construction, latrines, health education, community organization, and project administration. Working under the minimal supervision of a civil engineer, they provide technical advice and support as the communities work through the steps of installing their water systems themselves.

* * *

In December 1980, the villagers of San Juan and Chuacorral inaugurated a joint water system. Like the people of Pacul, these men and women had participated fully in each phase of their water project. Two months later, the joint water committee met in a makeshift schoolroom built with materials collected by their communities. They discussed how to raise enough money to build a more permanent schoolhouse, which they hoped would attract a full-time schoolteacher.

In the long run, their talk of schoolrooms, irrigation systems, electrification, and access roads may be the most eloquent testimony to the lasting value of participatory water projects. And in the short run—it should not be overlooked—their water was clean and running.

7

Conservation Kuna-Style

PATRICK BRESLIN AND MAC CHAPIN

When a Kuna Indian awakens on one of the small coral islands off the Panamanian coast where most of his people live, his gaze wanders past the thatched houses of his neighbors, out over the low-riding canoes of farmers headed for their mainland plots, and then across a mile or so of shimmering water to a mass of green forest rising, virgin and luxuriant, to the ridge of the San Blas mountains. At his back, the sun climbs above the calm Caribbean, and its first rays strike the tufts of mist snagged like fleece in the clefts of the hills. For generations, this dawn panorama, serene and unchanging, has greeted the Kuna people.

But if he were standing atop the 2,400-feet-high San Blas range, the view down the other slope would be less reassuring. Large swaths of thick vegetation have fallen victim to the machete and the torch. Ash-gray tree trunks stand above the denuded landscape, skeletal remnants of the once-towering jungle.

For several years now, peasants from the increasingly arid interior of Panama have been slashing and burning—implacable as soldier ants—toward Kuna land. Cattle drove many of them from their previous homes as ranches, producing beef for the international market, expanded onto farming land. And cattle are close behind them again. In three or four years, when the newly cleared and shocked land will no longer support subsistence crops of bananas, rice, corn, and manioc, farmers will plant pasture and try to sell their holdings to the ranchers. In a few more years, the ecologically fragile soils will be so leached that even cattle ranching will fail. The tracks of this future can be read on the San Blas' southern slopes and lower ridges, where the erosion that will inevitably claim all the cleared acres has already begun.

Panama's land-hungry peasants are involuntary recruits in a massive army on the march throughout the tropics. If unchecked, this process will complete the destruction of the world's tropical rain forests in our children's, if not our own, lifetimes. Some 900 million hectares of tropical moist forest remain; but it is disappearing, according to a 1981 United Nations satellite study, at a rate of 7.3 million hectares a year. Other, more pessimistic estimates put the annual loss as high as 20 million hectares.

If the tropical forests disappear, countless plant and animal species will vanish, many of them before man has had a chance to name, much less study, them. About half the world's estimated five to ten million plant and animal species are found in tropical moist forests. Yet according to the U.S. government's recent report, *Global 2000*, as many as one million of those species could be extinct at the end of the century.

In many parts of the tropical world, the assault seems uncontainable: expanding populations, central governments driving forward with development schemes, the spread of agriculture and ranching for the export market, the resulting concentration of land ownership that forces peasants to strike out for the frontier, all pose threats to the forests. But in Panama, a well-organized native people, with support from the scientific community and a host of international agencies, may be able to save one of the last remaining virgin rain forests in Central America. The Kuna have decided to turn part of their reservation into a forest park and wildlife refuge, with research facilities for scientists from around the globe. When the administrative and housing center opened to scientists in late 1984, Udirbi (in the early 1980s, the project site was named Nusagandi) became the first park of its type in the world created and run by an indigenous group.

The Kuna are one of the few indigenous groups in all the Americas to survive the impact of the white race with cultural and political autonomy intact. When the Spaniards made their appearance in the early 1500s, Kuna territory encompassed large tracts of the Darién jungle, spanning the isthmus from the Atlantic to the Pacific coasts. Over the centuries the Kuna have retreated into the Comarca of San Blas—a thin band of jungle running some 200 kilometers along the Atlantic coast, east to the Colombian border. Today, some 30,000 Kuna live spread out among more than sixty villages located on small islands hugging the coast or at the mouths of rivers.

Living in this jungle fastness, which until recently could only be reached by small plane or launch, the Kuna have evolved into the twentieth century largely on their own terms. Never conquered nor subjugated, they are the sole masters of their territory. According to Panamanian law, no non-Kuna can hold claim to land within the reservation. While tourists flock to the islands to photograph the Kuna and buy beautiful reverse-appliqué *mola* blouses, tourism is locally controlled and regulated. If travelers spend the night in San Blas, they stay in hotels owned and managed by Kuna.

Although the Kuna are in many ways insular, they are by no means strangers to the modern world. Since the 1930s, thousands of Kuna men have worked in what was formerly the Panama Canal Zone in Panama City. Kuna women dressed in their traditional wrap-around skirts, red-and-yellow head scarfs, and exotic *mola* blouses are a familiar sight on the bustling streets of the capital. And the Kuna are easily the best-educated tribe in Panama, even perhaps in Central America. Many Kuna students study at the National University and abroad, and the number of professionals has grown steadily during the past decade.

At the same time, the Kuna have not been so enticed by foreign ways that they have lost sight of their roots. They govern themselves according to custom, resolving disputes and making decisions in town meetings that are held nightly in most villages and in semi-annual General Congresses of local representatives. These traditional institutions bind the Kuna together as a nation and set the tone for everything in San Blas.

From the very beginning, the Kuna have approached the West more like careful department store shoppers than awe-struck primitives. They have an instinctual ability to search through the wares of Western culture, pick out those ideas and techniques that seem useful, and then tailor them to their own traditions. They approach the world with confidence assured of their own worth and even superiority. So conscious and proud are the Kuna of their culture, so fluent in discussing it, they can sound at times like a convention of anthropologists. And in all their discussions, the Kuna invariably stress the identification of their culture with a specific expanse of land—the Comarca of San Blas.

"We say that this land is our mother," Leonidas Valdez explained. Valdez is the second-ranking of the three *caciques* (chiefs), who are the principal spokesmen for the entire Kuna people. "And the land is also the culture. Here are born all things necessary to our culture: the fronds we use for the puberty ceremonies, all the foods gathered for our communal feasts, the materials our artisans use, what goes into the construction of our houses. All of it comes from the forest. If we were to lose this land, there would be no culture, no soul."

A threat to any part of the Comarca is instantly perceived by the

Kuna as a threat to their survival as a people. Growing out of a deep-seated respect for the land and a quiet determination to protect it, the Udirbi park is an example of how the Kuna utilize new ideas and techniques to serve old values.

Indeed, greater numbers of policymakers throughout the world are beginning to view their natural resources in a similar light. Until recently, people and governments in many tropical countries considered their rain forests obstacles to be conquered if their nations were ever going to break the shackles of poverty and under-development. In Latin America, the pillaging attitudes brought by the avid-for-gold Spanish and Portuguese conquerors in the sixteenth century have persisted into the present. After much of Latin America won its independence early in the nineteenth century, its urban intellectuals continued to regard the vast wildernesses of the southern pampas, the wastes of the Chaco, and the great jungles of the Amazon basin and Central America with a mixture of fear and fascination. The wilderness was supposedly the realm of the savage: it was the untamed, backward side of the Latin American character, which the intellectuals contrasted with the civilized traits of the Europeanized city. To the popular imagination, the jungle was dangerous terrain—teeming with mysterious and fatal diseases, predatory animals, and hostile Indians armed with venom-tipped darts. But there too were the futures of their countries, the riches that would one day lift them into the ranks of the wealthy nations. Latin America was the continent of tomorrow, and the path to development would inevitably cut through the wilderness.

Although the rain forests had been penetrated since colonial days in pursuit of gold, rubber, precious woods, cacao, and other riches, a full-scale assault could not be mounted until the middle of the twentieth century, when medical advances neutralized most tropical diseases. Equally important, national populations were growing rapidly along with popular aspirations for a better life. Pressure intensified on a land-holding system that left most productive land in the hands of a few rich families. As the clamor for land reform grew, governments sometimes found it politically easier to push colonization of untouched jungle than to attack the basis of economic and political power. During the past three decades, many Latin American countries have embarked on ambitious campaigns to open up their previously almost-inaccessible wilderness areas. Brazil hurled itself into the Amazon basin by carving out a brand new capital city 600 miles inland. Peru envisioned a road east of the Andes that would open up its Amazonian provinces.

In Panama, the zeal for development was personified in the figure of General Omar Torrijos, Panama's strongman ruler from 1969 to 1981. One day in 1980 his helicopter skimmed over the San Blas rain forest towards a meeting of Kuna leaders on the island of Narganá. The sight of so much virgin forest impressed Torrijos, and later that day, when he rose to speak in the Congress, he chided the Kuna leaders: "Why do you Kuna need so much land? You don't do anything with it. You don't use it. And if anyone else so much as cuts down a single tree, you shout and scream." A Kuna leader named Rafael Harris stood and responded:

> If I go to Panama City and stand in front of a pharmacy and, because I need medicine, pick up a rock and break the window, you would take me away and put me in jail. For me, the forest is my pharmacy. If I have sores on my legs, I go to the forest and get the medicine I need to cure them. The forest is also a great refrigerator. It keeps the food I need fresh. If I need a peccary, I go to the forest with my rifle and—pow!—take out food for myself and my family. So we Kuna need the forest, and we use it and take much from it. But we can take what we need without having to destroy everything as your people do.

According to Aurelio Chiari, administrator of the Udirbi project, who tells the story with great relish, Torrijos was left speechless. He could only stride across the Congress hall and wrap the Kuna leader in an emotional bear hug.

Increasingly, history and scientific research confirm the Kuna view of the rain forest: it is a source for a multitude of beneficial products, but at the same time it is something fragile that must be cared for. As developers lured by visions of great wealth have cut their way through tropical forests, the true ecological vulnerability of those areas has become apparent. To the layman, tropical forests conjure up images of inexhaustible fecundity, of lush, irrepressible growth. Plants spring up overnight, then push their trunks and stalks a hundred feet into the air and sprout leaves of elephantine size. The most varied forms of insect and animal life buzz, chatter, hoot, and shriek. Panama, for example, has more species of birds than the United States and Canada combined. A square mile of rain forest can contain as many varieties of plants as all of the British Isles.

Despite this amazing variety, the fecundity turns out to be literally skin deep. Top soil in the jungle is often just inches thick, and because of the constant rain—over 250 inches a year around Udirbi—it is rapidly leached of most nutrients when the forest cover is cut. The towering trees, the thick vines, the giant ferns must all draw their nourishment from shallow root systems that efficiently recycle whatever drops into their maw. It takes only hours for a fallen leaf in the grip of surface feeder roots to decompose back into its constituent elements.

When the forest is cut, left to dry out, then burned, there is a temporary enrichment of the top soil by the nutrient-laden ashes. But the continuous cycle of regeneration that supports the rain forest has been sacrificed. Food crops planted by settlers suck up the soil's limited store of nutrients; the tropical rains wash away more; and within three years or so, the soil is exhausted, capable only of supporting grass. If the land is hilly, erosion will soon eliminate even the grass.

Until recently, Kuna lands seemed safe from this specter of a grim and swift pasage from jungle to farm to pasture to desert. Although less than 100 miles from Panama City, the Comarca is sheltered behind a mountain range cloaked with almost impenetrable jungle. It was practically inaccessible by land until a branch road from El Llano on the Pan American highway opened about fifteen years ago. The road brought a gradual influx of settlers who opened farms along its flanks. But the real threat first appeared in the 1970s when the government launched its "Conquest of the Atlantic Coast," a campaign to open up the largely unsettled Caribbean side of the isthmus to landless settlers from the interior provinces. As part of that campaign, the El Llano road would be pushed over the ridge and down the northern slopes of the San Blas to Cartí on the Caribbean coast.

From the start, the Kuna were of two minds about the El Llano-Cartí road. Plane trips from Panama City were becoming ever more expensive as the cost of fuel rose in the mid-1970s, and the journey by launch out of the port city of Colón was lengthy and uncomfortable. The Kuna welcomed the prospect of easier movement for themselves and their goods between San Blas and Panama. But the tribe also worried about encroachments from peasant squatters moving steadily nearer to the southern rim of the reservation. With a fine sense of geopolitics, the Kuna realized that the point of maximum danger was a place called Udirbi, where the new road would enter the Comarca. It was there that they had to establish a presence.

In 1975, Guillermo Archibold, a young leader with experience in agronomy, went to Udirbi with a small group of volunteers to found an agricultural colony. Udirbi, named for a palm tree common in the area, is in pre-montane rain forest near the summit of the San Blas mountains. When not blanketed with rain clouds, the site offers a spectacular view across more than 20 kilometers of jungle out to the Gulf of San Blas and the densely populated islands of the Cartí group. The terrain is broken—a jumble of steep hills unlike the flat, sunnier land near the coast where Kuna farming is concentrated.

Archibold and the volunteers started by planting staple crops—corn, manioc, bananas, and yams. The results were disappointing, so they switched to tree and bush crops—coffee and cacao, peach, palm, cashew. Most would not grow in the cool, wet climate; those that did were stunted. Attempts to raise hogs, chickens, and cattle also failed. In early-1981, frustrated, the colonists consulted forestry specialists from the Centro Agronómico Tropical de Investigación y Enseñanza (CATIE), a regional agricultural research and teaching center based in Costa Rica. The CATIE foresters soon confirmed what the Kuna had already discovered the hard way: the land at Udirbi was unsuitable for agriculture and should be left in its virgin state.

It was then that the idea emerged to make the entire top of the mountain ridge at Udirbi into a park. Over the next two years, the Kuna consulted with scientists, foresters, and technicians from a wide variety of institutions: CATIE; the Smithsonian Tropical Research Institute (STRI) in Panama; the Center for Human Ecology in Austin, Texas; the Tropical Science Center in San José, Costa Rica; the Agency for International Development (AID); and the Inter-American Foundation (IAF). The foreigners quickly became enthusiastic about collaboration with the Kuna in developing a forest park, and the project picked up momentum.

Even as the Kuna reached out for assistance, they made sure that the project remained firmly in their control. AID provided funds to train Archibold and his followers in park management at CATIE's headquarters; during this time a plan took shape. By mid-1983, the Kuna had the key elements in place: they had selected a planning committee of young Kuna professionals and enlisted financial and technical support from local and international institutions. The Udirbi project was launched on a scale that outstripped earlier hopes. What had started almost a decade before as a spontaneous yet vaguely conceived indigenous effort to protect the reservation from invasion had become a full fledged and complex campaign aided by a prestigious lineup of international allies.[1]

Though they start from radically dissimilar world views and have become involved in the park for very different reasons, the scientists and the Kuna are discovering that they share a common goal—preservation of the virgin forest along the crest of the Continental Divide. For scientists, the Udirbi park offers a large expanse of previously unstudied forest with a great diversity of unique flora and fauna, including some eighty endangered species.

For the Kuna, the idea of preserving the virgin forest for research is not foreign, even though their rationale differs from that of biologists. They already keep small reserves of virgin forest on land that is often ideal for agriculture and located on the mainland near their coastal communities. According to the Kuna, these untouched reserves are domains belonging to potentially malevolent spirits prone to rise up in anger and attack entire communities if their homes are disturbed. No farming is allowed within the boundary of the spirit domain, and certain of the larger trees may not be chopped down. The Kuna believe that the spirits string their clotheslines in the branches of these trees and become justifiably furious when they are felled. These "spirit sanctuaries" are true botanical parks, since they may be used by medicine men to gather herbs.

Not only did the idea of a park at Udirbi fit with Kuna culture; the pragmatic Kuna were also quick to see that it would serve their goal of protecting the Comarca as well as, if not better than, an agricultural community. The main body of the park will cover some 20 square kilometers of virgin forest, with clearly marked boundaries permanently patrolled by Kuna forest rangers. A group of nine rangers has already been trained at the site and in Costa Rica. Some of them are Kuna members of the Panamanian National Guard assigned to the park. Others are trained as guides for the scientists who will eventually visit the site.

Except for technical assistance from CATIE, part of which is funded by World Wildlife Fund, the entire direction of the park is in Kuna hands. Guillermo Archbibold, the young leader who has been involved in the Udirbi project since the first days of the agricultural community, is the park's technical director, and Aurelio Chiari is the program administrator.

The presently rustic facilities at Udirbi were improved during 1984 to accommodate scientists willing to rough it to pursue their research. More permanent and comfortable facilities are planned to house between forty and fifty visitors as well as park personnel. The housing will be built on a high knoll at the original Udirbi site, with its spectacular view. The only infringements on the virgin forest will be nature trails and observation sites and several substations for scientific research. Architects are working closely with the Kuna to develop a design for the new buildings that will fit into the environment and reflect native culture.

These new facilities will serve not only scientists engaged in research projects, but a special kind of visitor the Kuna hope to attract —the "scientific tourist" drawn by the uniqueness of the region, the great beauty and variety of the plant and animal life. Bird watchers, for example, are most definitely welcome.

Thanks to the new road, the park will offer scientists and visitors an unusual combination: a pristine rain forest that is only two hours from a major city with a busy international airport. For scientists, an added bonus includes nearby laboratories and photographic-processing and communications facilities—much of which has grown out of the presence in Panama for more than sixty years of the Smithsonian Tropical Research Institute (STRI).

"There is a great unexploited potential for scientific tourism in Panama," said Ira Rubinoff, STRI's director. "Because this is a narrow isthmus, there is an enormous concentration of species of animals and birds. The bird flyways are funneled through here. There are few places like this left in the world, and the great attraction, of course, is that there is a good prospect for this being saved. That's the beauty of working with the Kuna. If their Congress accepts an idea like this, then they'll do it. You can count on it."

Brian Houseal, a young park management specialist who works as a full-time consultant for the Udirbi staff, emphasized that the Kuna's new park will not only preserve virgin forest and facilitate basic research but also provide unique opportunities for applied studies of agricultural techniques appropriate to tropical areas. "Again, there's so much we need to learn," he says. "The models of land use now current in the tropics are really not suitable. Some temporary use is gained from the land, but the end result is destruction. You just have to look at the other side of these mountains to see that. We need to study the techniques used by groups like the Kuna, who have lived in these areas for centuries without destroying them. They've developed technologies that are appropriate for tropical agriculture."

"We must control this chaotic use of tropical land," Rubinoff says. "The Comarca is a good example of using the tropics in a planned way. There are areas, like the park, which should be a reserve. There are other areas that are perfect for agriculture. But we need to learn how to use that land. At least now we know that the way to approach tropical lands is through seduction, not rape."

The Kuna, of course, have always known that. When the Kuna stand on their home islands and contemplate the jungle-shrouded slopes of the Comarca, they gaze, according to oral traditions, at the "green-clothed" body of the Great Mother, who is Earth. Those stories say that in the beginning she came naked. Her union with the Great Father produced all of the vegetation (which became her "garments"), the animals, and finally humans. Each season, the Earth replenishes her supplies of living things: plants grow and flower and yield fruit; fish are delivered from the Earth's body in rain-choked rivers and turbulent seas; and animals fall from the clouds that float low over the jungle. The act of periodic regeneration, together with nurture and maternal protection, are themes that the Kuna repeat in their culture.

If the Udirbi project ultimately succeeds in preserving the virgin rain forest of San Blas for scientific study and for future generations, the main reasons will be the Kuna's careful husbandry of their values and their special relationship with the land—reverential, affectionate, and intensely personal.

NOTE

1. The institutions that initially funded the project include the Inter-American Foundation, Centro Agronómico Tropical de Investigación y Enseñanza, World Wildlife Fund, Smithsonian Tropical Research Institute, and the Agency for International Development.

PART 4

Organizations and Making Money

During the 1970s, social reformers in Peru and Chile tried to create and organize a sector of small- and medium-sized businesses that were owned and managed by their workers. It was hoped that these firms would become an engine for economic growth, providing new and stable jobs for underemployed, often recently migrated, urban workers. The new sector would fill the gap between the small workshops that typified the unorganized, informal economy and the large industries that dominated the national economy. . . .

—Martin Scurrah and Bruno Podestá

8

What To Think About Cooperatives: A Guide from Bolivia

JUDITH TENDLER
with Kevin Healy and Carol Michaels O'Laughlin

I visited four peasant cooperative associations in Bolivia and came away perplexed. On the one hand, the four groups—which are described below—were decidedly successful in certain ways. On the other hand, they lacked some of the basic qualities considered vital to this kind of success. In fact, they had various traits and problems that we usually associate with failure. My puzzlement over this strange combination of success and inadequacy, and my struggle to reconcile the two sides of the picture I saw, were the inspiration for most of what is written here.

A word, first, about the nature of the success I witnessed, before describing the seeming mismatch between success and inadequacy. The most obvious achievement of the Bolivian groups is that they still exist, almost ten years after their creation. Though they have not yet suffered the ending of outside donor funding, their survival and active life are something of a record, when compared to many other endeavors to organize rural cooperatives in Latin America. A second category of achievements of the Bolivian groups is the benefits they provided to peasant-farmer members and, in many cases, nonmembers: (1) better prices, greater reliability, and honest weights resulting from cooperative purchasing and marketing of their crops, using coop-owned trucks; (2) better prices, honest measures and weights, and unadulterated products available at coop stores supplying consumer staples and agricultural inputs (the price differential tended to diminish after awhile, in marketing as well as retailing, either because coop prices drifted back toward prevailing prices or because private merchants adjusted their prices downwards to meet the coop competition); (3) savings in transport and other expenditures for farmers who previously had to travel some distance to buy consumer staples and inputs, and now could buy them nearby; (4) transport savings to producers resulting from the establishment of coop processing facilities (rice mills, cacao-processing plant) where before there were none; (5) availability of credit to those who previously had no access to banks; and (6) new opportunities for employment and apprenticeship in coop service operations, of which agroprocessing created the most jobs.

In addition to these benefits, two of the coop associations provided benefits to whole communities through community infrastructure projects undertaken in their early years—schools, potable water, irrigation, road grading. Another association initiated a campaign to combat cacao blight, which could have a significant impact on grower incomes. And the agricultural equipment-rental service of one association allowed peasant farmers to move from shifting to stable agriculture, and from rice-growing to cane-growing, with corresponding increases in income. Many of the benefits named here were reaped by nonmembers as well as members.

These direct benefits of coop activity tended to diminish as the groups struggled with the problems of running a business. Perhaps more enduring than the direct benefits were some less tangible results. In each region, the coop association represented one of the few institutions voicing the economic interests of peasant farmers. As organized groups, with one or another successful business ventures to show for themselves, the associations were able to (1) make effective claims on public-sector goods and services available previously only to larger farmers (official lines of subsidized credit, agricultural research and extension services, favorable tariff treatment for imported equipment, etc.); (2) gain entry to private-sector industry associations (of rice-millers, rice cooperatives, grape growers, grape distilleries), from which the coop associations gained valuable information about prices and marketing, and in which they could wield some influence on the side of peasant interests; and (3) set an example of how banks and public-sector agencies could relate to peasant groups, creating some confidence in these powerful institutions about the possibility of working with such groups and giving both sides experience with what such a relationship could be like. Again, these benefits were available to members and nonmembers alike.

Viewed against this picture of benefits, the inadequacies of the coop associations were striking. The most impressive inadequacy was in the area of management and administration. Prices charged for merchandise and services were sometimes too low to cover costs, credit collection was casual, inventory and sales records were often not kept, coop leaders were frequently the largest borrowers from coop credit funds, and acts of malfeasance were common.

The second surprising inadequacy of the coop associations had to do with membership growth. Membership seemed to stop growing at an early stage, even when the associations were expanding their services and income-earning activities. Each association had an average of twenty member coops with seventeen members apiece, totaling only 350 members. At most, coop membership reached only 25 percent of the families in a community, and a much smaller share of the population of the area served by the association of coops. Given that each association group had received roughly $350,000 from the Inter-American Foundation, the small size of membership could mean an average investment of $1,000 per member family—in addition to significant investment in the form of member and other donor contributions and IAF staff expenditures. Measured against the low-cost model of development assistance aspired to by the IAF, these costs would appear to be disappointingly high—an appearance modified significantly when nonmember benefits are taken into account.

The final shortcoming of the four Bolivian groups had to do with leadership. Leadership and management positions usually rotated among the same few persons, who were among the better-off members of the community. Though entrenched and better-off leaders are not necessarily incompatible with success, they are usually thought of as leading to trouble—e.g., misappropriation of coop goods and services, programs that benefit only a select few, and corrupt behavior that flourishes in an environment where there are no "democratic" pressures to be accountable.

It is obvious why the first inadequacy, weak management, would be cause for surprise. We are used to seeing this problem singled out, after all, as the cause of coop failure. It is not obvious why we are bothered when coops have small and declining memberships, little participation, and entrenched leaderships. What does this matter, if they succeed in generating some significant benefits? The problem lies partly in our vision of coops as participatory and democratic. If they do some good, it is hard for us to believe that they are low on participation. In reaction to this contradiction, we tend to see more participation and less control by entrenched leaders than actually exists or, more skeptically, we suspect that significant benefits for the poor have really not been achieved. Also, when we find that our favorite qualities are lacking in coops, we tend to prescribe or fund remedies for catching up—more training in cooperativism, more rotation of leadership, more drives to expand membership.

CAST OF CHARACTERS

Of the four groups visited, El Ceibo and Bella Vista are located in the same region. The Alto Beni is a subtropical region where the government carried out large colonization projects in the 1950s and 1960s, after which the public sector virtually withdrew and vigorous spontaneous migration followed. Cacao, coffee, bananas, rice, and corn are the principal crops; cacao, introduced by the colonization project, is the only export crop produced by any of the groups studied (coffee is marketed only domestically).

El Ceibo (Central Regional de Cooperativas "El Ceibo," Ltda.), a 350-member association of eighteen coops located in the cacao-producing area of the Alto Beni, was founded in 1976 by four small village groups that banded together to market cacao. Ceibo now buys 60 percent of the cacao marketed in the Alto Beni and, with its own 10-ton truck, markets it in La Paz, an eight-hour truckride away. On the backhaul from La Paz, Ceibo brings consumer staples that it wholesales to the small consumer stores of its member coops. Ceibo also operates cacao-processing and drying plants, where it ferments and dries about 40 percent of the cacao it buys (it purchases the rest home-dried); and, it has a small chocolate factory in La Paz, which absorbs less than one percent of the cacao marketed. Ceibo is now embarking upon an agricultural extension program to combat cacao blight, which has decimated much of the cacao plantings in the area.

Of the four groups, Ceibo has taken on the smallest number of activities, concentrating almost exclusively on cacao marketing. It is the only one of the groups without a credit program, and the only one without a retail consumer store operation; it is also the only one to have succeeded at a wholesale store operation. Partly because it attempted less, Ceibo seems to be the most successful of the groups in terms of its finances and its impact on the region. IAF support for Ceibo, starting in late 1980 and amounting to $200,000, was for (1) operating capital to purchase cacao, (2) construction of a second drying plant, (3) purchase of a second truck, (4) cooperative education, and (5) the salary of an administrator for the cacao-processing operation.

Bella Vista (Cooperativa de Ahorro y Crédito "Bella Vista," Ltda.), situated in the higher coffee-producing zone adjacent to El Ceibo, started in 1969 as a savings and loan cooperative that was closely guided by a Franciscan priest. Receiving outside funding in the late 1970s, Bella Vista expanded into the marketing of coffee and rice, acquired a small rice mill, opened a large consumer store, and continued its savings and loan operations. With about 200 members dispersed throughout the area, Bella Vista is the only one of the four groups that is a large single coop; the others are associations of small affiliated coops based in communities of less than one hundred families. Partly because of the geographic dispersion of Bella Vista's membership, it was the most precarious of the four groups; it also experienced a major loss of capital and in community confidence because of political repression resulting from its role in organizing a strike of the Alto Beni's farmers against increased trucking rates and other policies of the military government. IAF support for Bella Vista, starting in 1978, amounted to $185,000, and was used for (1) the purchase of a 14-ton truck, (2) operating capital for marketing, (3) operating capital for a consumer store, (4) a fund to promote eradication of coffee rust (a plan that did not materialize), and (5) cooperative education.

CCAM (Central de Cooperativas Agropecuarias Mineros, Ltda.), an association of twelve member coops with a total of 309 members, is located in the eastern lowland region of Santa Cruz, a center of Bolivian agricultural growth during the last twenty years. Growth was stimulated by heavy government investments in colonization, transport and power infrastructure, agroprocessing, and credit and other subsidized inputs for commercial agriculture. CCAM's members produce mainly rice and corn, with the better-off minority growing sugar cane and occasionally vegetables. Founded in 1972 and assisted for many years by a Maryknoll priest, CCAM was the most highly capitalized of the groups, mainly as a result of various donations for equipment. The association started out with rice marketing, and then acquired (1) a large rice mill and, later, storage and drying equipment; (2) an agricultural-equipment rental service (including a bulldozer and motorgraders used for opening and maintaining access roads, as well as land clearing); (3) trucks for a transport service; (4) a wholesale and retail consumer goods operation; (5) an equipment-repair shop; and (6) a credit fund for production loans. Of these activities, the rice mill is the most profitable.

In the early 1980s, CCAM became the only one of the four groups to receive funding from a large donor, the Inter-American Development Bank ($500,000). CCAM was also the only group to secure short-term production credit from a local private bank for lending to its members; it succeeded in repaying the loan. (From the same bank it also obtained operating-capital credit for its rice mill.) IAF support to CCAM, amounted to $206,000 between 1974 and 1983, and was used for (1) operating capital for the consumer-store operation, (2) grain storage and drying facilities for the rice mill (still to be completed), (3) a revolving-credit fund for production loans to members, and (4) the replacement of pontoon bridges washed out by floods.

COINCA (Cooperativa Integral Campesina), a 400-member association comprised of twenty coops in the southernmost department of Bolivia (Tarija), was founded in 1975 by a Jesuit social action agency, Acción Cultural Loyola (ACLO)—the only one of the four groups to have been created by an intermediary or "facilitator" organization. Tarija is a highland valley area of much older settlement than the Alto Beni and Santa Cruz, and suffers acutely from the twin problems of minifundization and soil erosion. Tarija's peasants produce potatos and corn; the better-off grow wine grapes, citrus, and vegetables—mostly on plots of no more than a few hectares, compared with the 12- and 25-hectare average plots in the Alto Beni and Santa Cruz. Tarija's peasant farmers are unique in their long use of chemical fertilizer on their potato crop, making fertilizer supply one of the mainstays of COINCA's activities.

COINCA operates a revolving loan fund for production credit to members (severely decapitalized through inflation, low interest rates, and delinquency), an agricultural-input supply operation, and a small winery (its most profitable operation) along with a technical assistance and credit program for grape growers, who are the better-off 30 percent of members. COINCA succeeded in obtaining government credit and assistance for a poultry-raising project for member coops and was the only group to sponsor some collective production projects (many have not done well). Partly because of the philosophy of its founder organization, ACLO, COINCA undertook more activities than any of the other groups, perhaps contributing to its being less successful than El Ceibo and CCAM.

IAF support for COINCA, starting in 1976, has amounted to $415,000, and was used for (1) a credit fund for production loans, (2) operating capital for a consumer store operation, (3) construction of a headquarters and store building in the capital city of Tarija, (4) purchase of a vehicle, (5) administrative salaries (COINCA was the only group with a paid, outside professional manager, agronomist, and accountant), and (6) an education program. (The winery operation was funded by a German volunteer agency.)

Coops with entrenched leaderships, small and declining memberships, and weak participation also cause us concern because of the faith we, as donors, have placed in them. We see coop groups like the Bolivian ones as more desirable and genuine approaches to the alleviation of rural poverty than many programs of the public sector—particularly in countries with weak, hierarchical institutions serving the countryside or with repressive regimes that are unsympathetic to a more proportional distribution of public-sector goods and services. If the membership of even the successful peasant federations is so paltry after so many years of our support, then how can we maintain our faith in these groups as a hopeful alternative to the deficient public sector?

Finally, we are uncomfortable with an entrenched and better-off leadership, because we think it leads to an elite-biased distribution of coop benefits. This kind of distribution, after all, is what has disappointed us so many times about the programs of the public sector. If coops are to have an impact on the rural poor, in other words, we expect them to be larger and growing, more democratic and participatory, with a leadership that rotates more vigorously and reaches more broadly into the community.

My search for ways to see the inadequacies of the Bolivian groups as more in harmony with their achievements led to four kinds of explanations: (1) the inadequacies turned out to be not as problematic as they are usually thought to be—or, resolving the problems was not always a prerequisite for doing well; (2) some of the problems were the side effects of *improvements* in management; (3) some of the inadequacies were more troublesome when they occurred in combination with certain crops, social structures, and tasks; and (4) certain tasks were distinctly more vulnerable to management inadequacies than others. All this is not to say that the shortcomings of the Bolivian groups are not to be taken seriously. Rather, the causal link between problems and failure—and between "prerequisites" and success—turned out to be looser than we are used to thinking it to be.

SPILLOVER AND ARRESTED GROWTH

After almost ten years of life and several years of IAF support, the Bolivian farmer associations were not only small, but they did not seem to display much impulse to grow. By 1982, moreover, all three of the associations had informally expressed a desire to stop growing at about 400 members. Why this arrest in membership growth, especially in cases where coop income-earning activities were expanding at a steady pace?

People did not join the Bolivian coops, or ended up leaving them, for various reasons: (1) coop work obligations were burdensome, (2) hopes for patronage refunds were not fulfilled, (3) episodes of corrupt and incompetent leadership caused disillusionment, (4) it was not always in the interests of leaders and members for membership to grow, (5) the agricultural-production services provided by these associations were largely irrelevant to people with little land or none at all; (6) people did not have to join in order to reap some of the most important benefits of coop action—the so-called "free-rider problem," and (7) certain improvements in management caused membership to be less attractive, or actually led to the cutting off of membership growth. The last two reasons are the most important and the least obvious, so I give them special attention here.

All the Bolivian groups engaged in agroprocessing, marketing, and consumer stores. Each of these activities served nonmembers as well as members, meaning that benefits reached far beyond the 350 member families. It was not benevolence that caused the coops to allow their benefits to "spill over" to those who did not join. Rather, it was the simple economics of their task: to achieve the volume of business required for the economic operation of a rice mill, a store, or a 14-ton truck, these small coops and their associations needed a larger number of buyers and sellers than the membership provided. Economies of scale, in other words, "forced" the groups to allow some of their benefits to be enjoyed by nonmembers.

In addition, three other "structural" traits of certain coop tasks caused them to spill benefits to nonmembers: (1) for activities that provided public goods (roads and road maintenance, potable water, schools), limitation of use to members or any other particular group in the community was not feasible or customary; (2) for some activities, members could not realize full benefits unless nonmembers participated too (control of contagious crop and livestock diseases); and (3) in some cases, innovations had a propensity to spread by themselves (agricultural practices that can be easily copied by observing neighbors, seeds and other inputs that are commonly traded among neighbors, and improved pasture grasses and other plants that spread like weeds). In all these cases, small and nongrowing coop memberships would not necessarily be a cause for concern, since the activities engaged in assured the spillover of benefits.

The spillover activities of the coop associations contrasted sharply with other activities like credit to individuals, collective production projects, and paid jobs in coop enterprises. These goods and services were not ruled by economies of scale, were usually in scarce supply, and hence were available to members only. Though this exclusive access was good for attracting new members—since it handsomely rewarded those who joined—it did nothing to help spread benefits the way spillover activities did.

The free riders

Spillover may be good for reaching large numbers, but it is bad for the growth of members and their capital contributions. People do not want to contribute to a coop if they can get their benefits without joining. Cooperativism, like labor unionism, is quite familiar with this "free-rider problem" and has laid down some basic rules for avoiding it. One such rule is that purchasing and marketing operations should provide benefits to consumers only in the form of profit distributions or patronage refunds (which can be limited to members)—and not in the form of better prices (from which all buyers will benefit, member and nonmember alike). In this way, the coop can take advantage of the nonmember's contribution to business volume and economies of scale without having to provide a reward through better prices.

Why didn't the Bolivian groups try to cut down on spillovers and reduce the adverse impact on membership? First, the income-earning activities of these groups did not generate enough profits to distribute—a not unusual outcome; when profits did materialize, they were often commandeered to cover losses in other coop activities or to capitalize expansions. Second, and also common, the Bolivian groups found it hard to charge prices that covered their costs if those prices were as high as prevailing prices—even if it meant they returned profits to member-patrons at the end of the year. To adhere to prevailing prices, they thought, was to behave exactly like the "exploitative" middleman whom they were supposed to replace—and hence would stand them in bad stead with the community. In this sense, the Bolivian associations were behaving contrary to what one might expect of a small group with a better-off, entrenched leadership: they were setting prices with a social conscience. (Sometimes, unfortunately, these "socially conscious" prices did not cover costs.) Patronage refunds and prevailing prices, in sum, do not always represent realistic policy choices for rural groups like the Bolivian ones, even though they may be the best way to attract members and keep away the free riders.[1]

Success and dependence

Small membership is bad for coops because it translates into very little self-generated capital, which is supposed to form the basis of cooperative independence.[2] Like many coops assisted by outside donors, the Bolivian groups enjoyed the luxury of not being dependent on member capital for their growth. Good performance in their ventures earned them outside donations for projects far beyond what they could have raised through increased capital contributions from members. That the groups were financially dependent as a result was not really a concern for them or for their coop promoters. Indeed, they saw their "dependence" on outside donations as allowing them to be independent of the public sector in their own countries.

In order to gain a different perspective on the financial dependence of the Bolivian groups, it is helpful to remember that the model of an independent agricultural coop, financed out of capital contributions from members, is more descriptive of North American historical experience than of current Latin American reality. In North America, rural coops were formed mainly by medium and large farmers with the capacity to make significant capital contributions, whereas in Bolivia and many other Latin American countries, farmers of these means often constitute only a better-off few. In Latin America, in other words, the financially independent coop may be an unrealizable goal—if we expect these organizations to draw their members from among the poor.

The acid test of the strength of donor-funded coops occurs, of course, when outside funding stops. None of the Bolivian groups had reached that point, even though some are over ten years old. Critics of the groups argue that they would be nothing without their outside funds and patrons, while supporters argue that self-sustaining success requires many years of outside support. Though the Bolivian groups might indeed have collapsed or severely contracted if their outside funding had been withdrawn, it is impossible to know what strength and resources they would mobilize if this state of affairs were actually upon them. Until the acid test takes place, moreover, these "financially dependent" groups end up providing some important services to the peasant economy over a long period—as well as building skills among the peasantry and the strength to deal with a powerful, nonpeasant world. The success of many such groups, finally, is often crowned with their "adoption" by the local public sector—at least in terms of financial support—so the acid test never takes place. Some of the concern about financial dependence, therefore, may be pointless.

Good management versus growth

In addition to the spillover dynamic, there was another good thing about the arrested growth of the Bolivian groups. Some loss of membership and discouragement of potential members was a result of certain attempts by the coop associations to improve management. CCAM and COINCA, for example, placed a moratorium on accepting new groups after the associations' third or fourth year of existence. They did this to reduce the losses arising from delinquency in credit and store operations—two activities particularly vulnerable to management inadequacy. The associations themselves contributed to these problems by being casual about delinquency, accounting, and the charging of interest. But they now wanted to reform their ways, after witnessing the erosion of capital caused by their laxness.

Growing memberships made it difficult for the Bolivian groups to work on these problems.[3] Because each new coop usually wanted a store and access to credit, the only way for the associations to start reducing their credit-caused problems was to refuse to accept new member groups or, at least, to not vigorously promote them. Also, some would-be members, and even old members, lost interest in membership upon learning that credit would no longer be so easy. From the coop's point of view, of course, this loss represented a desirable process of self-selection, whereby would-be delinquent borrowers were discouraged from joining.

Given the credit problems of the Bolivian groups, characteristic of most coop credit and store operations, it is not surprising that El Ceibo was the only one of the four groups to show an interest in expanding its membership: it was the only group without a credit program and the only one to operate its store system under a unique barter relationship by accepting cacao in exchange for merchandise. These differences meant that membership expansion was not as troublesome for El Ceibo as it was for the other groups.

CCAM and COINCA took a vigorous approach to the problem of store credit by "de-linking" store expansion from the creation of new coops. They centralized their store operations in one place under their direct control; and they severed the wholesale relationship with affiliated stores or exercised greater control over the stores' prices, profit margins, and management practices. In that these latter improvements involved less "local control" of the affiliated store, they made the member coop look more like a buying and selling outpost of the association—at least with respect to the store activity—than like an independent and democratic community body. The marketing operations of El Ceibo also resembled this more centralized, less "democratic" way—with member coops seeming more like "buying agents" for the association than genuinely participatory community bodies. Though the cooperative as buying agent may not jibe with our image of cooperativism, it may nevertheless be consistent with achieving a broader reach for otherwise limited coop benefits.

It is not new to say, as I have here, that the growth of high-spillover activities like marketing and stores can be choked off by the need to create a new cooperative every time the association wants to expand its service into a new community. In the late nineteenth and early twentieth centuries, the coop movement in the United States experienced considerable controversy over the question of federated versus centralized coop associations. Proponents of the federated, "bottom-up" form saw it as the only way to achieve truly democratic organizations. Proponents of the centralized, more "top-down" associations pointed to the difficulties of creating numerous, capable local organizations and of thereby achieving the volume of business necessary to obtain significant bulk discounts. Many of the more centralized associations, like the Grange, commonly sold through field agents or local entities and sometimes even private merchants. This was the only way to achieve scale economies, they thought, without having their efforts unduly constrained by the slow process of creating myriad affiliated organizations from scratch.

The Bolivian associations might also be able to expand their services with greater facility, and benefit more people, if they resorted to this more "centralized" approach in some activities—training persons who reside in unserved communities, for example, as paid field agents for marketing. And the centralized coop association, though perhaps more "top-down" than the federated ideal, still represents a highly decentralized and local institution in comparison to the public sector and its "local" agencies. It is this comparison to the state, in turn, that is behind the argument of many coop supporters in favor of coops as a "better" approach to improving the conditions of peasant farmers.

Barter is another way to reduce the management problems of store operations, illustrated by El Ceibo's combination of consumer merchandising with the purchasing of cacao. Barter, of course, is also the time-honored practice of many private merchants in rural areas who sell consumer staples on credit and receive payment in harvested products. In the hands of private merchants, the barter relationship is considered by many to be exploitative of the peasant.

A more drastic approach than barter to problems of store credit is to ban credit completely and sell only for cash—as dictated by the principles of Rochdale cooperativism. Though the Rochdale approach makes excellent management sense, the barter model of El Ceibo and the "exploitative" rural middleman may be preferable on distributional grounds: rural stores are often the only places where the poorest community members ever get access to credit and, therefore, are their lifeline to consumer necessities during hard times. Here is another case, then, where the pursuit of good management and healthy cooperativism is at odds with social equity—and where donors, therefore, should pay special attention to finding ways to preserve the more equitable results.

To sum up, arrested growth of coop membership need not always be a cause for concern. It may sometimes be a welcome sign of improved management—as long as benefits spill beyond members and the growth of coop activities is not tightly linked to the formation of new coops. When growth is arrested by activities that are particularly vulnerable to management problems—namely, stores and credit funds—donors might consider shifting their funding to other activities that are less demanding of socially difficult behavior, more compelling of management skills, less vulnerable to management inadequacies, or less linked to membership growth.

THE STRUCTURE OF TASKS, SOCIETY, AND THE ECONOMY

Entrenched and better-off leaders, living off coop spoils, have been the bane of cooperative history—in both North and Latin American. The principles of Rochdale cooperativism were designed to prevent this: coop officials must be elected by the membership, new elections must be held yearly, and elected officials cannot hold paid positions in the cooperative. The leaders of the Bolivian coops and their associations looked exactly like what these principles were meant to avoid: they were the better-off members of the community, the same few were re-elected year in and year out, and these leaders or their relatives held the few paid positions in the organization. If other groups with leadership like this came to unfortunate ends, how were the Bolivian groups able to do better?

We have already identified two reasons why entrenched leaders are not necessarily a problem. First, if one views the member coop as a local buying and selling outpost for the coop association, then an entrenched person in charge is not necessarily so bad, and may even have some advantages. Second, some activities like marketing, processing, and stores force coops to spill their benefits widely. For these activities, therefore, the reach of a coop's benefits will be in some ways beyond the self-interested control of the entrenched leaders. But why would entrenched leaders choose spillover activities in the first place if they were only looking after their own interests? This is where a strong influence will be played by social, agronomic, and economic conditions—in conjunction with the nature of the coop's task.

Fragmentation and leadership

The role played by the social environment is the most obvious. Three of the four Bolivian groups were comprised of member coops based in small hamlets of twenty to one hundred families. (The fourth, Bella Vista, was a large coop with no affiliates.) Each association was headed by leaders who rose through these member coops and continued to live in their home communities; even those few leaders who were exceptions to this pattern maintained strong ties to their communities, continuing to cultivate and live there part time. Like the other members of their small communities, these leaders were farmers—not merchants, traders, teachers, and shopowners who were often found at the head of rural coops.

Though the leaders of the Bolivian groups were definitely from among the better-off members of their communities, they shared as farmers the same economic interests as their poorer farming neighbors—the desire for better crop prices, lower transport costs, access to production credit, and consumer staples and agricultural inputs at lower prices. This contrasted with the merchant and trader leaders of coops with headquarters in larger rural towns. As businessmen, they would not be at all happy to see their coop charging lower prices than their own for consumer staples, or offering higher prices to growers, or introducing low-cost credit. The pursuit of self-interest by this latter kind of coop leadership has, in various instances, most certainly conflicted with the interests of farmer members.

That an entrenched and better-off leadership is less of a problem if it is based in small, dispersed communities, where mostly growers live, takes us back to the problem of membership growth: putting together and running an association of 350 members is more difficult if twenty different coops in twenty different communities must first be created, than if one can be put together in one central town. Thus the Bolivian associations' success of avoiding non-farmer leadership was partly at the cost of a much more difficult organizational task.

Crops and their social character

The agricultural economy of each coop environment determines whether leaders define their interests as consistent with those of the community. Of the four groups, El Ceibo seemed to exhibit the most socially concerned behavior and generated the greatest amount of spillover, even though its leadership was as entrenched as that of the other groups. At CCAM, in contrast, one heard criticisms of "elite dominance" and "rich peasants looking only after themselves"; the leadership had motorbikes or pickup trucks and second houses in the busy cantonal capital where association headquarters were located. Why El Ceibo did better than CCAM at being egalitarian is revealed by the strikingly different socio-economic structures of the two areas.

Unlike the Alto Beni, home of El Ceibo, CCAM's Santa Cruz exhibited a strong socio-economic differentiation on the basis of crop. In Santa Cruz, poor peasant farmers grew rice and were usually situated far from roads. The better-off farmers, in contrast, grew sugar cane and had good access to roads. Rice was grown under the shifting slash-and-burn system, requiring the eventual abandonment of one's land and the perpetual moves to new areas of virgin forest on the nearby frontier.[4] Sugar cane was competitive only when grown on land cleared of tree stumps using mechanized land-clearing and land-preparation techniques. Cane also needed to be near good transport because of its perishability, once harvested, and the low value of cane in relation to its volume. The differences between sugar and rice meant that the only way for a peasant to improve his income markedly in Santa Cruz was to have well-located land, access to machinery for land clearing and preparation, and credit to hire labor. Even getting this far, a peasant still could not market his cane without buying a quota at the local mill, which generally was not interested in selling quotas to small farmers.

In the Alto Beni, there was no such differentiation by crop. Everybody could plant the high-value crop (cacao) from the start, no matter what his location or means. Though cacao was also perishable, it had the advantage over sugar cane of being amenable to home-processing if one did not have ready access to transport. (Most Ceibo members sold their cacao home-processed.) As a perennial crop, of course, cacao requires more capital to establish than annual crops like rice—leading one to expect economic differentiation between better-off growers of cacao and the poorer growers of annual crops. But cacao, known as a small-farmer crop, was considerably less demanding of capital than sugar cane and was perfectly competitive without mechanization. And most growers in the Alto Beni had access to capital for starting cacao—in the past, through government credits provided by colonization projects, and later, through assistance to new settlers from their established relatives.

Finally, the remoteness of the Alto Beni from its consumer markets and the resulting difficulty of transport made marketing the most important problem. The marketing problem was a great equalizer, since it afflicted better-off and poor farmers alike. The gains farmers dreamed of had to do with reducing their transport costs and increasing their selling prices for cacao—and not with shifting to higher-value, more capital-intensive crops. (Likewise, farmers expressed little concern about gaining access to credit.) In comparison to sugar cane in Santa Cruz, then, cacao's characteristics lessened the social and economic gap between better-off and poorer farmers in the Alto Beni. Correspondingly, there was no differentiation by crop between El Ceibo's leadership and its rank-and-file. This was in contrast to the distinct differentiation at CCAM between the cane-growing leadership and the rice-growing rank-and-file, not to mention the rice-growing nonmembers.

The cane-growing interests of CCAM's leadership led to coop activities that, coincidentally, had an inherently low spillover potential. A peasant farmer wanting to shift from rice to cane—as all rice-growing peasants in Santa Cruz who accumulated a little capital wanted to do—could be helped by four types of coop activities: (1) agricultural equipment services (cane was competitive only on land cleared of trees by bulldozers and ploughed by tractor); (2) credit to hire labor (of the three regions, agricultural wages were the highest in Santa Cruz); (3) transport on which one could be absolutely reliant (because of cane's perishability); and (4) access to a cane mill (cane growers could not sell cane without buying a quota from the mill). CCAM's activities were concentrated in precisely these four areas: it was the only one of the three groups that ran an agricultural equipment-rental service, obtained credit at a private local bank for lending to members, and had a fleet of its own trucks, which were used mainly for cane transport. (CCAM also used a large amount of donated capital to purchase a cane quota.) None of these activities had the forced spillover potential that processing, marketing, and stores do.

Because the agro-economic environment of the Alto Beni defined an "equalizing" crop and activity (cacao and its marketing) as the most urgent need of farmers, El Ceibo was automatically drawn to a high-spillover activity that brought benefits to better-off leaders, poorer members, and poorer nonmembers alike. In Santa Cruz, in contrast, CCAM was drawn to the low-spillover activities of credit, agricultural equipment services, and transport dedicated to a minority of peasant farmers—dictated by the region's high labor costs, the possibility of improving peasant incomes by changing crops, and the need for mechanization to bring about and sustain that change. CCAM's entrenched and better-off leadership also contributed to make things work out this way, of course, but certainly not without the help of these structural conditions.

Remarkably, this same set of structural conditions worked in exactly the opposite direction in the case of CCAM's rice mill, despite the association's cane-grower leadership. While the difficulty of cane-milling excluded that activity as a way for the leadership to pursue its own interests, rice-milling presented a much easier venture. Since the cane growers also grew rice, rice-milling was not an unlikely next step for them to take in the cooperative venture. Though the rice mill would also benefit the poorer rank-and-file and nonmembers—and hence might not have been as desirable to the cane-growing leadership as the more focused equipment-rental, transport, and credit services— the mill also turned out to yield more profit and fewer problems than these other services. To sum up, four "structural" factors in CCAM's environment combined to draw the association into successful rice-milling—a high-spillover, and "equalizing" activity: (1) the impracticality of going into cane-milling, (2) the widespread cultivation in Santa Cruz of a crop (rice) for which the processing task was particularly easy, (3) the centrality of this crop to poorer-farmer income, in addition to its being cultivated by the better-off cane-growers, and (4) the fact that agroprocessing was an easier task than the credit, transport, and equipment operations taken on by CCAM.

Another example of the interaction of the agricultural environment with social impacts comes from El Ceibo. In the Alto Beni, cacao disease became so serious in the late 1970s that it reduced yields by more than half over a period of only four or five years. Eradication of cacao disease therefore came to be an urgent concern of the Alto Beni farmers; knowledge of eradication techniques and the ability to apply them represented a conspicuous way to increase grower income. Campaigns against contagious crop diseases, of course, have high spillover effects because everyone must participate in order for anyone to be protected. In addition, demonstrations of the new technique (mainly radical pruning) are like a public good—anyone can attend or can copy from his neighbor. Like the Alto Beni's marketing problem, then, cacao disease was a great equalizer. It attacked large and small producers alike and required participation by small producers in order for the crops of better-off producers to be free of disease. And because a contagious crop disease was such a pressing problem in the Alto Beni, El Ceibo was drawn into an activity with inherently high spillover benefits.

Fertilizer supply is another example of how the agricultural economy of a region and the economics of a particular task combine to determine the benefit distribution of an association's activities. Of the four groups, COINCA was the most involved in agricultural input supply, particularly fertilizer. Fertilizer supply was the centerpiece of its early success; in the beginning, it had sold fertilizer at half the prevailing price and, even when that differential disappeared, it still marketed a product with the rare reputation of being unadulterated and honestly weighed.

When coops supply fertilizer, there is a good potential for spillover benefits because significant discounts can be obtained on large wholesale purchases. The coop, as in the case of COINCA, wanted to sell to as large a number of users as possible. (Fertilizer supply was also an easier management task in comparison to the supply of consumer staples.) In addition, Tarija was one of the few places in Bolivia where peasants have been using chemical fertilizer for quite some time on a traditional crop—potatoes. Fertilizer was not used at all in the Alto Beni or in Santa Cruz, even for the cane grown by upwardly mobile peasants. In these areas, there were almost no crops with a yield response as high as for potatoes; and the abundance of land, in contrast to Tarija, made it cheaper to exhaust land and move on than to invest in returning nutrients to the soil. Even though fertilizer was used widely for potatoes in Tarija, moreover, it was not used in wine grapes, Tarija's "upwardly mobile" crop. Like rice in Santa Cruz, finally, Tarija's potatoes were a cash crop grown by better-off as well as poorer peasants. This means that any improvement in the price, quality, and availability of fertilizer would be in the interest of the better-off coop leadership as well as the poorer farmers.

The socio-economic environment of Tarija dictated that COINCA go into fertilizer supply and that this activity could have a broad social impact. The CCAM case was different: the socio-economic environment produced a leadership that was distinguishable from the rest of the membership by the crop it produced and by coop activities that tended to increase the distance between leaders and poorer farmers. Rice-milling was the significant exception.

Structural conditions, finally, also led COINCA into making wine and providing credit and technical assistance to grape growers, much as such conditions led CCAM into rice-milling. As an activity, the task of wine-making had the same desirable traits as rice-milling. But the distributional traits of wine-making were just the opposite of rice-milling: it kept benefits limited to a minority of better-off grape-growing members rather than spilling benefits widely.

In Tarija, in sum, two "easy" tasks were undertaken—fertilizer supply and wine-making—as dictated by the agro-economic environment. One had highly desirable distributional qualities and the other, just the opposite. The same kind of leadership produced both activities.

Entrenched leaders and trouble

Though entrenched and better-off coop leadership is often a cause for concern, it is nevertheless what one usually encounters in agricultural coops. That this kind of leadership occurs whether or not coops are successful or socially responsible suggests that we need to find other causes for the problems usually attributed to this phenomenon. Though donors have little power to change the nature of coop leadership—and it may not be their place to try to do so—they can exercise some control over the more undesirable effects of entrenched leadership. This can be done by choosing tasks to finance, and environments in which to finance them, that will bring out the similarity of interests between the better-off leadership and the rest, rather than their differences.

Because we associate trouble with entrenched or elite leaders, we have perhaps failed to notice a few distinctly positive aspects of such leadership. First, entrenched leaders can provide continuity to a coop as a service and income-earning enterprise—a continuity that is quite valuable, in light of what we have learned about the frequent disruption of public-sector programs caused by high turnover of their managers and staff. Second, better-off community leaders often have considerable entrepreneurial experience and drive, which can make the difference between success and failure of a coop business venture. In this sense, the coop "exploits" the skills and interests of its entrenched leaders. Third, in many Latin American communities, a community leader is expected to perform at least some socially responsible deeds. The coop provides an opportunity for the leader to meet these expectations as a way of achieving and maintaining status in his community. By drawing on entrenched community leaders, then, the coop can be seen as hitching certain socially obligated persons to its cause.

Our thinking about the problems of entrenched leadership by a few better-off persons has been confused somewhat by our concern about "the bottom 40 percent." With some exceptions, the Bolivian groups provided few direct benefits to that group—the landless and near-landless poor. But this was less a result of the coops being run by a better-off and entrenched leadership than of their being organized around the supply of services to agricultural producers—and thus "irrelevant," as some of the Santa Cruz landless said, to their needs. Agricultural coops, in short, are not the best way to reach the landless, unless through the employment effects of increased farmer incomes—a "trickle-down" approach to poverty that most proponents of coops do not accept. If a criticism of coops is to be made, then, it is not that a better-off entrenched leadership ignored the poorest, but that donors chose to support an inappropriate instrument for reaching the poorest.

SUCCESS AND INADEQUACY

How were the Bolivian coop associations able to grow and take on more activities while plagued by weakness in management? A clue can be found in the four tasks undertaken by all the groups—credit, consumer stores, marketing, and agroprocessing—and the fact that performance was consistently better (or worse) at certain of these tasks than at others. Agroprocessing ranked as the best-performed task— followed, in descending order, by marketing (including trucking operations), stores, and credit. Management inadequacies, in other words, seemed to be partly related to the nature of the task. Problems were consistently more prevalent in some activities than in others, leading one to suspect that some tasks were easier than others, or less vulnerable to bad management, or more demanding of good management. That might be why success and inadequacy could coexist.

That agroprocessing would be the least vulnerable to the management problems of rural coops comes as a surprise. Processing and other forms of manufacturing have often been considered by coop advisers to be too difficult for struggling agricultural groups like the Bolivian ones—in terms of the technology of the task, the complexity of the market, and the large investment required for fixed capital. Credit programs and consumer purchasing operations, in contrast, require almost no such technological and market expertise and little or no investment in fixed capital. But in terms of management, processing turns out to be remarkably "easier" than credit and stores. In some ways, moreover, it is more tolerant of lax management; and in other ways, it is more likely to induce good management. In order to explain why, I outline briefly the major problems of credit and stores.

Credit and stores

The most striking management problems of coop credit and store programs fall into three areas: (1) the setting of prices for merchandise and credit (interest rates), (2) credit-repayment policy (most stores sold on credit, at least to start out), and (3) accounting practices. Like many other coops, the Bolivian groups frequently charged prices for their services that were too low to cover costs. According to coop rhetoric, prevailing prices reflect the machinations of "exploitative" middlemen, who will be replaced by coops that charge lower and "just" prices. This rhetoric has invested coop prices with strong social symbolism, making it difficult to charge prices that cover costs.

Two instructive exceptions to the problem of inadequate pricing were the prices charged by CCAM for rental of its bulldozer and by El Ceibo for transport of cacao. The only piece of agricultural equipment that CCAM charged cost-covering rates was its bulldozer; unlike CCAM's other equipment, bulldozers were not available locally for rental from private suppliers. In setting its rental price, therefore, CCAM was not constrained by a prevailing bulldozer-rental price that it felt obligated to undercut, regardless of cost. El Ceibo, in turn, was able to "charge itself" a full cost-covering rate for truck transport when it bought the cacao and incurred the transport cost of marketing itself (an "internal cost"). This contrasted with the case where Ceibo transported cacao or other produce for producers, without buying the product. In this latter situation, the transport charge was quite direct and visible, paid by the farmer accompanying his produce. But when the transport cost was "internal," it was less visible to the farmer, since it was one of several components in the margin between Ceibo's buying and selling price for cacao. With the more visible "external" transport price, Ceibo felt obliged to charge an inadequate one-third less (and lower than prevailing prices) than it charged itself for the "internal price" of transport, as reflected in the marketing margin. Ceibo could get away with charging the higher price on internal transport, it explained, because nobody would know or complain. When the price charged was "hidden" along with other costs in the marketing margin—or when there was no prevailing price to undercut—it was easier for coops to use criteria of cost and financial viability in determining the prices they charged.

Casual repayment policy, as seen above, also contributes to the problems of credit and store operations. Coops find it very difficult to be tough about repayment because it means being hard on their own people—particularly their leaders, who are often the largest borrowers and who play an important role in making decisions about who gets credit. Rigorous repayment policy spoils the comfortable and rewarding aspect of credit and store programs—the act of giving—because delinquent borrowers must be denied new credit and purchases. Together with the difficulty of charging adequate prices, these repayment problems cause the operating capital of coop credit and store operations to dwindle rapidly.[5]

Whereas the difficulties of price-setting and credit policies were partly social and political, those of bookkeeping and accounting for store and credit programs were more a result of inadequate skills. A store manager had to keep track of many small transactions with different units of measure and different prices; the same had to be done with inventory (it rarely was) and for sales on credit. A credit manager needed even more fluency with arithmetic in order to make the various interest calculations for each repayment installment. Though these accounting requirements do not seem overwhelming, they turned out to be so for groups with no experience at it and with little training in arithmetic. As a result, the accounting was often simply ignored. COINCA lent from an IAF-financed rotating credit fund for three years without recording any of the transactions, and Bella Vista's large consumer store could not take time out to record transactions or give receipts because there were always "too many customers waiting in line."

Agroprocessing and marketing

When viewed against these problems of credit and stores, agro-processing begins to look less complex—but in an administrative rather than a technical sense. In contrast to stores, processing and marketing involve the simple aggregation of units of a homogeneous product—unmilled rice, cacao beans, wine grapes—with a standard measure and price. This contrasts with the consumer store's breaking down of things into small amounts, and its myriad measures and prices—a more complex process that presents greater opportunities for graft. Graft is also less likely with agroprocessing because the product belongs to the farmers, and they will be directly affected if they do not get their return. Misappropriation of credit or store merchandise, in contrast, does not affect coop patrons directly—even though it is bad for the coop and, in the long run, for its patrons. There are strong social pressures against graft in agroprocessing and marketing, then, that are not present in store and credit operations.

Setting adequate prices is easier when coops are engaged in agroprocessing and marketing. All growers, of course, will want the coop to sell their crop at the highest price possible. In marked contrast to credit and stores, the marketing coop can charge what the market will bear—since the buyer is an impersonal outsider, or even an adversary, for whom the coop has no particular concern. Similarly, there is little social constraint on the prices charged by the coop for the various components of its marketing or agroprocessing services—transport, labor, fuel, depreciation of equipment, overhead—because these prices are not directly in view. They are aggregated into a total that is reflected in the margin between the coop's buying and selling price, as seen in El Ceibo's "hidden" price for transporting cacao.

Though the coop's marketing margin is clearly of concern to growers, and very much in view, the costing of each item in that margin is less evident. Prices charged for credit and merchandise (and hauling and equipment rental), in contrast, are more visible and easily subjected to invidious comparison with prevailing prices.

Agroprocessing and marketing are in no way burdened with anything similar to the difficult social problem of being tough about credit repayment. Improvements in the management of agroprocessing and marketing usually are "technical" tasks—greater utilization of capacity, better scheduling of buying and selling operations, and arrangements for timely delivery of working capital. Though all of these problems can be major, they are not politically or socially difficult to handle.

One of the most remarkable differences between agroprocessing and credit or store operations is the effect of mismanagement on capital. If stores and credit operations cannot deal adequately with prices, repayment, and accounting, they will lose their operating capital and jeopardize the very existence of the operation—as happened with CCAM and COINCA. But if the management demands of a rice mill or a cacao-processing plant are not met, the coop will not lose its capital. It will simply earn less income, or none at all, while the plant stands idle or is poorly used. In this sense, agroprocessing is more tolerant of lax management than credit and stores, regardless of how easy or difficult it is.[6]

Agroprocessing, and its embodiment in equipment and buildings, is endowed with a certain protective isolation from meddling. Decisions about plant operation are less interesting or less within the understanding of members than the topics of who gets credit, what kind of merchandise should be bought for the store, what rates should be charged for credit, and what prices should be charged for merchandise. The separate and "unknowable" nature of a production task also makes it easier for coops to justify handing over the activity to an outside technician. The four processing operations of the Bolivian groups—two rice mills, a winery, and a cacao-processing plant—were run as separate businesses, which members could "join" without subscribing to other coop activities. CCAM's winery and the large rice mill were run by paid outside professionals—an enologist and an experienced rice-mill operator—who kept an iron control over the books. Agroprocessing performed better, in sum, because the inaccessibility of the technology, together with the inconspicuous nature of the prices charged for the various components of the marketing margin, helped to keep meddling opinions and disruptive political pressures at bay. Agroprocessing was desirable, in other words, because it kept "participation" out.[7]

Agroprocessing has another positive feature. Like any construction project, coop processing plants usually elicit large member contributions in labor and in materials such as sacks of concrete or loaned tools and equipment. (This is in contrast to the ongoing labor contributions required of members for collective plots and for storekeeping, which are often disliked by members and potential members.) New coop members are frequently allowed to pay their capital subscription in labor and materials—as occurred with the construction of Bella Vista's rice mill. Credit and stores, as well as trucking and agricultural-equipment rental, offer no such opportunity for member contributions—except for cases where the coop constructs the store building rather than occupying an existing structure. The membership, therefore, does not feel the same pride of ownership for the credit fund and the store's inventory as it does for the processing plant. Processing installations, finally, enable coop associations to get credit at local private banks; both COINCA and CCAM obtained commercial credit—an unusual achievement for coops still dependent on donor financing—by pledging, respectively, their winery and their rice mill as guarantees.

Another way of expressing the argument is that agroprocessing does better than credit and store operations because it requires a project that finances capital, rather than operating, costs. Donors have been criticized for indulging in just these kinds of projects and neglecting the less glamorous projects where operating costs are central and not overshadowed by capital costs. In various ways, however, the Bolivian agroprocessing plants were not stereotypical capital projects. The technologies were "appropriately" rustic, the construction techniques were labor-intensive, and the operation of the plants generated the most employment of all coop activities. The plants also represented linkages forward from agricultural production, providing growers with the opportunity to appropriate more of the value added to their crop. In addition, the profits of the processing operations were crucial to covering the losses in the areas of credit and stores, allowing the coops not to be completely undone by the costly learning process of these latter activities.

The processing plants, in sharp contrast to credit and stores, were more tolerant of lax management, because it would not necessarily lead to a loss of capital. At the same time, lax management would result in a failure to earn income from one's investment. In this sense, the processing task contributed to eliciting good performance: one could not utilize plant capacity fully and earn income from it without good management. On the other hand, when donor funds are provided for budget support and operating capital, the recipient gets the income and a first round of benefits without having to first perform. All these qualities make the "capital-intensive" agroprocessing project look more appropriate than it would seem—at least when compared to the less capital-intensive credit and store programs or to general budget support. Given certain conditions, then, the donor weakness for capital-intensive projects may not be all that reprehensible.

Agroprocessing is not without its disadvantages. Along with marketing, the agroprocessor runs the risk of making one large mistake in judgment that can cause a tremendous loss. Bella Vista, for example, withheld its rice from the market in the expectation of a large price increase and ended up having to sell below the original post-harvest prices. Similar tales of woe are a common theme in the history of cooperatives, both successful and failed. With credit and stores, in contrast, loss of operating capital through poor management is gradual—perhaps one reason why it is tolerated for so long. The agroprocessing (and marketing) accomplishments of the four groups did not come easy, then, but these activities also did not suffer from the problems and sustained losses that credit and stores did.

Whether or not a coop should go into processing will be dependent on the crops its members produce, the nature of available technology, and the market. Rice-milling cacao-drying, and wine-making were all accessible technologies, and their markets were not difficult to enter. (Cane-milling was not; though it would have been a "natural" step for CCAM's cane-grower leadership to undertake, it was more complex and capital-demanding, and the market was more formidable than the rice-milling operation for which CCAM settled.) Another example of accessible processing activities comes from the history of U.S. agricultural coops in the late nineteenth and early twentieth centuries, when coop processing was succesful only in dairy products and fruit drying (raisins, figs, and nuts). As in the Bolivian case, rustic technologies were already available for such production, and processing was already being carried out by farmers at home.

In deciding whether to support coop proposals for processing operations—which sometimes seem frighteningly ambitious—donors can learn to distinguish between the easily-mastered technologies (and markets) and the more difficult ones. A cross-project look at what has worked can also provide some help—with the Bolivia projects suggesting grain milling and the initial stages of cacao (and coffee) processing —and the U.S. experience suggesting fruit drying and, based on the experience of many other countries as well, dairy products. Each case, however, has to be judged on its merits. Processing will not always be appropriate.

The problem of free capital

With our knowledge of the winning qualities of agroprocessing, we can now understand better the problems of credit and stores. Grant-funded credit operations do poorly, in part, because the coop association does not have to pay the money back. It is not forced, therefore, to take on the disagreeable task of being tough about borrowing requirements, repayment, and interest rates. Thus it was that CCAM started to get tough on borrowing qualifications and repayment, and to charge prevailing interest rates, only when its IAF-financed credit fund was so decapitalized that there was no other alternative but to seek a private bank loan for more capital. "Free" donor capital, then, seems to be a culprit in the credit problem. But the agroprocessing projects also received free capital from donors, yet this did not create the same serious problems—except for some casualness, on occasion, about excess capacity. Indeed, free donor capital for agroprocessing seemed to facilitate rather than hinder improved management, by providing time for the coop to make mistakes and learn the business.

How could it be that free capital was a problem for credit but not for agroprocessing? The elements of an answer already have been indicated: in order to carry out the proper decisions about price and collection policy, credit and store operations must behave in ways that are socially costly and unpleasant. Agroprocessing has no such problems. Either its cost components are hidden from view, or the socially popular sales price for the marketed product (i.e., the highest possible) also happens to be the right price in income-earning terms. Or, decisionmaking is of a technical nature with no direct impact on members and of little interest to them. Credit and purchasing operations, in contrast, need the help of outside pressures "beyond their control." The repayment discipline imposed by a bank loan, and the fear of losing assets or further bank credit if repayment is not made, can help coop managers carry out unpopular and uncomfortable decisions.

Having to repay credit for loan funds and purchasing operations also helps coops to make better choices about which activities to take on. Coops tend to want credit, stores, processing plants, and marketing operations all at once—because that's what coops are supposed to do. But credit, though it sounds very good, may actually not be as important for some groups as other services. CCAM in Santa Cruz, for example, was the only group among the four in Bolivia that actually went to the bank to obtain credit for lending to members— charging a market interest rate to members, pledging its assets, and repaying on time. This is a good test of how serious a constraint credit was in Santa Cruz, in comparison to the other regions, to improving farmer incomes. Compared to Tarija and the Alto Beni, land in Santa Cruz was plentiful and labor was costly. This meant that credit was more crucial for increased agricultural production, because the credit-financed hiring of additional labor and renting of agricultural equipment were necessary in order to expand the area under cultivation. In the other areas, where land expansion was less feasible and labor was less costly, increased production would have to rely on improved inputs and cultivation practices. These "land-augmenting" techniques would not be as demanding of capital, particularly where labor was less costly.

When credit is not a prime constraint, coops may be less willing to take the plunge into bank credit. Providing credit funds to coops as loans rather than grants, therefore, may constitute an excellent mechanism of self-selection: those groups that are still interested, even after knowing the conditions, may be more up to the difficult task ahead. Given that credit operations require such strength of organizational character, it may be best to simply eliminate credit from support to the groups that do not need it as urgently as other services. It may appear cold-hearted, of course, to suggest that fledgling peasant coops be subjected to repayment discipline in order to help them make some choices. But it should be remembered that the complaint of most peasant farmers who want credit is that the bank will not lend to them, will not treat them well, will cause them many costly trips back and forth, and will not disburse the credit on time for clearing and planting. They are more concerned about gaining access to the bank, in other words, than about getting special consideration on repayment conditions and interest rates.

Loss, learning, and change

Requiring repayment is not the only way to provide coops with more outside support and guidance for the taking of difficult steps. Well-timed donor warnings about suspending disbursements on a grant—or refusals to consider grant amendments or additional grants—can have the same effect. Two marked improvements in the management of the studied groups occurred as a result of such feared deprivations.

COINCA received a highly unfavorable audit report some years into the first IAF grant; the audit focused, not surprisingly, on problems in the area of credit and stores. (The winery received a clean bill of health.) Since COINCA believed that the IAF would provide no further disbursements or grants until it made the audit-recommended improvements, the audit provoked a crisis that resulted in certain improvements in management.

In an analogous sequence of events, Bella Vista found that it could not complete its payments on an IAF-funded truck because of a tenfold increase in the price of the dollar (in which the truck payments were denominated) over an eight-month period. Previous to the crisis, Bella Vista had been rather lax about charging adequate trucking rates and using the truck to full capacity. With the suddenly increased repayment burden caused by the devaluation, Bella Vista decided in desperation to raise its hauling rates and embark upon a new program to market bananas, a major crop of the area. (Bananas are particularly appropriate for excess-capacity problems of trucks because they are marketed throughout the year; previously, Bella Vista had marketed only coffee and rice, both of which have only three-month harvest periods, that partly overlap.) Though the IAF did not actually suspend disbursement to Bella Vista—the value of its Bolivian-currency disbursement simply diminished drastically—the effect was the same: Bella Vista would not be able to keep the truck from being repossessed by the supplier unless it raised truck income enough to cover its installments.

These crisis-induced improvements in management had one feature in common: the coop associations knew exactly what to do to make things better once the crisis was upon them. COINCA had to stop lending to borrowers who were delinquent on past loans, to keep better records of loans made and payments received, to charge interest and penalties on delinquent accounts, and to keep better records of store inventory. Bella Vista had to raise truck rates and fill up the excess capacity of the truck through more aggressive marketing operations. It was not increased learning that brought about these decisions, in other words, but markedly changed external conditions. Such "reactive" improvements in management are not unique to the Bolivian coop associations. The reactions are like the "satisficing" behavior of private firms, portrayed in the recent economics literature as being more realistic than the "maximizing" model in describing how firms behave. The satisficing firms, like the coop associations, do only what is necessary to get by. They will even show a "preference" for spending as opposed to profit-making—on labor costs, management perquisites, and other ways of improving the work environment—unless jolted to do better by sudden competition or other external events.

If certain management problems are the result of an undemanding environment rather than a lack of knowledge, then people do not necessarily have to be trained or convinced in order for things to improve. Instead, one may be able to reduce the problems by "changing" the environment—a power that donors often have, since they are an important part of a coop's environment. The IAF sometimes ignores its power to change an environment for the good. It has a distaste for intervention and is more preoccupied with the vulnerability of coops to the uncontrollable parts of their environment—the sudden price changes, the shortfall in fertilizer supply, the failed harvest, the opposition of powerful intermediaries, political repression.

For donors to exercise their power wisely requires two kinds of knowledge. First, they need to know which kinds of project agreements are most conducive to good management and allow time for learning. When few strings are attached, for example, agroprocessing seems to do better than credit and stores. Second, they need to know at which moments in a coop's development, and for what kinds of activities and problems, will radical reductions in donor permissiveness lead to constructive results. The need to make these kinds of judgments suggests that donors devote more time to analyzing a project after it is underway than, as is usually the case, beforehand.

Easy successes

One final point about the ways that donors can constructively intervene and the best moments to do so. All of the studied groups produced impressive early successes. El Ceibo quickly captured 40 percent of the cacao market of an entire region, paid growers almost twice the price paid by the large middlemen, and still earned a handsome profit. COINCA succeeded in obtaining such a large bulk discount on a fertilizer purchase that it could sell fertilizer to growers at half the prevailing prices. CCAM opened roads to distant communities with its bulldozer and motor graders, supplying them with their first consumer stores, trucking services, and reliable access to markets. These remarkable successes led to subsequent and more ambitious grants from a pleased IAF.

If the groups had done so well with so little to start, it seems reasonable to have assumed that they could have moved forward easily. Almost without exception, however, the later years turned out to be more difficult, with less impressive results, than the early ones. Prices charged or paid crept closer to prevailing prices; transport operations started to run losses as equipment got older and maintenance became more expensive; decentralized store operations shrank or closed up; credit funds decapitalized. Early coop success, then, did not necessarily augur a vigorous future. In fact, a coop that fails (especially one with years of free donor funding) may have lived several seemingly healthy years before its failure. This is strikingly illustrated by the data on U.S. coops that failed, which show a ripe average age, "at death," of ten years.

El Ceibo provides one of the most striking examples of the difficulty of holding onto a spectacular early success. As noted, Ceibo made a handsome profit with its first foray into large-scale marketing of cacao, but it had no experience managing so much money. A good part of the profits was therefore unwisely invested in urban real estate, another part was robbed (allegedly) from the manager as he traveled with it in cash from the Alto Beni to La Paz, and the rest was used to set up a small chocolate factory in the nation's capital that made little contribution to coop or grower income (though it had important symbolic value). Though the first success had generated enough capital to sustain itself, the inability to manage that capital resulted in two or three dark years for El Ceibo. Even when things improved again, with Ceibo controlling more than 60 percent of the cacao market in 1982, the association was still not able to come up with the finance for its dream project costing $20,000—a cocoa-butter plant in the producing region.

The reasons that coops have difficulty in maintaining their early successes may seem obvious, but they bear stressing because donors sometimes overreact to the first blush of success. First, the early years are more successful because it is easier to spend money than to earn a sustained return from it. Second, some time will usually pass before management inadequacies take their cumulative toll on the returns of a new organization. Third, uncontrollable events in agriculture and marketing will bring some bad years sooner or later, and those costs must be covered by returns from the early and subsequent good years.

If success is easier in the beginning, then donors should exercise some control over their enthusiasm at these first signs of success. They should not rush in with subsequent grants designed to build more elaborate organizational structures on top of that first experience. The subsequent grant might be better viewed as covering a settling period—rather than as carrying a torch forward to ever larger operations and new activities. Restraint does not necessarily mean doing nothing, but it does require using more discretion to decide which combinations of activities should be financed, and under what conditions. Instead of committing additional funds to replenish or expand a grant-funded credit operation, for example, one might try to place it on a repaying basis. Or, new grant funds could be used to improve coop access to local banks—e.g., by providing technical assistance in the form of a local person or organization with good connections or in the preparation of project proposals for local bank funding. Or, instead of financing an expanded marketing project, the donor might decide that the coop was now capable of trying for its own bank credit and might want to instead finance another activity—like agricultural extension, or land titling—with high social and economic payoffs but lower probabilities of obtaining financing elsewhere. Early successes, in sum, should be looked upon as more fragile than they appear.

CONCLUSION

I have made various suggestions about how donors might improve the way they make decisions about coops and other projects that seek to improve the conditions of the rural poor. These suggestions, if followed, do not necessarily require a cooperative as their instrument. Sometimes, as we will see, the coops are a good form in which to undertake the pursuit of our goals, though the form will not always fit our image of what a good coop should be. Sometimes, moreover, we will want to conduct the pursuit of our goals through coops for a limited time only, after which the coop may tend to stagnate, decline, or limit its benefits. At this point we may want to facilitate a transfer of the activity from the coop to the state (or to another entity), or at least support some interaction between the two. To do this would be to support a sequence of institutional developments in which coops are an early stage. This means that our support of coops may not be worth its while unless the subsequent steps in the sequence also take place.

Finally, our experience with coops can teach us a great deal about decentralized community or regional initiatives. Sometimes, non-cooperative forms of these endeavors will be an even better approach to the task. Normally, we tend to ignore or reject these other institutional forms because they do not have the "good" qualities we associate with coops—they may be controlled by elites, they may be weak on management, they may involve only a few people. But since our study has shown that coops themselves often have these same "failings"—even when they yield substantial benefits—then we need not be so restrictive in our search for alternatives. At the same time, we will have to pay careful attention to the structural factors that contribute to the good results.

Unfortunately, I have not come up with a better description, or term, for what "coops" actually are when they are doing the good things that the Bolivian groups were doing. Though this kind of naming would help us recognize the kinds of groups we want to support, it would also be inconsistent with the findings of my analysis. What determined the various accomplishments of the Bolivian groups, that is, was not only their organizational form. It was also a combination of structural factors—the sequence in which activities were undertaken, the social structure of the communities, the varying characteristics of the principal crops grown, and the traits of the various activities undertaken by the coops. Since these combinations are different for every group, the same organizational form can easily give rise to different results—some satisfying to us, and some not.

NOTES

1. Most coops tended to pay and charge prices that were closer to the prevailing ones as time went on—in order to meet their unexpectedly higher costs or because prevailing prices of private operators had come down in response to coop competition.

2. In addition, the Bolivian coops were not too demanding of existing members to pay in their capital subscriptions and dues.

3. The management problems attendant upon membership growth were nowhere as great for activities like processing and marketing.

4. Under ideal conditions of population density, slash-and-burn systems are self-perpetuating and do not require abandonment because of soil regeneration during long fallow periods. But population densities in Santa Cruz, as in other rapidly growing frontier areas, are beyond the "carrying capacities" of the land, causing fallow periods to be too short and leading to eventual deterioration of soil quality. In Santa Cruz, the problem is exacerbated by a second growth of *barbecho* (weed-grass) that makes subsequent crop cultivation impossible under the slash-and-burn system.

5. Credit funds were afflicted more rapidly than store capital, since the discrepancy between coop and bank interest rates was greater than that between coop and private store prices. Also, it was hard for credit funds to keep up with inflation, unless principal and interest payments were indexed to inflation—another price policy that coops would have considered "evil." Stores, in contrast, could protect themselves better from inflation by "indexing" the prices of merchandise on the shelf, though there was some reluctance to do this on social grounds, as well as some ignorance in the more remote areas about current price increases.

6. If the fixed investment in the plant is financed with bank credit, of course, the capital may indeed be lost if the loan cannot be repaid. This was not a concern for the Bolivian groups because, like most coops, their processing facilities were acquired with grants from donors, rather than with loans.

7. The "technological" insulation of agroprocessing versus credit and stores is not unique to this coop activity. In general, development projects and programs that are "technology-intensive" are often less vulnerable to political meddling than are those where a knowledge of technology is not required in order for someone to offer opinions and wield influence.

9

Community Stores in Rural Colombia: Organizing the Means of Consumption

JAN L. FLORA AND CORNELIA BUTLER FLORA
with Humberto Rojas and Norma Villareal

During the 1970s, the movement to organize cooperative institutions and improve the welfare of Colombia's rural poor reached a crossroads. Efforts at land reform through the Asociación Nacional de Usuarios Campesinos (ANUC) were meeting stiff opposition from large landowners and were declining in number and intensity. Meanwhile, high national rates of inflation were increasing the costs of food and other staples and severely undermining the living standards of small farmers and agricultural workers. Many campesino groups responded to these challenges by setting up community-run stores that would stock basic items—such as rice, beans, corn, salt, candles, and soda— for sale at reduced prices. It was assumed that by doing their own packaging, buying in bulk, and relying on enthusiastic volunteers, these stores could eliminate most of the markup normally charged by retailers. It was also hoped that these stores would provide a new market for local farmers, raising incomes while improving the availability of fresh foods and the quality of local diets. That is, an attempt was underway to raise the living standards of the poor by organizing the means of consumption rather than the means of production. By the end of the decade, community stores were springing up throughout the countryside.

Although some of those stores—usually situated in out-of-the-way hamlets—arose spontaneously and now operate independently, many are tied into informal networks through distribution centers associated with the Catholic Church or regional peasant organizations. These central stores provide wholesale goods, credit, and technical assistance to the outlets started by local community groups. Salaried *promotores* (professionals) travel from site to site and offer a variety of services—

from helping campesinos open a store, to advising them about long-range goals, to setting up a system of accurate bookkeeping.

In an attempt to learn how this movement was faring, we studied, during June and July of 1983, four regional organizations in Colombia that service networks of community stores. Most leaders of three organizations—the Grupo Asociativo de Versalles, the Center for Peasant Marketing in Valle (CEMECAV), and the Foundation for Rural Development (FUNDER)—trace their roots to and were trained by the Jesuit-run Advanced Peasant Institute (IMCA) in Buga, Valle. The first two groups are located in the Cauca Valley, the country's richest agricultural region. FUNDER operates in Huila, in the Magdalena Valley, which lies over the Central Cordillera to the east. The fourth group, the Foundation for Communities of Risaralda (FUNDACOMUN), emerged from the secular, government-sponsored *Acción Comunal* (Community Action Movement). It is located in the Department of Risaralda, downriver from the Cauca Valley where the valley floor narrows to almost nothing. All four organizations have received grants for their community store operations from the Inter-American Foundation.

We also compiled case studies of several beneficiary stores associated with each of the central stores. Our selection was made after consultation with the leaders of the central organizations and was intended to examine two sets of characteristics: (1) successful vs. struggling enterprises;[1] and (2) a cross section of stores by community size and location. We then conducted a pilot study of COINCA—a consumer store in the highly commercialized, mountainous region of Cundinamarca and about two hours by bus from Bogotá—to refine our interview instruments. (This study also provided useful control data to compare with our later surveys, since COINCA is an economically successful, legally registered cooperative that had received no outside assistance.)

In our interviews, we found that the leaders of the central organizations and the local community-run stores tended to share similar initial values and goals. Both assumed that campesinos are eager to unite and cooperate around the immediate need of provisioning their families and that a community, by setting up and running a consumer store, can save the money, master the skills, and generate the enthusiasm to tackle longer-range development projects. The actual record of achievement, however, tended to fall short of that ambitious mark. Two factors seemed most responsible: early expectations often contained internal contradictions that were exposed only when the community store opened, and the store's actual operations were modified by having to compete in the marketplace.

COMMUNITY SERVICE AND ECONOMIC SURVIVAL

Community-run stores are not just businesses: their economic goals are shaped and conditioned by a social vision of cooperative action. The people who start these stores do, of course, begin with a definite economic agenda. They want to lower or stabilize consumer prices by reducing "exorbitant" profits by storekeepers. They want to ensure fair trade practices by instituting the use of reliable weights and measures. They want to provide local farmers with the opportunity to realize a better return for their produce. They want people with seasonal incomes to have access to credit so that they can purchase staples year-round. They also want to accumulate profits to fund other joint enterprises—from building a schoolroom for their children, to offering adult training programs, to sponsoring religious activities.

Unfortunately, many of these goals operate at cross purposes. That is, maximizing one aim may limit the others and may even undermine the solvency of the community store. The desire to keep prices low, for instance, minimizes profits for investment in community programs. Indeed, if profit margins are not calculated carefully to include indirect as well as direct costs, the store may lack the operating capital to restock. This bottom line means that credit usually must be sharply curtailed and given to people who can best pay back rather than to those who need it the most. Since that usually undermines membership cohesion and complicates the accounting task, stores often stop providing any credit at all.

Such contradictions provoke an almost excruciating dilemma because the need to survive is not just an economic imperative. The founders of community stores—often drawing on Catholic social doctrine—have a deep commitment to service that is reflected by their initial decision to keep prices low and to reinvest any accumulated profits in new community programs rather than returning them as dividends. This commitment is all the more impressive since we found that members of the local groups generally contribute their own funds as start-up capital for the stores. The leaders of community stores also commonly express their belief that mere survival of the business is an inadequate measure of success. Larger goals—such as raising the level of peasant education, expanding into the marketing of agricultural products, and increasing the political presence of campesinos in the community and in the larger movement—have to be pursued. That is, the people who start the stores and the networks that service them share a single overriding aim: they want their enterprise to be a focal point for organizing and mobilizing further community action.

Yet, in Colombia, community-run stores typically attract and actively involve limited memberships. (Most never enlist the twenty-five people required by law to register as a cooperative.) This phenomenon seems puzzling since other organizations in these communities often have larger rolls, but several factors help to account for the apparent failures. First, the legal requirements—including strictly prescribed bookkeeping procedures and complex paperwork—tax the available resources and skills of a small group and discourage formal registration. Consequently, most groups adopt other judicial forms: from "precooperatives," to "associated groups," to "foundations."[2]

Second, shopping and, frequently, credit privileges are not contingent on membership in the group that operates the enterprise because the founders usually believe that a community store, by definition, should serve everyone. Most consumers have no material incentive to join the organization. There is, in fact, a disincentive since membership usually requires a substantial commitment of time and, often, of dues.

Third, the founding group limits recruitment to protect itself from "cooptation" by prospective members who hold different values or seek personal gain. COINCA, the only cooperative store in our sample, illustrates this. Indiscriminate recruitment almost led to the early death of the organization when townspeople with ties to family-run groceries joined and tried to take over the cooperative. The original membership of two hundred shrank to about one hundred by 1980 as greater care was taken to enlist only peasants.

COINCA also demonstrates how economic necessity—the final factor—affects membership size. In 1983, a shortage of operating capital arose from a rapid expansion of store operations and led to a sixfold increase in monthly membership dues—from 200 to 1,250 pesos. Membership declined to thirty-seven people. That is, the effort needed to make a community store work as a business and stay afloat exerts a counterweight that limits its social goal of attracting new members and broadening their involvement in the organization.

Inevitably, the managers and groups operating consumer stores have had difficulty in balancing this equation. In our field study, we examined thirteen community stores in depth and twenty-three others less extensively. In all but three cases, we found the enterprises struggling: either they faced bankruptcy because significant costs (particularly of credit) were not reflected in prices, or their leadership was being criticized for overcharging on goods or for restricting credit. Both difficulties often plagued the same organization as early and continuing threats to solvency led to sharp price increases—which often still did not adequately cover costs.

COMMUNITY SIZE AND PRIVATE COMPETITION

As previously stated, community size and location were key considerations in selecting which community-run stores would be studied in depth. We found that, depending on these two factors, community stores encountered different kinds of competition from private retailers. The nature of that challenge, in turn, affected a store's solvency and its ability to meet its social goals.

Isolated or Very Small Communities

The community stores with the best prospects for survival were started in small, out-of-the-way villages. Of the five stores we surveyed, two are associated with agricultural collectives established during the brief period of land reform in the late 1960s and early 1970s. Three of the communities are accessible only by foot or mule, and another can be reached only by a rough, unpaved road. Only one is located along a major highway and is readily accessible. None of these hamlets has more than a cluster of houses and a few services. Except for the settlements containing production coops, more people who shop at the stores live outside rather than in the village. In all cases, the community-run stores are the only groceries in the immediate vicinity.

The resulting lack of competition enhances the economic position of these stores in several ways. First, inventories can be limited to a few basic items, and customers are so well known that their weekly purchases can be predicted almost exactly. Just before market day the shelves are almost empty; on market day they are full; the following day supplies are sparse again. Capital is seldom tied up, and the risks of spoilage or overstocking are minimized. Second, small village stores can also curtail their hours of operation, reducing the amount of wages and benefits that must be paid to the storekeeper-member or making it feasible to rely solely on volunteer labor. Finally, these stores have more flexibility to raise profit margins without losing customers. We found one of the five groups exercising this option in order to raise capital for reinvestment in store operations.

Of the various examples we looked at, small village stores also came closest to reconciling their economic and social goals. The degree of community support was high, perhaps because the economic benefits were obvious. Campesinos no longer had to make the time-consuming and often arduous trip into town on market day to buy the few items their families would need during the coming week. Donations of rent-free space for the store and an abundance of volunteers to share the workload were common. This enthusiasm was also reflected in relatively high membership rolls: the village store that chose to raise its profit margins actually had more members than many of the consumer stores we studied in much larger communities. (Of course, larger memberships were also possible because these villages are comparatively undifferentiated: the emphasis on nonprofit or profit-for-community investments coincided with a general belief that the outside world was full of people anxious to exploit naive peasants.)

We also found that these stores were developing new skills in community participation and planning. Despite minimal levels of formal education, members were willing to consider relatively complex problems (such as cost-accounting) and made noteworthy efforts to apply what they learned to running their stores. One reason may be that these stores start small and expand slowly, which makes the economic principles governing their operations easier to understand. Usually, however, these new skills are related to store operations, and training tends to be concentrated within the membership ranks. Only one store was sponsoring a rich social program of outside activities, and it relied on its network sponsor for the necessary resources. The two stores associated with cooperative production enterprises allowed those institutions to promote educational and organizational activities within the community.

The small village store that deviated the most from these norms was situated near a major highway, and travel into larger communities with family-run groceries was relatively easy. Despite having the highest average levels of education among these five groups, its members seemed relatively uninterested in the day-to-day operations of the business or in its solvency. Indeed, the storekeeper-member had merged the community store with her own grocery and had located it in her home. This will seem less anomalous after looking at consumer stores started in larger communities.

Intermediate-sized Communities

The five stores in this group were located in large *veredas* (rural neighborhoods) or in *corregimientos* (township headquarters with police outposts). Four of the communities were situated in mountainous areas, one among rolling foothills. All were centers of commerce for several smaller, surrounding villages whose peasants grow diverse crops—from corn, to coffee, to blackberries, to tree tomatoes. One township was only two hours by bus from Bogotá's markets; another was a bustling outlet for settlements higher up in the Andes and contained a variety of retail stores and wholesale marketing operations for agricultural products. Most of these communities also had a rich infrastructure of voluntary organizations, many of them associated with the Catholic Church.

Community-run stores find it extremely difficult to survive in these medium-sized rural centers. Here, retail trade—particularly the relatively risky, low-markup variety—involves brisk competition, usually from "mom-and-pop" family stores. These enterprises enjoy several advantages. First, the business and home are under the same roof while a community store almost always has to buy or rent space. Second, a mom-and-pop store can rely on family labor, but the community-run groceries must pay their workers or resort to volunteers who hold other jobs and for whom the store remains a secondary priority. Third, the cost of wages and the difficulty in recruiting volunteers limits community store hours. Small family groceries are often open more than 100 hours per week since there is usually someone to mind the business, even if that person is also watching the children and cooking the evening meal. Finally, the community outlet requires accurate bookkeeping if it is to avoid corruption and remain accountable to its constituency (and to outside donors like the IAF). In the mom-and-pop store, owners answer only to themselves. They know how the business is faring not by examining ledgers but by seeing whether the family's bills are being paid and whether some money is being put aside.

Given the advantages enjoyed by their competition, why were there any community-run groceries in this setting at all? First, it should be noted that turnover is also high among mom-and-pop stores. Failures are related to the general difficulty of operating any sort of small business profitably, whether mom-and-pop or community store. But to the extent that some community stores managed to succeed financially, it is because they replicated or offset (at least partially) the favorable characteristics of the family store. For instance, one enterprise was known locally as "Don Julio's store," and most of the seven members in the organizing group were kin. Two of the community stores we examined had managers who took nominal salaries for long hours, and one of these men had donated part of his house so the store could get on its feet during its first eight months of operation without having to pay rent. In a third community, members voluntarily helped out on Sunday, the busiest day of the week. Only COINCA, the full-fledged cooperative of our pilot study, employed an accountant; the others relied on a central store network to keep their accounts or to provide technical assistance to the manager-bookkeeper. That is, most of the surviving community stores depended upon a few highly motivated leaders and members and on access to outside resources.

Even when these stores were holding their own, however, the struggle to meet the challenge of stiff competition was altering their operations in ways that tended to undermine membership morale and participation over the long term. The process can be summed up as follows. Members tend to be highly inspired when the store opens, and enthusiasm increases as benefits are realized. A policy of keeping prices low and using reliable weights and measures puts pressure on other retailers. Prices for consumers can even drop dramatically in the short term if a price war breaks out. Usually however, an informal truce is quickly reached since most small businesses—family-run or cooperative—are undercapitalized and cannot afford to sustain losses for long. The need to stay solvent leads the community store to tighten its credit policies or even to increase its prices while private retailers adopt fairer trade practices. It becomes harder, in purely economic terms, for members to distinguish between the benefits offered by the community store and its rivals. At the same time, the day-to-day operations of the store become so complex and time-consuming that decisions are left in the manager's hands. If membership apathy becomes too great, the leaders and managers of the store may tire of bearing the burden, and the store will fold. Or, the store may evolve into a version of the family stores with which it competes.

The community store we studied that had just gone out of business revealed that outside support does not guarantee success and may even be counterproductive. This was the only store that did not arise solely from local initiative and did not rely on members contributing substantial amounts of their own capital. A loan offered by a central network made the idea of starting a community store attractive. Unfortunately, the members of the founding group confused the loan with a donation and never really established their grocery as an economic enterprise. The inability to make that transition led to the business's folding when the start-up capital was exhausted.

Despite these difficulties, the example of COINCA shows that community stores can, given the proper circumstances, not only survive but can surpass their competition. The cooperative now has eleven employees and handles 60 percent of the grocery business in La Florida. It took over a steadily larger share of the market as family stores went out of business. Of course, COINCA enjoys several advantages that may make its success difficult to replicate elsewhere. The coop has been able to exploit its central location within a highly commercialized region where harvests occur throughout the year, and it has considerably enlarged its capital base by expanding its activities into marketing operations for local farmers. The closeness to the Bogotá market and the community's year-round production of blackberries has made it possible to dovetail marketing with restocking operations. COINCA is the only community store we examined whose trucking operation has broken even; the same trucks carry produce into the city for sale and return laden with groceries for the store. COINCA has also used its dual service capability to capture business: unlike any of its private competitors, it offers free delivery of groceries at the same time trucks pick up blackberries at the farm gate. Finally, the cooperative also has a number of well-trained leaders who now have up to ten years of experience in making the business work. Again, it must be remembered that even COINCA's success has not prevented a steadily dwindling membership.

County-seat Towns

Three county-seat community stores were examined. One was located in a bustling, working-class town of about 30,000 citizens along the Cauca River in Risaralda. The second was in a nearby mountainous community with an active coffee trade. The third was based in Algeciras, an assembly point in Huila for products brought from the eastern plains. The first two stores were associated with the Community Action Movement while the third emerged from the now-defunct ANUC.

At first glance, these stores seem to enjoy the favorable position enjoyed by COINCA: they have the potential for sufficient sales volume to realize economies of scale, and once that advantage is secured, they no longer have to compete with mom-and-pop stores but with larger enterprises that also have to pay rent, wages, and employee benefits. Nonetheless, these stores had difficulty making that transition. The two linked with the Community Action Movement actually had a negative net worth and had suffered from periods of bad adminis-tration that forced their principal creditor—FUNDACOMUN—to exert pressure to change the management.

In this case, part of the problem was related to the fact that the groups sponsoring the stores—the County Associations of Community Action Boards—were really collections of conflicting interests: they were comprised of representatives from various local boards that were scattered in settlements throughout the mountainous area. Peasant representatives were cut off from regular contact with each other and with the stores. Consequently, the stores' operations were supervised by two representatives who lived in the county seat. One was a county employee who was in charge of repossessing tax-delinquent farms. Understandably, he had difficulty gaining the support of the peasant members from rural Community Action Boards.

There was also a second reason for the faulty management. The active members of each association perceived the community store as an instrument of political patronage rather than as a business. Thus, rivalry between two community leaders, each seeking to strengthen his or her political base, made it difficult to settle disputes over store operations on the technical merits of what would be cost effective.

The one store in this group that is solvent is not tied to the Community Action structure. The "ANUC store" is basically run in a family-store fashion by the administrator, his wife, and the two remaining ANUC members. For all practical purposes the grocery has ceased to be a community outlet: it is more like a family operation with a hired manager. Although all three of the county-seat stores depended on outside grants—either from the government, the IAF, or both—to get off the ground, this is the only one that succeeded in converting its start-up funds into operating capital.

Only one of the county-seat stores we looked at was responding to the social goals of its central-network sponsor. Classes in accounting and in dance have been organized, and both men and women have attended. Many of these students—notably several young women—have gone on to work with their County Association and their local Community Action Boards. This community store and its activities program, however, are heavily subsidized by FUNDACOMUN, and the original hope that consumer-run stores would generate profits to finance other community action projects has proven utopian in all county seats. Moreover, participation and training of members within the store's structure have also been severely limited because of the complexity of day-to-day operations, and management has been consigned to a few members or to a paid staff.

CENTRAL STORES: RAISING THE ANTE

The four regional organizations that we studied operated central stores to supply their grassroots affiliates with wholesale goods, credit, and technical assistance. Although these services often improved a new community store's competitive position and prospects for survival in the short term, the long-term outlook remained clouded. Instead of resolving the contradictions between social and economic goals at the local level, central stores tended to absorb and reproduce—often more virulently—those conflicts within their own business operations.

As businesses, the central stores have no intrinsic price advantage in competing with private wholesalers to supply community stores. Both buy from the same middlemen, and none of the four central stores has achieved sufficient economies of scale to purchase goods directly from the processor. They have not developed effective mechanisms for marketing their customers' locally grown produce within the networks.

Their chief advantage over other suppliers—access to grants from outside donors—is offset, even dwarfed, by the task of building and maintaining peasant organizations. A substantial portion of those funds is used to subsidize credit to beneficiary community stores, usually by stocking a new grocery's shelves. Although this start-up capital is given as a loan, credit terms are usually soft. In practice, loans often become grants. After a community store gets off the ground, the central store faces the added expense of providing bookkeeping and technical assistance so the local group can meet its legal requirements and learn how to survive as a business. Should the store begin to prosper, central store organizers want the group to be independent and encourage it to buy goods as cheaply as possible, whatever the source. The local stores that are the most successful as businesses thus have an incentive to buy elsewhere, while the stores with the worst credit records have nowhere else to turn. Central store networks face the constant danger of hemorrhage from pumping capital into the least efficient community groceries. Meanwhile, central stores find themselves competing with market-oriented wholesalers who do not carry the same burden of social investment, who sell to customers that are already capitalized, who can cut off a buyer when bills are not paid on time, and for whom marketing and profits are the bottom line.

Increasingly, that competition and the need to conserve resources has pushed the central stores into more traditional, market-oriented behavior. Some of the central stores that we examined were beginning to sell to mom-and-pop as well as community stores and were rationalizing their credit and pricing policies on economic rather than social grounds. A similar reordering has occurred in transportation services. Central organizations commonly have used grant monies to purchase vehicles, on the assumption that this investment will eliminate the markup charged by intermediaries for carrying goods to the central store and from there to the local outlets. In practice, however, it has proven extremely difficult to calculate how to use a vehicle efficiently enough to cover maintenance, labor, and fuel costs: drivers still have to be paid for empty backhauls that also burn gas. One remedy has been to rent the vehicle or vehicles to a reliable member who then supervises hired drivers and schedules the most profitable runs rather than those routes that would serve the neediest stores. Even those central stores that obtained vehicles with the specific intention of supplying isolated stores no longer use them for this purpose. Either their trucks and jeeps are rented out, or they stand idle.

Sometimes, however, that economic rationalization has allowed the central store to provide better service to its grassroots affiliates. This can be illustrated by comparing the experience of two central stores. The first chose to focus most of its efforts on keeping prices down in its county seat by slashing profits to the bone. This sparked an interminable price war with rival grocers, and although the county-seat community store achieved a larger sales volume than any of its competitors, per unit profits remained too low to fund technical assistance, training programs, or new organizational projects. The second central store—the most successful of the four we surveyed in providing higher-quality food at lower prices—concentrated on rationalizing its wholesale merchandising by simplifying its sales inventory to a few items, by selling to mom-and-pop as well as community-run groceries, and by hiring a purchasing agent with previous experience in the private sector. Sufficient funds are available to support an organized educational program that utilizes professional staff and is tailored to the business needs of individual community stores. For instance, the head of the purchasing department also helps local stores improve their marketing. He recently conducted the leaders and workers of a county-seat community grocery on a tour of a large supermarket. Shortly afterward, the county-seat store converted into a self-service facility, reducing labor costs while increasing sales. Similarly, the central store's accountant visits each associated community store every two weeks to assist local bookkeepers in drawing up their monthly balance sheets. The goal has been to develop necessary skills so that the local groups can eventually keep their own books. The other central stores we examined were simply absorbing this burden by keeping accounts for local outlets, with no relief in sight.

MEANS AND ENDS

Although central stores and their grassroots affiliates are hardly extinct in Colombia, many community groceries have short lifespans, and the ambitious goals of network organizers have dimmed. By those organizers' own accounts, mere survival is not enough. Only two of the fourteen community stores—including COINCA—that we looked at in depth have been successful enough to launch second generation social programs. Even then, it took four years in one case and nearly a decade in the other. Moreover, the stores we examined tended to draw their leadership from other organizations rather than spawn new leaders. That is, a community store may be a vivid example of self-help in action, but the success of that enterprise tends to reflect prior levels of organization rather than the mobilization of new resources. Indeed, store management usually includes a steadily dwindling number of active leaders who find themselves saddled with business responsibilities, with little time and resources left over for new organizing. Understandably, morale is often low, the sense of frustration high.

What can be done? For one thing, central organizations can target their resources more carefully. That may mean separating economic and social goals and asking how each can best be furthered. Sometimes the community store will not be the answer, or at least not the only answer. In medium-sized communities it might make more sense to try to organize mom-and-pop stores and use credit or other services as an incentive to promote socially responsible pricing. Similarly, forming a citizens' committee made up of members of community organizations to monitor the use of accurate weights and measures might be a more efficient way to guarantee fair trade practices than starting and staffing a community store.

There may even be virtue in necessity. As previously noted, store management and member participation tend to narrow over time, anyway. One central store organization hit hard times and turned over ownership of three outlets to highly motivated members. Thus far, those stores are still operating and serving their communities. In such cases, community stores provide training in merchandising and bookkeeping that allows their managers to successfully compete in the private sector.

Given the number of caveats, should intermediary organizations continue to emphasize their community store operations? The answer is a cautious yes. Community stores will continue to spring up spontaneously anyway, and they will need a variety of services to get on their feet. In the larger towns, when more informal means such as citizens' watchdog committees fail, it may be necessary to help start a community store to stir competition, promote fair trade practices, and hold down prices. In out-of-the-way hamlets, a community store may be invaluable because it will be the only store. That store can also be a vital tool for organizing the small community and mobilizing its resources.

However, as the experience of the Grupo Asociativo de Versalles shows, new stores need a solid foundation. Organization should begin with an in-depth study of the rural neighborhood that singles out potential leaders. Establishment of the store should then be incremental, allowing members to learn, at their own pace, the cooperative and technical skills needed to operate a business. The Grupo Asociativo has also developed a valuable method of recruiting new leaders by establishing soccer teams in conjunction with the community store. Team participation promotes cooperation among the players, builds local pride, and gives leaders higher visibility. (Two comments should be added. First, this method of organizing has an obvious gender bias, and alternative ways to recruit women need to be discovered. Second, this method is not limited to promoting community stores: it can be a valuable tool in other kinds of development activities.)

Finally, it seems obvious that central organizations badly need to rethink their wholesale marketing operations. As previously mentioned, those operations have no intrinsic advantage and several disadvantages over those of traditional intermediaries. It takes considerable time and often the waste of resources that comes with trial-by-error learning to master the complexities of marketing. Those groups that have already gained those skills and are sound fiscally should probably continue; those in trouble or considering entering the field should carefully reexamine their alternatives. In general, central organizations should realize that the primary "good" that they can offer is not money or in-kind credit but knowledge. It is vital that the members of the local store invest some of their own resources so that they will have a real stake in the enterprise and its operations. Since so few community stores ever develop sufficiently to sponsor secondary social and educational programs, the temptation exists to siphon off supplemental funding from central organizations for such programs to cover up business inefficiencies. Additional social programs should be funded directly and operated apart from the community store structure.

NOTES

1. Although we interviewed the officers of one community store that had just closed its doors, it proved extremely difficult to obtain reliable information on failed outlets.

2. It should be added that how the store is organized is not merely a question of competing legalisms. Several of the groups we looked at chose to register as "precooperatives" although that meant more paperwork and more stringent bookkeeping than the other judicial alternatives. This form also stipulates that members must contribute their own start-up capital for the store. That requirement cuts two ways: it can act as a drag on membership recruitment, but it can also be a barometer to gauge membership commitment

and enthusiasm. There is also a time limit on how long a group can remain a precooperative. As a result, at the time of our interview, many groups were changing their status to that of "associated group," which mandates no mechanism for distributing profits to or even returning the initial investments of members.

10

The Experience of
Worker
Self-Management in Peru
and Chile

MARTIN J. SCURRAH AND BRUNO PODESTA

During the 1970s, social reformers in Peru and Chile tried to create and organize a sector of small- and medium-sized businesses that were owned and managed by their workers. It was hoped that these firms would become an engine for economic growth, providing new and stable jobs for underemployed, often recently migrated, urban workers. The new sector would fill the gap between the small workshops that typified the unorganized, informal economy and the large private industries that dominated the national economy.

Although the aspirations in both Chile and Peru were similar, the two movements had very different origins. Worker-owned enterprises first appeared in Chile while Eduardo Frei was president. They multiplied under the Allende government in the early 1970s when several large firms were nationalized and when many others were placed under state receivership because of bankruptcy, owner abandonment, or labor problems.

Following the coup d'état of 1973, the government decided to sell its public industries to the highest bidders. A small group of professionals, who had worked for the government's Technical Cooperation Service during the 1960s forming and advising urban industrial cooperatives, hurriedly drew up a plan to help workers purchase their own firms. The proposal, which also included loans for working capital to existing production cooperatives and small technical assistance and training programs, was funded by various international agencies. Workers borrowed from these funds to finance approximately one-third of the cost of buying fifteen large, state-owned

---

A list of the acronyms used in this chapter can be found at the end of the chapter.

companies and used their accumulated pension rights and severance pay to cover another six percent of the purchase price. The government provided the rest of the money through loans from an institute for financing cooperatives.

These fifteen businesses were much larger than any previous worker-owned firms in Chile. Although the size of the new enterprises made them difficult to run, consolidation of the firms into a whole "sector" seemed possible. A board was set up under the auspices of the Catholic Church's Foundation for Development to manage loan funds, to prepare bids, and in general, to nurture both pre-existing and newly purchased production cooperatives. In short, from the outset, the attempt to organize the new sector in Chile was an ad hoc, private response to a public crisis. The government's initial attitude toward these enterprises wavered between suspicion and indifference.

Meanwhile, in Peru, a similar, though less dramatic effort was under way. In 1974, the government passed the Social Property Law to create "social property" firms and integrate them into an economic sector. Property would be "social" in the sense that the people who worked in a company would operate but not directly own the business: all firms would be owned by all of the workers in the sector. Internally, each enterprise would resemble a cooperative and be organized by one-man one-vote rule; collectively, the firms would be grouped by regions to elect assemblies that, in turn, would elect a national governing assembly. The legislation was influenced by foreign models (especially the worker-run factories in Yugoslavia) and by Peru's previous experience with cooperatives and agrarian reform.

To avoid individual or group ownership, the government would finance the new sector through the National Social Property Fund (FONAPS), which would charge each social property firm a variable "rent" to compensate for differences in profitability, natural monopolies, and preferential access to raw materials. Any excess profits were to be channeled to FONAPS where, combined with loan repayments, they would form an ever-increasing fund for establishing new enterprises. (To minimize opposition from established businesses, severe restrictions were placed upon converting privately owned companies into social property firms.) Thus, in contrast to Chile, the government was not only not hostile to the establishment of the new sector, but was the driving force behind it.

To understand Peru and Chile's experience with worker self-management—and, in particular, the creation of public and private institutions to support the enterprises—it is useful to consider the cases of two workers who found themselves participating in the worker self-management sector.[1]

A STOVE FACTORY IN CHILE

Ernesto Gutierrez was born and grew up in a shantytown on the edge of Santiago de Chile. His father, who had migrated from the countryside after many years of short-term jobs between periods of unemployment, finally landed a steady job as a factory watchman when Ernesto was ten years old. The third child in a family of six brothers and sisters, Ernesto left school when he was fourteen to help support his family.

He was lucky enough to get a job in a medium-sized factory that produced gas stoves. Shortly afterward, he joined the union because practically all of his co-workers belonged and approved. Although the union leaders appeared to favor the Chilean Communist party, most of the employees were not active in a political party, and support for the Socialist and Christian Democratic parties was tolerated.

The campaign that elected Salvador Allende as president of Chile at the head of the Popular Unity coalition aroused considerable interest and discussion among the employees in the factory. Even those workers who had voted for the Christian Democrats seemed well disposed toward the new government. Most people expected that wages and working conditions would improve and that workers' concerns would have high priority, although there was some concern about the possible reaction of business and the armed forces.

The owner of the factory, a Chilean of European descent, was upset by the election and made it clear that he would not let the union interfere in factory operations nor would he accept any disrespectful behavior from "upstart" employees. The union leaders, for their part, felt able to be more demanding in contract negotiations with the owner and expected the Labor Ministry to vigorously enforce employer compliance with collective bargaining agreements and government regulations.

During the next two years, the demand for the company's products increased, but raw material shortages and deteriorating relations between the union and the owner led to numerous work stoppages and slowdowns. Events came to a head near the end of 1972, when the owner stopped coming to the factory. At first work continued normally, but by the second week, when there was still no news and bills had to be paid and decisions made, the bookkeeper tried to contact the owner at home. Neighbors said that the owner had sold his house and moved with his family to the United States. The bank confirmed that the firm's accounts had been closed and its money withdrawn.

Faced with an impending crisis, the union local called a series of meetings and consulted its national confederation. After several discussions with government officials, the company was declared to be *intervenida*[2] and a recent university graduate was appointed to run the factory. Although well disposed toward the workers, the "intervenor" lacked experience and was frequently absent. Thus, the firm's everyday operation and management were left to the workers. Concerned about their jobs, the workers, under the leadership of the union, assumed new responsibilities and strove to increase production, despite the shortages of materials and spare parts.

After the military coup in September 1973, the intervenor disappeared and was replaced by a young military officer who was even more inexperienced in managing a factory. After some initial distrust, a modus vivendi was established with the workers. As long as employees showed up on time, were respectful toward authority, and avoided any political activity, the officer would not initiate any reprisals. Production and sales, however, were low, and salaries did not keep up with inflation.

Several months after the coup, the former owner was seen talking to the officer, and the rumor spread that the factory was about to be handed back. Still, nothing happened. Six months later, the workers were told that the government had decided to sell the company to the highest bidder.

After the coup, the union's leadership had passed quietly into the hands of a coalition of Christian Democrats and independents. Concerned about who might buy their factory and about the possible loss of autonomy that had been gained from a series of "absentee owners," the union officials considered purchasing the factory. One person said he knew an engineer who had promoted industrial cooperatives during the former government of Eduardo Frei. Through this contact the workers received a loan of $250,000 from a Church-sponsored savings and loan association. By combining this money with their accumulated rights to pensions and severance pay, the workers purchased the firm for $300,000.

Simply purchasing the firm, however, did not end the workers' problems. Ernesto and his fellow worker-owners now confronted challenges and responsibilities for which they were unprepared. What alternative legal forms might their enterprise take, and what were the advantages and disadvantages of each? What steps were needed to set up the desired form? Were there any legal problems or lawsuits pending, and what could be done about them? In order to purchase the firm, the workers had ceded their rights to pensions and severance pay. What would happen to people when they retired or if the firm went bankrupt? How would the workers repay the money they had borrowed to buy the factory? Would there be enough working capital to buy raw materials and pay wages? The machinery was old and needed replacing: what would be the best technology to purchase? How could they afford it? How should the factory be run? Was a manager needed? If so, should the manager come from the ranks or be hired from the outside? To whom could they turn for help and advice?

A GARMENT FACTORY IN PERU

Fortunata Huamán was born in the Peruvian Andes where, during her childhood, she looked after the few animals on her family's tiny farm. She and her four brothers and sisters rarely saw their father, who was usually looking for work in the city. Soon after her eighth birthday, Fortunata and her older brother were sent to an uncle who lived in a squatter settlement in the desert on the outskirts of Lima. Her household chores were heavy, but she did have a chance to attend school with younger children. She never got beyond the fourth grade.

When she was fourteen, Fortunata was hired as a maid by a middle-class family. Although the pay was extremely low, she did receive room and board, and her employer taught her the basics of dressmaking. Two years later, Fortunata used that skill and the recommendation of a cousin of her uncle to find a job as a seamstress in a small workshop. Even though she earned a smaller net income in her new position after she paid her bus fares and room and board, at least she was independent and hopeful of advancement.

At first it was difficult to adjust to the discipline required in the workshop, and it took some time to adapt to the habits of other employees, most of whom had grown up on the coast. But gradually, she felt the sense of belonging to a group of women who shared the same problems.

Things seemed to improve until, in 1974, the workload began to slacken. Then, one payday, the owner announced that because of a lack of "liquidity," the women would only receive half their pay. One of the other employees had heard that the owner was parcelling out sewing to seamstresses who worked at home for lower piece-rates and without social security or pension rights.

The situation continued to worsen. Some paydays were missed altogether, and the firm ran up a sizable debt with its employees. When one woman became ill and applied to the social security hospital, she was refused treatment because her employer was behind in her insurance payment. Finally, the owner tried to browbeat some of the women into resigning voluntarily. Faced with these threats, the "industrial community,"[3] which had been formed by officials from the Ministry of Industry over the owner's opposition, began to demand the right to participate on the board of directors and to inspect the firm's books. The owner responded by closing the factory for a month's "vacation."

During their forced vacation, Fortunata Huamán and the other members of the industrial community's governing committee frequently visited the Ministry of Industry to enlist support but were shuffled from one official to another. When the women returned to work, they found that half the machines were gone. Then the owner announced that he could not employ everyone. He offered to pay—on the spot—half their legal benefits to all employees who resigned now and the other half in six months, insinuating that those who did not quit might be fired. Some people resigned, but about twenty decided to stay on under the leadership of the industrial community.

Several weeks later, the owner announced he was shutting the factory and cancelling the women's back pay and other legal benefits. In the meantime, the workers had learned that the owner had set up another factory with the machinery that had "disappeared," with new laborers receiving lower wages and lacking an industrial community. Alarmed, the women decided to take over the factory and sit in.

For several weeks, a core of about fifteen workers occupied the building. Their cause was publicized by sympathetic newspapers, and they received support from unions and other worker-owned firms with which they had no previous contact. The leaders of the industrial community managed to find, a lawyer, and with his aid and after innumerable meetings in government agencies, the bankruptcy court awarded temporary administration of the firm to the industrial community.

Now that the business belonged to the remaining workers organized as an industrial community, they faced a range of problems similar to those of Ernesto Gutierrez and his fellow workers in the stove factory in Chile. How could they prepare themselves to carry out their new responsibilities?

THE NEED FOR A SUPPORT STRUCTURE

It is difficult for any new business to succeed, but worker self-managed firms have a special underlying logic which separates them from traditional private or state-run enterprises. The workers are also the owners: they directly or indirectly (through elections and general meetings) make decisions usually reserved for management and shareholders. To operate their business, some workers must learn new skills or sharpen old skills: an accounting system must be set up; marketing strategies have to be developed; and quality control mechanisms have to be designed to make products more competitive. The workers must have a basic understanding of how the firm operates so that they can set policy for whoever manages the business.

If the new enterprise is to function smoothly, workers have to learn how to accomplish these tasks together. Such cooperative behavior is atypical of most workers' prior experience in traditional, hierarchical firms, and reaching a consensus that balances the desire for higher individual incomes with business' financial solvency can be difficult. For instance, if outmoded machinery needs replacement, everyone must be willing to defer short-term wage increases to invest in the long-term survivability of the enterprise. Such decisions require extraordinary self-discipline on the basis of evidence which may not be immediately apparent to the workers who must make the sacrifices. Even if direct income is not at issue, indirect social services may be. Many worker cooperatives offer additional benefits to their members in the form of health clinics, revolving funds for housing loans, consumer stores, and day care. But these services can drain scarce resources.

Since they have special needs, worker-owned firms often find it difficult to get assistance from institutions that are geared to deal with traditional private and public firms. For instance, self-managed enterprises usually begin operations heavily in debt and without an established credit history or a tested management. Loans for operating or investment capital may be impossible to obtain from private lenders. Most of the firms in Chile and Peru that would compose the new worker self-managed sectors were businesses which had previously gone bankrupt, had their operations suspended, or had been abandoned by their former owners. In other words, it was not only necessary to reorganize the firms' operating procedures to cope with a new business structure, it was also necessary to revive companies which had faltered or failed when they were run according to the dominant rules of the game.

When private groups in Chile and the government in Peru began to promote worker self-managed sectors in 1974, they also tried to set up institutions to provide the services those firms would need to survive. In Chile, a board was established under the auspices of the Catholic Church to funnel technical and financial resources to worker self-managed firms. From the beginning, this agency had difficulty reconciling conflicting demands and integrating the sector. The small- and medium-sized firms which were founded before the coup desperately needed working capital and resented that most of the money from foreign donors was being used to buy new firms. The new and old firms were so different in size, production activity, and market that coordinated planning was difficult and the possibilities of vertical or horizontal integration were minimal.

Dwarfing these internal problems, the country remained in crisis. When the board first met to hammer out an agreement between the various worker self-management factions, the meeting was interrupted by troops who were called out to maintain "order." The delegates at the meeting emphasized the need to avoid potentially divisive debate which might split the sector or raise issues which would prompt a government crackdown. During the years it existed, the board was often ineffectual. Strong measures that might damage the board's tenuous consensus were precluded.

The internal difficulties in organizing the sector were aggravated by the condition of the Chilean economy. The government withdrew from the Andean Pact and drastically reduced tariffs, exposing manufacturers to foreign competition and throwing the whole industrial sector into a deep depression. Bankruptcies mushroomed. On top of this, in 1975 a large savings and loan cooperative, IFICOOP, was taken over by the government and dissolved, forcing several production cooperatives into bankruptcy and eliminating an important source of working capital for others. (The government used the default of one of IFICOOP's large debtor cooperatives to justify the closure: the government was acting only to protect other debtors from IFICOOP's inevitable bankruptcy. Yet, when the accounts of the savings and loan were settled, there was actually a surplus.)

By mid-1977, the situation was critical. Many self-managed firms—including some of the biggest—had disappeared, and most of the rest were teetering. Early attempts at increasing productivity by training workers through the Cardijn Foundation[4] failed when the foundation was dissolved under political pressure from the government.

There were, however, some positive signs. In late 1977, the board responsible for governing the sector was reorganized as the Institute for Self-Management (INA). To reduce the friction that had arisen between the professionals who had originally tried to organize the sector and the rest of the movement, representatives from unions and worker self-managed firms joined the institute's board of directors. Despite procedural delays, the government eventually granted INA a legal charter.

Meanwhile, a second problem had arisen. The Labor Savings and Loan Cooperative (ACL), which was designed to be the sector's financing mechanism, was hamstrung by government regulations limiting its loans to under $16,000. To some extent, this hindrance was circumvented when the sector purchased the Social Interest Financial Institution (FINTESA) from a savings and loan cooperative. FINTESA had a broader legal mandate and promised to be a more effective instrument for coordinating the sector's financial strategy.

In 1978, INA designed an emergency program to assist troubled firms with funds received from the United States and West Germany that were to be channeled as loans through FINTESA. The sector was divided into three groups: those enterprises with a good chance to survive with some financial assistance, those that might survive, and those that were certain to fail. Medium-term loans were granted to firms in the first two categories in an effort to stabilize and consolidate the sector while minimizing decapitalization so that future expansion could be financed when the economy improved. Funds were also allotted for a more integrated technical assistance program which would concentrate on organizational development. This program was to be designed and run by the Center for the Study of Cooperative Development (CEDEC), while previously scattered and ineffectual training efforts were to be coordinated through INA.

In 1979, an economic recovery began and the worker self-managed sector seemed to be holding its own. By 1981, however, the Chilean economy was foundering again. Exports were down; interest rates reached record levels (50–60 percent); and internal demand was falling. The number of self-managed firms fell from its 1974 peak of sixty to about twenty-five in late 1981. Of these enterprises, no more than a dozen were expected to survive, and many were already technically in default.

Despite an influx of new donor capital, FINTESA—which was expected to service the union movement, peasant cooperatives, and industrial self-managed businesses at below-market interest rates—was foundering. Most of its outstanding loans were to self-managed enterprises that were unable to repay. Then, a major fraud involving the leading self-managed firm shook the ethical and financial foundation of the whole sector. INA, with most of its assets inconvertible in the short term, had guaranteed but could not cover FINTESA's unpaid loans to the self-managed sector. On the edge of bankruptcy, the institute sharply curtailed its activities. Conflicts between the various partners in FINTESA, and between the self-managed firms and INA and FINTESA, finally required mediation by the Catholic Church. In short, the self-managed sector never consolidated and was on the brink of total collapse.

In Peru, the attempt to set up a coordinated support structure for the new worker self-managed sector followed a different course to a similar end. The government created the National Social Property Commission (CONAPS) to implement the 1974 legislation that mandated the new sector. The commission's president had ministerial rank and its members were drawn primarily from government agencies. CONAPS' early strategy was to establish as many firms as quickly as possible. However, to implement its program, CONAPS had to work through the state bureaucracy. These ministries had independent priorities and there were inevitable delays.

Just as the legislation did not anticipate the need for an adequate organizational structure to launch the new sector, it also underestimated the time lag in converting an idea for a project into an independently functioning business. Self-managed firms did not spring into being. Instead, struggling companies with management boards dominated by government appointees were emerging: a strange hybrid between state and self-managed enterprises.

After 1976, the government appointed two CONAPS managers who would eliminate the amateurish and even demagogic style in which the sector and its firms had been run. The new appointees tried to impose economic and technical rationality on the sector, but at the price of reduced worker involvement. By 1980, a return to civilian rule was imminent, and the government made a last attempt to revitalize the sector. Workers elected their own boards of directors; regional and national assemblies were inaugurated; and worker control over FONAPS, the sector's financial institution, was confirmed.

The transfer of power was hasty, and it destabilized rather than consolidated the sector. The assembly elections prefigured the impending national elections and reflected partisan political concerns. There was not enough time for a genuinely representative leadership to form, and many of those who were elected were later accused of corruption. The legitimacy of national assembly elections was questioned, and for a time, there was an acrimonious public debate between competing factions. Meanwhile, FONAPS faced a liquidity crisis, largely because of past unpaid loans.

In some ways, this disarray was misleading since the focus of worker self-managed enterprises had already shifted. After 1976, government interest waned, and private initiatives began. As a result of bankruptcies (often fraudulent), prolonged labor conflicts, and factory takeovers, many companies were acquired by workers who were either unionized, organized as an industrial community, or both. Although many of these firms could have, few joined the social property sector: either the new businesses were considered financially unsound, or their workers feared external controls.

Legally, these firms were required to become worker production cooperatives, but few felt strong ideological or historical ties to the cooperative movement. These firms generally had a militant and integrated membership with ties to labor unions. Most of the new production cooperatives were affiliated with the Committee of Worker-Administered Firms (CEAT).

To help support these firms, three private institutions were formed with foreign financing. CIDIAG was started by a group of former officials from the Ministry of Industry. Although it has been relatively successful in gaining worker confidence, it was not until the early 1980s that it began to provide effective technical assistance, especially in the management of CEAT's revolving fund. The second group, INDA, is a splinter from CIDIAG, concentrated on providing loans, especially for working capital. A series of speculative ventures to generate profits to compensate for below-market-cost loans to self-managed firms led to huge losses, and the loan fund was later liquidated. The third organization, INPET, was founded by former generals and high-level civil servants to provide legal services. Later, INPET began a technical assistance and training program and started a small loan fund. Because of its more modest beginnings and a long-range strategy aimed at gaining worker trust through tangible results, today this is the largest and most consolidated of the three institutions. Partly because of the competition among these three support institutions for clients, and partly in an attempt to avoid isolating themselves from the union movement, the firms in CEAT remain a loose coalition.

SOME LESSONS OF THE CHILEAN AND PERUVIAN EXPERIENCE

Although the attempts to foster worker self-managed firms by creating a network of private and public support groups had diametrically opposed origins in Chile and Peru, there were convergences. The Chilean effort began in crisis and faced economic and political hurdles that were perhaps insurmountable. Similarly, Peru suffered from the effects of recessions in the world economy during the 1970s, and initial government sponsorship of self-managed firms faded into eventual indifference.

In both Chile and Peru, the effort to organize an integrated sector began outside existing worker self-managed firms, admittedly with the best of intentions. In both cases, the attempts were largely unsuccessful, although the exceptions are interesting. The firms with the best chance to survive in Chile into the 1980s could all trace their origins to the period when self-managed enterprises were first emerging, while all of the companies purchased after 1974 failed. In Peru, worker self-managed businesses have sprung up outside the auspices of the government and have begun to attract a private support structure. This suggests that the firms that have the best chance to survive originate "organically"—under unique circumstances, perhaps, but from the workers themselves.

Without diminishing the importance of external factors such as the health of the national economy and the attitude of the government, some of the failures in Chile and Peru were due to an inadequate relationship between self-managed firms and their support structure. This can be seen by exploring the record of the Chilean and Peruvian institutions that provided credit, training, legal advice, and technical assistance.

Credit

In both Peru and Chile, most worker self-managed firms were either new, were decapitalized by the bankruptcy of their previous owners, or had outmoded equipment which needed replacement. The borrowing needs of these enterprises were acute, but the workers' capacity for self-management was unproved, and financial institutions did not believe these businesses were credit worthy. Workers also lacked adequate alternative sources of capital such as personal or family savings.

The professionals who promoted self-management in both Peru and Chile responded by establishing financial entities dedicated predominantly or exclusively to providing loans to worker-owned enterprises. In Chile, an existing development finance institution was bought and transformed; in Peru, a quasi-public development finance institution (FONAPS) and a private loan fund (FONSIAG) were created.

These lending institutions were capitalized totally or partially by private, foreign donations or transfers from the state treasury, and—despite the precarious solvency of most borrowing firms—offered loans on favorable terms at below-market interest rates. This financial strategy generated a problem common to development finance institutions: the onset of decapitalization. If loans do not carry an interest rate that at least matches the rate of inflation, the lender suffers a loss (which is magnified by administrative overhead and the costs of servicing loans) and will eventually exhaust its funds.

The financial development institutions in Peru and Chile used two approaches to avoid decapitalization, without much success. First, they sought "inexhaustible" sources of funds, such as central reserve banks or foreign philanthropic organizations. However, in practice, no bank or international donor was willing to supply funds indefinitely, especially with results that were not encouraging. The financial development institutions in Chile did have access to funds from international donors for some six years, but the money finally dried up in 1981 when most of the businesses in the self-managed sector had gone or were about to go bankrupt. Although FINTESA—the sector's primary lending institution—had grown by 1982 into the twelfth largest of eighteen financial institutions in Chile, its assets were tied up in unpaid loans to the insolvent firms. In Peru, government funds never matched the level of rhetoric and remained frozen as government interest grew progressively lukewarm during the late 1970s.

Some development groups used a second strategy to avoid decapitalization. They tried to generate new funds—either by attracting deposits from or making loans to the general public, or by investing in speculative ventures. The money available to earn new money was limited, however. These development institutions were obliged to devote most of their resources to their clients in the cooperative or social service sector. The leaders of these institutions also were inexperienced in commercial banking and were unable to successfully compete with traditional banks in making profitable loans to the private sector. When some institutions tried to maximize their scarce resources through speculative ventures, the slide toward decapitalization accelerated.

Problems were also experienced by the borrowers. Many of the self-managed firms were totally reliant on the financial support institutions for loans. Knowing that the lenders had received their funds from donations or subsidized loans on condition that the money would be assigned to self-managed firms, the workers frequently felt "entitled" to the money they borrowed. As a result, the self-managed enterprises often felt no obligation to repay their loans or did so only after meeting other obligations. The financial institutions attributed this phenomenon to the workers' immaturity, irresponsibility, or lack of solidarity.

This basic difference between the support institutions and the enterprises was aggravated by the underlying condition of most of the borrowing companies. Most firms were saddled with large debts, obsolete machinery, and too little working capital. They needed a combination of medium- and long-term capital (to replace outmoded equipment, expand their plant, or diversify production) and short-term working capital (to provide an adequate cash flow and to increase production by exploiting idle capacity).

Unfortunately, the financial institutions had, at best, only limited funds for medium- and long-term loans. In Chile, at least, the first priority for funds during the early 1970s was for buying new firms rather than stabilizing existing production cooperatives. Even when credit became available, production cooperatives suffered a competitive disadvantage compared to private firms with equity capital which implied no repayment and on which dividends could be skipped when necessary.

When short-term loans were available, the repayment schedule for working capital often was less than the time needed to rotate the funds and generate the income necessary to retire the loans. The resulting penalties and additional financial expenses increased the real cost of the credit and limited the firms' ability to generate their own working capital.

In fact, the financial institutions resorted to such hidden charges as penalties and commissions to recoup money from loans that were offered at unrealistically low rates. This attempt to compensate grew out of the early and widespread amateurism in the financial institutions. Set up in order to help a specific sector, lending authorities tended to define their task in political, social, and philanthropic rather than financial terms. From this point of view, subsidized credit was considered equivalent to a donation which might or might not be repaid. On the basis of this fatalistic assumption—often more implicit than explicit—loan recovery became a hope rather than an expectation.

Within the firms, it was only a short step to use credit to sidestep rather than solve organizational problems—frequently saving incompetent or unscrupulous managers from the logical consequences of their actions. Employing the logic of subsidy, the financial institutions did not evaluate projects by their profitability and thus failed to implement a system for monitoring loans and advising firms. They were unable to assure the productive use of the money or its future repayment. As a result, self-managed enterprises continued to borrow in the belief that if they could not pay their loans, they need not pay.

The fact that the Chilean Foundation for Development and its successor, the Self-Management Institute, failed to keep adequate financial records to oversee or evaluate the funds they were funneling into the self-management sector is symptomatic. Audits were virtually impossible. Not only did this hamper sectoral planning, it wasted an opportunity to use loans to educate and train workers and managers in the responsibilities of running their own business.

There were attempts in both Chile and Peru at midstream corrections. In Chile, loan funds were targeted at those firms with the greatest chance to survive. In Peru, more experienced technicians were appointed to FONAPS, and they tried to introduce greater rationality into the system.

Unfortunately, the new "rules of the game" were often introduced abruptly and exacerbated tension between the firms and the support agencies. In Chile, workers who were about to lose their jobs pressured the primary development lending institutions into channeling funds intended for consolidating firms with better survival prospects into the revival and reorganization of businesses about to fail. In Peru, the technical staff soon clashed with the new majority of worker representatives on the FONAPS board and resigned.

The accumulation of indebtedness was slowed but not halted. Over time, the firms' assets were tied up totally or substantially in underwriting their loans. When the financial institutions—which were largely staffed by ex-civil servants from the Ministry of Industry in Peru and the Industrial Development Agency (CORFO) in Chile—discovered that their external funding was finite, the failure to develop strategies to maintain and increase their loan funds placed the lending agencies in a double bind. Loans could be recaptured only by bankrupting and auctioning off the very firms the agencies were supposed to support. The companies' dependence on the financial institutions was transformed into an interdependence where neither the firms nor the institutions were autonomous or viable.

Philanthropic organizations contributed to this paralysis in various ways. First, they funded institutions that lacked employees with sufficient financial knowledge and experience. Second, they approved projects that had no prospect of achieving self-sufficiency in the medium term on the (unspoken) understanding that additional future funding was available. Third, they did not exercise sufficient or timely supervision or follow-up in order to detect emerging problems. Finally, they never fully understood what was necessary to develop a financial system that would promote the firms' autonomy and consolidation. The basic problem was that support for self-managed enterprises did not transcend the desire to save jobs. Firms were not equipped to become more productive; they were maintained, and their continued survival depended on donations and subsidized credit.

Training

Workers in self-managed enterprises are typically unprepared for the tasks and responsibilities that come with ownership. To give them a competitive boost, support institutions provide training programs to equip the firms' labor force with the skills that the marketplace demands. Usually, these programs concentrate on three areas:

motivational development, technical training, and managerial expertise.

Because worker participation is usually a new experience, worker-owners need a set of new ideas to help interpret their roles. This new conceptual framework—which in its most elaborate form approaches an ideology—helps build a consensus among the labor force and reinforces acceptance of commonly agreed-upon rules of the game. The particular content of this motivational ideology can vary widely, as the diverse experiences of the Hutterites, Israeli kibbutzim, and the workers in Yugoslavian self-managed companies indicate.

The early training programs in both Peru and Chile tried, with varying degrees of success, to supply such a motivational under-pinning. In Chile, three institutions were charged with developing training programs during the early 1970s. Each of their curricula provided a separate social and political rationale. Not only did this make it difficult to organize the worker self-managed enterprise into a sector, but ideology was offered at the expense of technical and administrative skills. Within five years, the three support groups had dissolved without creating a permanent training program.

In the late 1970s, INA integrated a training program into its effort to channel financial aid to those firms with the greatest apparent chance to succeed. This second training phase was more pragmatic than the first, focusing on teaching literacy and technical, entrepreneurial, and administrative skills. The program was well received by workers but was terminated because participating firms could not pay for the service when INA was forced to curtail its activities because of financial difficulties.

The early training programs in Peru were also strongly ideological. However, as government support for a new "social property" sector waned, and new worker self-managed businesses spontaneously arose, the range of ideologies broadened. One immediate effect was to make the coordination of sector-wide policies even more difficult than in Chile. As technicians succeeded the social reformers who staffed the government support institutions, they tried to increase managerial competence within firms. Somewhat heretically, this drive for efficiency emphasized centralized control over worker participation and training. The private support groups that emerged to service new worker production cooperatives at first promoted competing ideologies that sometimes sparked crippling conflicts within individual firms and tended to increase friction between firms, but over time, adverse external pressures tended to highlight common problems at the expense of ideological differences, and pragmatic cooperation began to emerge.

The experience in both Chile and Peru suggests that worker self-managed firms may need a justifying rationale if they are to cohere, but ideology is no substitute for technical training. In the more successful programs, job-related technical training tended to promote worker satisfaction and provide a sense of job security, thereby reinforcing the idea of worker participation in the firm.

On the other hand, technical training can be too narrowly drawn, particularly when applied to managerial improvements. In a small firm, the workers must organize themselves to collectively run their business. In larger companies, the workers must be able to supervise managerial and technical personnel. Both tasks require workers to make new decisions as owners. Traditionally, management programs teach skills for particular slots in an organizational hierarchy; e.g., bookkeeper or salesman. One reason these programs succeed is that there is normally agreement about what a bookkeeper or salesman needs to know. But there is less certainty about how to teach the general principles of business operation to the members of a production cooperative. Self-management training programs often fail because there is no consensus about what a cooperative's general assembly or governing board needs to know.

Although many of the training efforts in Chile and Peru have fizzled, some of the more successful programs have begun to integrate the diverse aspects of training with an effective methodology. Using inductive techniques, the workers study and analyze what is concrete and familiar (machine, workshop, or job), gradually and accumulatively incorporating more complex realities. For example, a training program in Lima taught workers the concept of the break-even point by organizing groups to collect information about the costs, output, sales price, etc., of their most important machine. The data were then used to illustrate the distinction between fixed and variable and direct and indirect costs.

Training efforts organized by CEDEC in Chile and INPET in Peru have used these experiential techniques to teach job-related skills in a way that helps workers to better manage themselves. A firm's technical leaders (manager, foreman, line supervisor) and its political leaders (president, members of the governing board) are included in the program so the problem-solving methodology can be internalized within the firm. When this kind of training succeeds, conflicts between "participatory" laborers and "authoritarian" managers are minimized, and the factory or shop is transformed into a classroom where people learn how to analyze and adapt their everyday work habits. Since the content of programs emerges inductively, it is possible to tailor the training to an enterprise's specific and most-urgent needs.

Technical Assistance and Legal Advice

A worker self-managed firm usually begins with problems that must be addressed immediately (such as a lack of funds to meet the payroll or sudden resignation of key technicians) even if the workers are inadequately trained to solve them. Coordinating longer-term training programs with the more immediate needs for technical assistance was a problem in both Peru and Chile.

Technical assistance from support institutions was initially overlooked in Chile, where the overwhelming priority was to help workers buy firms before the companies could be sold to outsiders. After the enterprises were purchased and began to have problems, the need for technical assistance became more apparent, and responsibility for providing the needed aid gravitated toward the development finance institutions. These institutions were understaffed, however, and the same people who evaluated loan applications were expected to help the firms with their organizational and managerial problems. These professionals not only were cut off from vital information (it was not in a firm's interest to spotlight its problems if that would jeopardize a loan), they were themselves usually inexperienced in dealing with the problems of self-managed firms. As a result, assistance tended to be improvisational and occasional.

As self-managed firms encountered more problems, two other efforts to provide technical advice were started. Neither was successful. The umbrella organization managing the sector (INA) ostensibly offered technical assistance, but it never organized a systematic or permanent support structure. One private group, CEDEC, did eventually organize a technical aid program that also offered legal and entrepreneurial advice, but this plan promised medium- and long-term benefits when most firms were facing imminent bankruptcy. Self-managed firms could not afford to pay for the advice they needed, and the support institutions lacked funds to subsidize a more thorough program.

Firms in Peru have had difficulty obtaining technical aid that was consistent with workers managing their own enterprises. Initially, the government officials who were charged with servicing the sector were more concerned with ideological than technical issues. Their immediate objective was to mobilize a sector from scratch, not service its organizational and technical needs. As these appointees were replaced by technicians, centralized and efficient management was emphasized—rather than participatory management.

Despite frequent failures, there have been positive experiences with technical assistance in both Peru and Chile. One private institution in Peru that provides workers with advice has developed a particularly effective "delivery system." In response to a firm's request for help, a written report and perhaps a verbal report are presented. Beyond that, however, training programs are organized for everyone in the firm to explain how the study was made, the alternatives considered and rejected, the arguments in support of recommendations, and the tasks required for implementation. As a result, workers are better able to implement a project's recommendations.

The experience of self-managed firms in both Chile and Peru underscores the fact that legal advice is important for a number of obvious reasons. First, many self-managed enterprises begin with workers taking legal action to defend their interests and acquire ownership of the company. Second, since self-managed firms are organized differently from traditional businesses, existing legislation may be prejudicial or indifferent toward their problems, creating the need for new legal formulas. In Peru, for example, a new body of Social Law was passed to help adjudicate disputes involving social property firms.

FROM DEPENDENCE TO INTERDEPENDENCE

Achievements in worker self-management in Peru and Chile have been limited at best. In both countries, smoothly integrated sectors of individual firms and complementary support institutions failed to develop. Why?

A large part of the answer lies in the condition of the two national economies and the levels of state hostility and/or indifference. Yet, a deficient relationship between the firms and their support institutions was also a factor. The various types of support—credit, training, technical assistance, and legal aid—were often uncoordinated. Organizations frequently offered only one service; and when umbrella institutions attempted to unify services, they usually compartmentalized responsibility for each function within a separate department.

The experiences we reviewed suggest an approach that integrates credit, training, and technical and legal assistance will generate the best results. It is easy to see why. Self-managed firms often must borrow. If adequate studies are not made to determine the amount needed and the turnover time to pay off the loan, and if workers are untrained to efficiently use the funds, a firm may end up saddled with a crushing debt. An undercapitalized cooperative may survive for years at low-income levels—and then go bankrupt with the "help" of a well-intentioned but poorly planned loan or technological conversion.

The actual lending of money, however, is an important exception to the principle of integration of services. Financial development institutions in Peru and Chile that provided both loans and other services often confused technical with sociopolitical criteria and donation with credit. Conflicts of interest developed, and both the service institutions and their clients eventually became insolvent. This suggests that the criteria, and perhaps the responsibility, for making loans should be separate from other forms of assistance.

A second factor that affected the quality of support institution service was personnel. Typically, these organizations have been staffed by former government employees and by professionals with a political commitment to the poor and to the remaking of society. The ex-government officials generally are highly motivated, but they often favor grandiose schemes more appropriate to national planning and operate in a bureaucratic style that emphasizes codified rather than innovative procedures. These professionals sometimes display an Olympian disdain for budgets and cost overruns, presuming that the state treasury (or its equivalent) will provide needed funding. Many politically motivated professionals, on the other hand, tend to subordinate technical and financial criteria to ideology. Institutions staffed primarily by this group frequently operate in fiscal and administrative chaos and offer services that are technically mediocre or unsound. Admittedly, support institution professionals cannot be divided neatly into separate categories, but these two types occur frequently enough to be easily recognizable.

Finally, there is a danger of mutually damaging conflict between worker self-managed enterprises and their support institutions when both compete for the same scarce resources. Most self-managed firms begin with a desperate need for reliable assistance from support institutions. Understandably, the firms want the best help for the lowest cost with the fewest limitations. Meanwhile, support institutions prefer predictable clients with manageable demands, so service tasks can be simplified and rationally planned. When the sector as a whole is not expanding and the number of potential clients is frozen, support institutions have little incentive to further client independence or to cooperate with other potentially competing support groups.

Ideally, the relationship between self-managed firms and their support structure could be symbiotic. In the real world, each party often views the other as parasitic. Certainly, the economic and political crises in Peru and Chile during the past decade have increased antagonisms; relations between many support groups and self-managed enterprises degenerated into power struggles, mutual

destruction, or typically, chronic instability and conflict. In the words
of one worker, "When we sit around the table with representatives [of
a support institution] to discuss the problems of the firm, some have a
machine gun, some have a knife, and some are completely unarmed."

How can an antagonistically dependent relationship be converted
into a viably interdependent one? Although failures have been
frequent, the record of worker self-management in Peru and Chile
suggests that those support institutions that give individual firms the
best chance to survive and grow offer integrated services and use
participatory methodologies that preempt potential conflicts and
misunderstandings. Such institutions tailor their services not only to
meet the specific need of the firm, but to emphasize organizational
development so training is combined with consulting, an integrated
vision of the firm is promoted, and workers learn the skills to solve
their own problems.

Institutional Acronyms in Chile

ACL   Ahorro y Crédito Laboral Limitada
             (Worker's Savings and Loan Limited)

CEDEC   Centro de Estudios para el Desarrollo Cooperativo
             (Center for the Study of Cooperative Development)

CORFO   Corporación de Fomento
             (Industrial Development Agency)

FINTESA   Financiera de Interés Social, S.A.
             (Social Interest Financial Institution)

IFICOOP   Instituto de Financimiento Cooperativo
             (Institute for Cooperative Financing)

INA   Instituto de la Autogestión
             (Institute for Self-Management)

Institutional Acronyms in Peru

CEAT   Comité de Empresas Administradas por sus
             Trabajadores
             (Committee of Worker-Administered Firms)

CIDIAG   Centro Internacional para la Información y
             Desarrollo
             (International Center for Information and the
             Development of Self-Management)

CONAPS   Comisión Nacional de Propiedad Social
              (National Social Property Commission)

FONAPS   Fondo Nacional de Propiedad Social
              (National Social Property Fund)

INDA   Instituto para la Investigación y Desarrollo de
              la Autogestión
              (Peruvian Institute for the Research and
              Development of Self-Management)

INPET   Instituto Peruano de Empresas de Propiedad
              Exclusiva de sus Trabajadores
              (Peruvian Institute for Firms Exclusively Owned
              by Their Workers)

NOTES

1. The following examples are slightly fictionalized composites drawn from actual cases.

2. This was a procedure whereby bankrupt or abandoned firms or those taken over by their employees were temporarily placed under state supervision until their future was determined (that is, until they were bought by the workers, nationalized, or returned to former owners).

3. This comprised all workers—from manager to doorman—in businesses with more than five employees. The community, through a profit-sharing arrangement over time, would acquire 50 percent of the ownership and control of each firm.

4. An institution for training young workers.

PART 5

Investing in Culture

Development usually implies production. But for many multi-ethnic societies, even desperately poor ones like Bolivia, the need for cultural integration is no less acute than the need for economic growth—or rather, the two are linked. Each is a condition of the other.

—Patrick Breslin

11

The Technology of Self-Respect: Cultural Projects Among Aymara and Quechua Indians

PATRICK BRESLIN

Of Bolivia's estimated six million people, 60 percent are Indian, and the rest are *criollo*. As is often the case in Latin America, the line that separates the two is drawn more by culture and history than race. An Indian is a person who comes from an Indian community, wears Indian dress, and speaks one of thirty Indian languages—most often, Quechua, Aymara, or Guaraní. A *criollo* is a white or mestizo—usually an urban person—who bears the language and traditions of the Spaniards.

Since the Conquest, "Indian" has also meant the people who are exploited. Avid for the mineral wealth of the Andes, the Spaniards herded Indians into silver mines, and then onto the haciendas that grew up around the mining centers. Institutionalized systems of mandatory labor preserved the serf-like condition of the Indian for more than a century after independence. A common practice called *pongiaje* (from the Aymara word for door), required that every night an Indian protect the landowner's house by sleeping curled in the doorway. Even today, the word *indio* is so weighted with connotations of oppression and degradation that it is considered an insult. The more neutral term, *campesino*, has replaced it in polite language.

Despite advances since the 1952 revolution, chasms of distrust separate Indians from criollos. Many Bolivians insist that the political instability and economic chaos for which their country is famous are only surface manifestations of these deeper rifts. They see scant possibility for genuine national development until there is both self- and mutual-respect among the groups that cohabit the country.

Development usually implies production. But for many multi-ethnic societies, even desperately poor ones like Bolivia, the need for cultural integration is no less acute than the need for economic growth—or rather, the two are linked. Each is a condition of the other.

The Inter-American Foundation has supported several projects in Bolivia which address the human as well as the material requirements for development. Jorge Arduz, president of one group that has received foundation support, expressed the need this way: "The important factor in any kind of development is the human factor. To be productive, man has to value himself, which means being able to understand where he stands in society and in history. That's why for us, cultural development goes hand in hand with economic development."

But how? What is the technology that restores respect after four hundred years of degradation? In recent years, many Bolivians—campesinos, community organizers, schoolteachers—have looked inward to their own traditions. These people approach their culture as developmentalists. They have found resources in their music, language, folktales, crafts, and dance. They see these cultural forms as the basis for educational programs that teach self-worth. By inverting the symbols associated with shame, they create a kind of cultural capital that is as important and valuable as land, water, or seed.

PROJECT AYNI: AESOPS OF THE ANDES

The Christmas tree light bulb in the control room window flashed red; and in the studio, three Aymara Indians leaned toward their microphones and began to dramatize the fable of the farmer and the fox. In the control room, an Aymara woman draped in an alpaca poncho expertly twirled the dials of the recording equipment, checking the oscillating needles and adjusting sound levels. The bowler hat that normally crowns her black, braided hair rested beside her on a shelf.

This scene is repeated three mornings a week in the La Paz studio of Radio San Gabriel. Fifteen-minute tapes are recorded and then broadcast to the *altiplano*, where an estimated two million Aymara speakers live—three quarters of them in Bolivia, the rest across the border in southern Peru. Four centuries ago—before the European conquest—this was a prosperous area. But today the highland home of the Aymara is one of the bleakest, harshest, and poorest rural aras of the hemisphere.

The people in the recording studio are members of the Centro de Promoción Cultural Campesino Ayni. These seven young Aymara leaders are trying to reanimate the centuries-old fables of the Aymara people, and they are using radio to do it. "The Aymara," said the Spanish Jesuit who directs Radio San Gabriel, "are like the Japanese. They are traditional and progressive at the same time."

Radio is *the* medium of mass communication in rural Bolivia. Newspapers circulate only in the cities, and then only to the minority who read Spanish. Television antennas are sprouting from rooftops in the cities; but in the countryside, only radio reaches into every community and into practically every home. Many Aymara—such as army recruits stationed in distant corners of Bolivia—write to their families in care of Radio San Gabriel. The station broadcasts a mail call, and the letters are promptly picked up at its office. It is the only station broadcasting exclusively in the Aymara language, and all but four of the radio staff of forty-eight are Aymara. Ayni's idea of broadcasting traditional fables blends well into San Gabriel's mixed format of cultural and educational programs.

The seven young Aymara who make up the Ayni group refer to themselves as "promoters of popular development." All seven come from peasant backgrounds. Although most completed primary school, only a few went on for more than a year or two of secondary school. Each participated in leadership training programs for campesinos and then began working on rural development projects. As Aymara, they are conscious of their long history as an oppressed people. They bitterly recall the haciendas and the degradation of enforced labor.

Ayni's members, like a small but growing number of Aymara rural leaders, share a vision that culture is a foundation upon which to build. They speak of educational and cultural revitalization. Some of their projects are as straightforward as construction of community cultural centers that double as meeting halls and classrooms or helping the Ministry of Education teach short courses on weaving, tailoring, electrical repair, and food preparation in rural areas. Others are as sophisticated as the Radio San Gabriel education project.

Felix Tarqui, Ayni's director, explained the group's evolution this way: "We are all campesinos. We each began to participate in a course that sought to prepare us for educational work in the countryside. But as we went along, we saw that for education to be effective, it must build people's capabilities, not reinforce feelings of inferiority. It must be based on the culture of the people being educated."

The public educational system is a controversial subject in Bolivia, and the Aymara speak of its failings with vehemence. "Education here attempts to colonize us," one Aymara organizer said.

"The rural school in Bolivia is simply a jail for children," said another.

"It is all in Spanish," complained an Aymara linguist. "How can it *not* be an alienating education?"

Ayni cannot replace the national educational system, but its radio program does provide an educational experience with which the Aymara can identify. Not only is it effective because it is in the language of its listeners, but—as the accompanying example illustrates—stories are perceived by the Aymara to be a method of teaching and learning. No Aymara is too "uneducated" to understand the implications of the laziness of the sons who do not follow their mother's instructions.

Another series of fables traces the adventures of a fox. No one misses the fox's symbolism as a deceitful middleman. In some fables, the allegorical fox represents the Aymara themselves, matching cleverness against the brute force of larger, fiercer beasts. The stories reinforce traditional Aymara values of shrewdness, hard work, and respect for elders.

To gather tales, the three Ayni members who work on the radio program first visited communities throughout the highlands. Once the program went on the air, however, they began to receive a stream of stories written and mailed in by listeners. Currently, two or three tales a day arrive by mail at the radio station—many painstakingly written out in a mixture of Aymara and Spanish. Other listeners, instead of writing down a story, come into La Paz to tell it.

The members of Ayni turn the narrative into a script. Lines are written for each character. Frequently, the same characters appear in several stories—for example, the wise grandfather and Susana and Paulino who come to him for advice.

> *Grandfather:* Paulino, you're wandering around like a stray mutt. Don't you have anything to do? Haven't you heard the saying: "Loafers, like dust, are gone with the wind?"
> *Paulino:* No, Grandfather. I never heard that.
> *Susana:* Well, now that you have, you must never be lazy.
> *Paulino:* Grandfather always has good advice. His experience makes him wise.
> *Susana:* That's right. We should always listen to his advice. Grandfather, what story will you tell us today?
> *Grandfather:* A story I heard in the province of Los Andes, about a widow who had three lazy sons. This was in ancient times. One day, she sent them to plant potatoes.

> *Mother:* My sons, it's time to plant the potatoes. Take these seed potatoes to the field. Plant them and then come right back.

Roberto: All right, Mother. We'll plant the potatoes.

[Musical transition]

Roberto: Whew, these seed potatoes are heavy.

Manucho: These hoes and picks are wearing me out, too.

Santico: Oooh, I'm beat! Why did Mama have to make us walk so far? I need to rest. You plow the soil.

Roberto: But, how can you want to rest, Santico? If we work together we can finish early.

Santico: No, I can't. Didn't I tell you I'm exhausted?

Manucho: Then let's forget it. The rest of us are tired too.

Grandfather: So the three lazy sons didn't plant the potatoes. Instead they cooked them and then, not being able to eat them all, amused themselves throwing them at one another. When it was late, they returned home where their old mother was waiting.

[Musical transition and sound of wind]

Grandfather: When six months had passed, the mother told her sons to harvest the potatoes. No one wanted to. So the mother went by herself. She had scarcely begun to turn up some plants when a man came along.

Man: Hey, woman, why are you gathering my potatoes when you haven't planted your own?

Mother: But, sir, I sent my sons here to plant . . .

Man: Your sons were loafers. The day we were all working, they didn't plant one potato. They spent the whole day eating and playing.

Grandfather: The poor mother returned home, filled with bitterness at her sons. Not having any food in the house, she cut a piece of flesh from her leg and silently served it to them. Soon after, she died and her sons realized what she had done. In a flash, they were transformed: one into wind, another into frost, and the third into hail.

Paulino: What punishment! No wonder our grandfathers are not loafers.

Grandfather: That's right, my grandchildren. Otherwise, as the story teaches us, they would have been swept away with the wind.

How is Ayni's radio program received by its Aymara listeners? At an isolated farmhouse southwest of La Paz, one woman said: "Most people around here listen to it. It's more than entertainment. It's important, because each story makes you think. And often, after listening, the young people ask for more stories."

Others are less convinced. From a community near La Paz: "Some don't like to hear that this is the way we were. They think it confirms the picture the whites have of us: primitive, superstitious, that we have strange beliefs. Some even think that it could therefore do us harm."

In Bolivia, the Aymara have the reputation of being much more impermeable than other Indian societies. They have protected themselves from the outside by sealing themselves off. Asked whether there isn't need for more intercultural communication, an Aymara rural organizer said, "For now, it's important to preserve the culture for ourselves. When we go somewhere, people look at us and ask us, 'Well, what people are you? Are you Quechua or Aymara?' And when we say, 'We're Aymara,' then they want to know what kind of people we are, what are our customs. We need to know them ourselves in order to be able to show them to others. Later on we can think more about carrying our culture to other people."

CENTRO CULTURAL LOS MASIS: HARMONIZING BOLIVIA'S CULTURE

When a group of youngsters play the haunting music of the Andes, Bolivia's discordant culture suddenly seems a bit closer to harmony. It is there in the instruments: the guitar brought from Spain; the *charango*, an Indian version of the guitar, its body fashioned from a humped armadillo shell; and the fur-trimmed drums, the *quenas* (flutes), and *zamponas* (pan pipes) that are as Andean as the snow on Illimani's peak. Together, they produce a rhythmic, piercing music tinged with the desolation of the altiplano.

Late one sunny afternoon in Sucre, Bolivia's nineteenth century capital, four teenagers headed out Calle Perez to the whitewashed, colonial-style building which houses the Centro Cultural Los Masis. Warming up for their music classes, they capered along the street, blowing riffs at one another on their quenas and zamponas. People passing them on the narrow sidewalk smiled.

There weren't always smiles for the quena and zampona. Sucre is perhaps the best preserved colonial city in all of South America, and it has always preened its Spanish heritage, which included a deprecatory attitude toward all things native. Until 1952, no Indian wearing traditional garments dared even enter the city's central plaza. Thus, when the young people who formed the original group, Los Masis, first began to play Indian instruments in Sucre, tomatoes sometimes came flying their way, and most people dismissed them as "hippies."

In those days musical performance meant an occasional visiting artist from Europe. "Serious" music did *not* include sounds such as those produced by the flutes and drums of the villagers of nearby Tarabuco, whose feet, shod with rattling spurs and three-inch wooden clogs, shook the earth as they stomped through their monotonous dances. But when word filtered back from Paris and Rome in the 1960s that groups playing Andean music were the rage, many Bolivians began to listen with greater interest.

In 1969, several university students in Sucre formed a group to play Andean music. They called themselves "Los Masis." Roberto Sahonero, one of the original members, explained the name: "It's a Quechua word. It means someone of your class, your equal; someone who's neither more than you, nor less than you. An intimate friend, almost a brother." During the next decade, Los Masis prospered. They released several records and traveled thousands of kilometers on concert tours.

Since it was composed of university students, Los Masis began losing members as they finished their studies and moved on to other careers. Tito Tapia, another original member, thinks it was this inherent instability of the group that motivated some members to begin teaching music and dance to children in Sucre. After 1975, they found themselves devoting more and more time to teaching, and in 1980, the group known as Los Masis played its last concert together. But by then, the Centro Cultural Masis was well established.

Since 1980 the center has offered nightly classes in guitar and Andean musical instruments. In its workshop, students are taught to make as well as play the traditional instruments. More important, they learn to value the culture that they symbolize. There are also classes in theater, mime, and the Quechua language. Students who can afford it are asked to pay $4 for the two- to three-month courses. Those whose interest in the music continues are encouraged to form their own groups.

The Masis center's impact on life in the Sucre area is varied. For example, the center has placed its mark on Sucre's carnival—a four-day, pre-Lenten celebration—by reviving the traditional synchronized dances. In the weeks leading up to the pre-Lenten festival, the center offers classes in traditional dancing, and the number of people participating has doubled every year. The center directs an exhausting regimen of physical training and nightly practice. This year, 500 children, teenagers, and adults signed up for five weeks of strenuous conditioning every morning from six to eight o'clock plus an hour of dancing six evenings a week.

The efforts of the Los Masis Center are felt especially in the poor barrios on Sucre's outskirts. There, many impoverished, Quechua-speaking migrants from the countryside face a daily struggle for survival in an alien world. Many of the barrio's residents are rural children sent by their parents to live with relatives during the school year. "A child will come in here crying because someone called him an Indian," said a foreign teacher in one barrio. "They have lovely legends, lovely traditions, but they're not valued, and so they don't value themselves. The problem is how to learn to value those things again, in the face of a modern world that devours tradition."

El Tajar is one such poor neighborhood—dark, low-roofed houses that are crowded along the railroad tracks below the city. One Saturday night, 250 people jammed the parish hall while dozens more strained at the doorways and open windows for a program that included works in progress by the center's theater group, educational slide shows on local festivals, and traditional music by four newly trained groups.

That night, after each of the center's barrio performances, three scholarships for music classes were awarded. In fact, students from all the nearby neighborhoods now attend classes at the center. And instructors from the center are beginning to work in more distant barrios.

The slide show at El Tajar was produced by the center's research unit, which documents the cultural legacy of the Sucre region. Similar narrated slide shows are presented in the schools. "Nanta Ruaspa," the center's twice-monthly radio program (in Quechua, it means "to open a road"), draws upon these materials. The program reaches listeners in both rural and urban areas. School children typically have been taught to esteem foreign culture and to denigrate their own. This is the first systematic effort in the region to treat the culture, history, and geography of surrounding communities as educational tools.

A group called "Raices," seven teenagers who have been playing together since they were ten years old, now teaches in San Juanillo, a poor neighborhood on the far side of Sucre. Raices is clear evidence of the center's ability to train accomplished musicians and to imbue them with respect for traditional culture. They have already won top prizes in regional and national festivals. Their repertory has grown from the days when, as one of them recalled, "If an audience asked for an encore, we'd play the same song again. We only knew two songs then." The group plays and dances in traditional Indian dress. It is the same clothing that, outside the center, still provokes middle-class disdain. The challenge, which Los Masis recognizes, is to generate the same respect for Indian dress on the street as it now generates on the stage.

The center's growth and diversification have more than met the hopes of the young musicians who gave up their own performing careers to found it. Asked if he missed his days of touring with Los Masis, Tapia said: "Yes, a bit, but teaching at the center keeps me in touch with the music. More important, I have the sense that there's something permanent. Behind me there are thirty-five or forty young people that I've helped to train. We've transmitted not only the music, but the tradition of teaching. Now Raices, who are only kids of sixteen—they're already teaching the younger kids."

BREAD AND ROSES

In 1912, mill girls in Lawrence, Massachusetts, went on strike under the banner, "We want bread and roses too." Many Bolivians, surveying their country's poverty and disarray, have concluded that bread and roses—economic and cultural development—are inseparable, and that in fact, the latter may well be a precondition to the former.

Ayni and Centro Cultural Masis are two responses to the cultural divisions that afflict Bolivia. Both projects emphasize Aymara and Quechua values of mutual assistance, solidarity, and equality. The members of Ayni and Centro Cultural Masis believe that until criollos better appreciate the values of the majority of the nation's inhabitants, Bolivia's future will remain bleak. Linguist Juan Yapita de Dios put it this way: "A great need here is to diminish the ignorance of the criollo, to educate him to the worth of the native values. It is the discrimination practiced by the criollo against the indigenous people and all the resulting distortions in education, in jobs, in possibilities for advancement which is the brake on Bolivia's development." Ayni and Los Masis contribute to that educational process by legitimizing Indian culture.

12

Wandering on the Boundaries of Development

ARIEL DORFMAN

As a child, one of my friends thought the Matacos were some sort of animal. He had been brought up on a sugar mill in the province of Tucuman, Argentina, where at night the adults would tell stories. One story dealt with something called Matacos, which were hunted down by the hundreds in the jungles of the Gran Chaco forest. He remembered, above all, an evening when a guest of his father related how Matacos had been picked off one by one by soldiers from the back of a moving train. This confirmed his impression that the victims were monkeys or other wild beasts.

That idea persisted until several years later. One morning he went out into the yard and saw his grandmother standing in front of two small, bronze-faced children, an impassive brother and sister. With a pair of large scissors, she began to shear off their black, dirty hair. "These Matacos," she announced, "are full of lice. This is the only way to get rid of them."

It was only then that my friend realized that the Matacos were Indians.

* * *

There is a vast region in the Argentine province of El Chaco, some two million hectares of dry scrub forest, known as El Impenetrable. I found nobody who could fix the date when the phrase first came into use, but everybody agrees that it describes no ordinary jungle. A thick,

A slightly revised version of this chapter first appeared in the *Massachusetts Review* Fall-Winter 1986, XXVII, 3-4; and is used here with permission of the author.

intertwined bramble of vegetation stretches densely for miles, with an occasional solitary tree jutting above the low bush, to form a suffocating wall of thickets you can neither enter without a guide nor leave alive were that guide to abandon you.

But it is not the forest alone that isolates the zone. The land cannot absorb all the water that flows into it—water from the sky during months of rain; water from swollen rivers that are fed by the remote Andes when they thaw, rivers overflowing and changing course unpredictably. For days, often weeks, the roads are cut off—they can be navigated for miles as if they were narrow lakes. Afterward, withering months of dry heat, even of drought, will come; but that does not matter, the local people know that soon enough they will have more water than they know what to do with.

Most people would find such a place, alternating between swamp and arid scrubland, not only impenetrable, but uninhabitable. What to others is inhospitable and menacing is to the remaining Matacos— 15,000 of the extant 23,000 are concentrated in this area—a last refuge, and perhaps, a last opportunity to survive.

It is here, on the northern frontier of El Impenetrable, bordering the brown, muddy currents of the tumultuous Rio Bermejo, that the village of El Sauzalito lies. It is here that a remarkable experiment is being carried out to try to save a people from extinction.

* * *

In 1879, Julio Roca, then Argentina's minister of war and soon to be its president, defined a new strategy toward the Indians, who still controlled vast territories of the republic. "It is necessary," he said, perhaps thinking of the newly invented Remington rifle, "to directly search out the Indian's hiding place and make him submit or expel him." The resulting offensive against the Indians of the Pampas was known as *La Campaña del Desierto* (the Campaign of the Desert), and it all but exterminated the nomad warriors who roamed the rich, fertile plains that were needed for grazing cattle and raising wheat. At the same time, though with less urgency and fewer resources, the Gran Chaco (called the Green Desert) was conquered, and the remaining tribes of Indians were pushed back. The offensive culminated finally in the expedition to the river Pilcomayo in 1912 and the massacre that was probably at the source of those stories my friend once heard around the bonfire in Tucuman.

The Matacos have their own version of what happened. Andrés Segundo is a fifty-four-year-old Mataco who learned how to write forty years ago. One of the first things he wrote down was his grandparents' memory of that expedition against his people, a recollection repeated today by his own children and grandchildren. He reads from his notebooks, and because his words are difficult to follow, I try to understand better by focusing on the print. Though the words are Spanish, the small, scrubby letters look almost indecipherable. As his fingers trace the hieroglyphics across the page, his voice is slurred, repetitive, incantatory.

> We did not know where the soldiers came from or why. They found where the aborigines [the Matacos never use the words "Indians" or "natives" to refer to themselves] lived and came with rifles, with bullets, beating people up. The Matacos went into the *monte* (the bush). There was one woman with a child. She was hurt. She threw the child away. That is what my grandfather told me. They hunted the aborigine as if he was a tiger. . . . We were not harming anyone. We lived from the land, gathering the things that belonged to nobody. I do not know know why the soldiers came.

The reason is in fact quite simple. They came because by then Argentina was producing goods for export to foreign markets, and a lot of Indian land was there for the taking. "The settlers would come," Manuel Fernández, another Mataco chronicler, told me, "and ask for permission to clear land or settle down. They might give the tribe a cow." The Indians interpreted this as a gesture of gratitude. The settlers understood that they had bought the land. To the Matacos, that was absurd: How could you sell the land? The Army arbitrated. . . .

Their territory began to dwindle—but even so, the Matacos were not to be left alone on what remained. The Argentine economy needed not only their land, but their bodies as well.

Andrés Segundo has also recorded this event. His uncle told him of the day that a stranger arrived. He had been sent by the owner of a remote sugar mill in search of field hands to cut cane. The long journey that followed is recorded on yellowing scraps of paper—how they walked for a month, whole families, until they reached the train. Andrés Segundo tells the tale in a monotone, almost without emotion, as if these catastrophes were natural and not manmade. It rained along the route, it seems (I write "it seems" because the details are blurred, as if it were still raining and there were mud on the words themselves). The little ones cried from the cold. A terrible wind swept down, trees fell, people were killed.

That was to be the first, but not the last trip. Trapped in the system of debt bondage, increasingly dependent on manufactured goods, the Matacos keep returning to the sugar plantations (cotton would come later). Part of the year they were seasonal workers, hiring out for low wages and cheap merchandise; the rest of the time they hunted and fished, and ate fruits and berries.

But even this divided, miserable life was endangered. By the 1960s, fewer workers were being hired—the era of mechanization had set in. (On the plane back from the Northeast, I happened to sit next to a major Argentine cotton exporter. Texas Instrument in hand, he calculated, for my benefit—punching plus and minus buttons, doling out percentages—how mechanization had made the migrants increasingly obsolete.)

The Matacos found themselves in a precarious situation. The *monte* was eroding, animal species were disappearing, the ecological equilibrium of the region had been fractured, wages were insufficient. ("There was no work," Andrés Segundo explained, "but we had to eat anyway.") Along with malnutrition, diseases like tuberculosis, Chagas, and parasitosis became prevalent. Infant mortality rose.

As the 1970s began, the future looked still bleaker for the Matacos. They had survived natural floods and disasters for centuries, but they could not withstand the manmade flood of modern civilization. Like so many other contemporary tribes of aborigines, the Matacos seemed bound for extinction.

* * *

There was no road to El Sauzalito twelve years ago. Had you been able to get there, you would have found a scattering of thatched huts in the middle of a clearing overgrown with weeds. Remove the steel machetes, some clothing, a couple of bottles and tin cans, and you might have thought you were visiting the Stone Age.

Today El Sauzalito is connected by a dirt road to Castelli, 200 miles away, and by radio to the outside world. In the center of the town is a plaza, with benches, planted flowers, gravel pathways. Nearby is a bungalow where the elected mayor and aldermen meet, along with an office for the justice of the peace and a civil registrar. A hospital, a grade school, and a high school have been built. Most (though not all) of the inhabitants live in brick houses. And there is electricity.

More important, instead of losing population, El Sauzalito is growing. Couples are marrying, children are being born. I met several young men who had left to log trees but were now returning home for good. The movement is centripetal, not centrifugal as before.

Just a few miles away, you can still find small settlements that remind you of El Sauzalito's recent past: sparse collections of huts barely differentiated from the surrounding *monte*. But the real distance is not measured in miles. To transform El Sauzalito, the Matacos have spent thousands of hours and unstinting energy, and resources have poured in from the outside. If the Matacos were to sink into apathy, if the resources were to dry up, this new version of El Sauzalito would slip back in time, slip away into the waiting overgrowth, and once again begin to die.

* * *

At the beginning of this century, a doctor by the name of Maradona wrote a book, *Através de la Selva* (*Crossing the Jungle*), in which he narrates his visits to various Indian communities of the Gran Chaco. "The Indian," he writes of the Mataco, "speaks softly and is even gentle in the way he treats you, but his savage, suspicious, and egoistic nature quickly prevails." On other pages, he mentions criminal personality and readiness to destroy. Other adjectives he uses are "indolent," "decadent," "ridiculous," "sanguinary."

The Argentine Constitution, of course, uses none of these words to describe the Indian. But by mandating that the Indian be converted to Catholicism as a way of guaranteeing peace (Article 67, Item 15), it legally affirms the inferiority of native civilization and culture and denies Indians the right to their own beliefs—a 1978 decree put the undersecretary for Indian affairs also in charge of the welfare of minors, elderly, and the handicapped. Indians are lumped together with those who are not adults, and with those who have already lived out their usefulness and are waiting for death.

* * *

When Diego Soneira arrived in El Sauzalito in 1973 as the representative of the Instituto del Aborigen (a sort of Bureau of Indian Affairs), he had already spent several years working in the area and was convinced that only a dramatic alteration in their way of life could save the Matacos. They had been, until then, constantly on the move, either as nomads in the jungle or as migrants on the plantations. Neither form of subsistence offered any guarantee of stability. What the Matacos needed, he thought, was to become the legal owners of their own land so they would never again be expelled from it. But this meant they had to till that land and become sedentary.

This was not going to be easy. Though they had learned something about growing subsistence crops from the outreaches of the Incan empire many centuries ago and later picked up a bit more from the whites, the Matacos are primarily hunter-gatherers. What had taken the human race many thousands of years to develop the Matacos would have to achieve in a generation.

Soneira was not the kind of bureaucrat who comes to visit the poor or the Indians armed with theories and suggestions that others must enact and then leaves for a comfortable home. He knew that if change were to have any chance of success, it would have to be carried out by the Matacos themselves and could not be imposed from the outside. And he knew this meant he would have to live as the Matacos did. A former priest who lost none of his missionary zeal when he gave up the priesthood, Soneira arrived in El Sauzalito to stay. Six other white persons—experts in health, agriculture, education—joined him, among them his new wife, Nene, and her mother Clemencia Sarmiento, known to one and all from then on as Mami.

Of course the Matacos were suspicious. They had no way of knowing that Diego was different from the other white men, who had brought ambitious proposals and then gone away richer than when they arrived and certainly better off than the Indians they left behind. In their first meeting with Soneira—which has assumed a sort of legendary, almost foundational status in the collective memory of El Sauzalito and is now narrated in a confused tangle of versions—eight Matacos were ready to cooperate; 150 others opposed his presence. (Each Mataco I spoke to included himself among the eight.) What *is* clear is that Soneira's group managed, after hours of discussion during a deluge, to pitch three tents in the middle of the bush (in the exact spot where the central plaza now proudly stands). As the days slipped by, Soneira and his companions gradually won the confidence of the Matacos—though he would be expelled twice from the town when they did not receive everything they wanted. Soneira eventually created the Asociación de Promotores Chaco, which brought in outsiders to help the Matacos develop agricultural projects. Today, there are nineteen *promotores* throughout the Impenetrable.

To focus only on the outside advisors, however, is unfair to the many Matacos who had concluded on their own that they were heading for a dead end. Without these Matacos, Soneira's plans would never have worked. Ernesto Reynoso, for one, the *cacique* (chieftain) of the Matacos, had watched his people's situation deteriorate year after year. Like Soneira, he had come to believe that land ownership was the best hope for the Matacos. Nobody had elected Reynoso to his post; no other candidate wanted the job. While he may tend to exaggerate his own role ("I made this place; I am the *tata*, the big father of this place; I am the authority here."), all agree that he *was* indispensable. Over the years, he was to prove himself a wily advocate, tirelessly pestering authorities to exact promises of aid, then knocking on doors to hold them to those promises. A stubborn rock of a man, he knew that if aid were to be continued, his people would have to show results. Behind him and beside him, therefore, stand many other Matacos. His pride in what has been accomplished is their pride. "These are the machines that did everything," he says, lifting up his arms. "And these legs, they did the walking. Everything you see—the plaza, the hospital, the fields—we made it all."

Reynoso's great-grandfather did not know a word of Spanish. He lived off the honey and the iguana and the fish. With machete, pickax, and shovel, his grandfather helped to build the railroad from Formosa to Salta. His father was a *bracero* in the plantations. Reynoso himself began to pick cotton when he was five years old. His wife died on one of those month-long treks to the cotton fields. "Someday," he told me, "we will have Mataco doctors. Who knows? Perhaps someday my grandchild will pilot a plane."

* * *

But the confluence of these two streams—the whites devoted to the Matacos and the Matacos' faith in themselves—might have been insufficient if another sort of downpour had not taken place. In 1975, the Argentine military overthrew the government of Isabel Perón.

How ironic that this event would help the Matacos, who, when they vote at all, tend to vote Peronist. The military government, as history has shown, was not overly interested in helping those who lived on the margins of society. Obsessed with security, however, they worried that the Gran Chaco was so underdeveloped and isolated that it would be vulnerable to foreign attacks—and the very notion that something "internal" could also be "impenetrable" was an insult to the macho geopolitical pride of the military.

The armed forces therefore supplied an enormous quantity of resources to the region—most quite useless. In the middle of the jungle, for instance, in an area with few natives, a small concrete town was built from scratch, replete with telephone lines, satellite-dish television, and air-conditioned buildings staffed by government employees who have nothing to do all day but wait for the next showcase visit.

But in El Sauzalito, funds could be used for plans that were already underway. Thus, when the governor of the province came for a visit and noted that a great deal had already been accomplished with little outside support, he offered Diego Soneira the post of *Intendente*. Though the military government's national policy ran directly counter to his own democratic ideals, Soneira saw the chance to further develop the area, pay the promotores salaries, and channel municipal money into essential infrastructure.

As Soneira reports it, he told the governor that there were two ways to approach the development of El Impenetrable. One alternative was to see it as an enormous enterprise. "In that case," he said, "your purpose is to make money, and you exploit things to produce an immediate benefit. Or you can see a vast school here. That means that, like any form of education, you will run a deficit in the short run, with the benefits coming many years from now. I am not an entrepreneur. If you want me and my people to work here, we must be allowed to make this place into a school that will give the Indians a chance to learn how to live on their own and not be condemned to live off welfare forever."

The governor, surprisingly, agreed.

* * *

It was inevitable that someday the vast school of and for the Matacos would run into trouble, because this effort is made up of two separate—one might almost say contradictory—learning processes.

The first, which has had priority until now, is to modernize the Mataco economy, allowing its members to cope with an overwhelming foreign civilization that technologically and organizationally is far more powerful than theirs.

The second, which was only implicit and thus far has found no institutional expression or funding, is to help the Matacos save their identity and sustain what makes them unique as they become integrated into a world whose rules they did not make.

To become modern and have an economic base of their own, the Matacos must break their traditional patterns of social organization. For hunter-gatherers, Nature is the provider: the future depends on reading the natural world carefully, not on the systematic planning of one's work. You collect enough to last for a brief period, and when that stock has been depleted, you go out and get more. Such a culture does not conceive of the idea, for example, that a crop can be ruined if you leave the fields for a week, that there are such things as capitalization, or credit to be repaid. The future is really not in one's hands. "This may happen," the Matacos told me. "And then again perhaps it may not."

Nor are the Matacos accustomed to fulfilling collective obligations. Formerly in their community, each family could leave without permission. Decisions were not made by a majority and imposed upon a minority. This is a perfectly logical structure if the renewable forest is always there, but it invites disaster if the earth must be worked, tractors allocated, seed and fertilizer distributed, if survival depends on taming Nature through mutual cooperation.

The Matacos have been relatively successful in this venture. This is evident in the number of buildings and facilities, in the increased standard of living, in the many hectares (still insufficient) now under irrigation, in the crops exported and the timber sold, and above all, in their capacity to organize. They control and regulate their own economic activities through the Asociación Comunitaria, with a subcommission for each industry—agriculture, lumber, tree-felling, repair work, and soon, fishing. The association allows the Matacos to plan their work, distribute the benefits, do the accounting, discuss and solve their difficulties. The promotores, to be sure, are still on hand with suggestions, expertise, techniques, as an unavoidable bridge to a confusing outside world, and they may remain until a new generation is educated. Yet, the Matacos are obviously weaving their uncertain way toward relative autonomy.

Achieving this first educational objective, however, has forced the Matacos to deal with the second, which has been perpetually postponed. The promotores did not initiate this experiment as a way to ingest one more aboriginal tribe into the stomach of the twentieth century. The idea was that the Matacos should modernize without losing their values and perspectives, their own culture.

The difficult question, of course, is the same one that is heard in many other places in the Third World: "Can it be done?"

* * *

The day I arrived in El Sauzalito, a little Mataco girl had just died. She was the sixteenth child to die in the last four months.

A few hours later, I met the doctor who is supposedly in charge of the community's health. I had heard stories about him—a man who turned away the sick if they called outside the regular schedule, a man who did not visit other communities, a man who supposedly had said that the only way to make an Indian work was to fire a couple of shots at him. But even those stories did not prepare me for the person who swaggered through the door. He began by verbally abusing the whole experiment: it was, he said—his eyes protruding from a thin, bony face—"a total failure." Instead of advancing, the Matacos were going backwards. He branded the recent decision to plant cotton as ludicrous and stated that what was needed was a *criollo* landowner to establish some order. Finally, he turned around, crouched slightly, and using his buttocks as a metaphor, wiped them with his hand to show how worthless he considered everything.

"Why are you here then?" I asked.

His answer chilled me. "I am not human," he said. Perhaps he meant "humanitarian"—but the word he may have used mistakenly suited his manner quite well. "I didn't come here to save anybody, but for my own benefit. I'm almost 60. If I had retired as an ordinary doctor, I would be a beggar. That's why I agreed to come to this place. So I could retire with the pension of a hospital director."

The doctor personifies, in my opinion, two undeniable facts about the Mataco condition. First, many outsiders come to such places not to help those who live there but to help themselves. Second, and perhaps more significant, the Matacos had been trying to get the doctor replaced ever since he arrived. They had received repeated assurances that he would soon depart, but there he sat, symbol of all the things— far too many things—that the Matacos do not control and yet are essential to their well-being. The Matacos can do little about the world economic crisis or that of the Argentine economy—even though these crises mean that their products fetch lower prices, that inflation eats up their benefits, and that subsidies and services become even scarcer.

The apparent hostility and complexity of the outside world creates among the Matacos an added dependency on the external buffers that protect and benefit them. Without the promotores or outside aid, the Matacos could not have begun their journey toward autonomy; but now they tend to think of those factors as permanent. Wherever I went, I had to submit, with some embarrassment, to a long litany of needs and petitions and complaints, as if each person were demanding that I solve individual problems.

This is not, of course, unique to the Matacos. The dilemmas of paternalism and dependency are present in most development projects. It is not my purpose to explore here how those problems can be overcome. What does matter is to note that if all power—both evil and good—seems to come from outside, then the Matacos' sense of self-worth is weakened. Everything they learn tells them that the road to autonomy, the road to success, passes through the abrogation and eradication of their past identity.

* * *

The anthropologist Edward Spier, in his classic study of the Yaqui Indians, coined the phrase "enduring peoples" to designate those human groups who have "experienced incorporation into nation-states, and have existed within or outlasted nation-states." He examines the Catalans and Basques of Spain; the Welsh and the Irish; the Cherokees, the Hopis, and the Senecas of the United States; the Lowland Mayas of Mexico; and finally, the Jews of many different states.

In all of these cases, he finds that a people will persist despite drastic changes in genetic constitution, place of residence, language, customs, and beliefs—if they continue to hold a common identity, that is, a stock of symbols and experiences that allow them to have a common understanding of the world and of their relationship to other cultures. Peoples who are unable to maintain the consciousness of their ethnicity are unable to remember their past collectively or use it to interpret the present, and will probably be absorbed.

Can the Matacos endure?

Do they have within their culture the resilience and flexibility to go through the rites of modernization without disintegrating as an independent cultural entity?

There is at this point no way of telling for sure. What I saw and heard was not overly encouraging.

In 1944, the Matacos were converted to Christianity by missionaries of the Anglican Church. For the first time, the Indians received some elementary education, health care, and protection from the incursions of the army and the white settlers who would often kill a Mataco or two for fun. The Indians were also taught to forget their own legends and stories, to feel ashamed of their past, and to stop dancing and singing to their traditional music.

I asked the Matacos I met to tell me stories and myths from their past. They either pretended not to understand my question or told me they could not remember. When I repeated several legends or described beliefs about the dead and their spirits—things I had read in collections edited by foreign anthropologists—people nodded, agreeing that these were stories they knew. They did not, however, admit to telling their own children these tales, to sharing that body of sacred law that contains moral guidance and threads of communal identity. Some promotores told me that something similar happens with songs and dances: the Matacos sing hymns at church, but the old instruments and melodies are being put aside and forgotten.

The only Mataco I met who was prepared to recount and discuss the old myths was, strange as it may seem, Ernesto Avendaño, the Anglican pastor of El Sauzalito. Perhaps he was sure enough of the divine origins of his own beliefs to be able to admit knowing those stories. He explained, in any case, that they were mere superstitions and were no longer necessary to his people. The songs, he added, were learned as apprenticeship to witchcraft, but all of that was a thing of the past.

This rejecting attitude of most Matacos—or at least the attitude they profess—creates a delicate situation for the promotores. Patricio Doyle, a former Catholic priest who focused on the cultural future of the Matacos, does not want to interfere with their religious beliefs or their form of worship. But he does want to discover what remains of their values, skills, and legends, what the Matacos can build on as they become part of the Western world and the Argentine nation.

He is now working on a *revistita*, a small magazine in Mataco and Spanish that will belong to the community itself and serve as a vehicle for amplifying the multiple voice of the Matacos. He hopes the Matacos will begin to express their present problems as well as what belongs to their past and their collective memory.

He has also managed to persuade two experts in the development of art and recreation among marginal groups to come from Buenos Aires and work with the local people; presumably the project will be funded by the Ministry of Education.

And yet, Patricio Doyle, who has spent many years among the Matacos, does not speak their language. Nor, for that matter, does any other promotor, not even Diego Soneira. Nor do any of the white children. Some words are understood, some conversations can be followed vaguely, but not one of the people who have come to help the Matacos survive as a cultural entity is fluent in their language. No matter how they have tried, they have been unable to learn it or even find Matacos who will teach them.

I heard the language often during my stay. Once, I remember, I was at a meeting that Mario Pisano, a promotor, held with the residents of nearby Vizacheral to discuss future fishing activity. After some words had been exchanged in Spanish, one of the men suddenly switched to Mataco, and the rest soon joined in with a flowing antiphony. Before one person had ended, another had begun, as if speaking to himself and yet to all of them, as if somebody inside were listening, murmuring very low—only ears accustomed to the bush could distinguish each sound—and on it went, a honied, intertwining superimposition of voices, until they stopped. They had reached some sort of conclusion, one and all of them, and Spanish was once again the language to be used. I felt, during these moments, as if they were defending their last refuge on earth, those thickets of syllables that only they could understand.

It almost seems as if the Matacos are unwilling to teach the promotores their language. Once you give strangers your language, it is as if you have given them your jungle, your land, your trees. It is in the language, after all, that places and birds, animals and customs are named and invoked.

Perhaps I had caught a glimpse of the real Impenetrable—the language, the one place in the world that belongs only to the Matacos.

* * *

The Matacos have beautiful legends.

Like all peoples, they narrate the origins of the universe, the reason why there are men and women, how animals appeared, why it rains and why honey exists, the struggles of heroes, and the voyages of tricksters. Some of their legends seem to be recent because they exhibit a considerable awareness of white, dominant people.

In one legend, the Matacos explain why they are so few and other tribes so populous. According to this tale, the different races and nations crawled out from underground through a hole dug by an armadillo. All the men and women of each race were able to escape and populate the earth. But when the Matacos' turn came, only a few appeared before a pregnant Mataco woman got stuck in the hole and was unable to move—and so many Matacos remain unborn.

Another legend says Christians and Matacos resided together long ago in one house "where everything could be found." Everything that was good—the axes, tools, horses, cattle, beautiful clothes for women—was taken by the ancestors of the Christians, and the Matacos were left with only clay pots, dogs, and "other inferior things."

The clay pot, which the Matacos make with great skill and elegance, is the protagonist of another short tale. A clay pot began to compete with an iron pot, saying that it could cook as well and as quickly over the fire. But the iron pot won, and so the pot made of earth cracked and was thrown away.

The Matacos have beautiful legends, but they feel defeated. A people will survive only if they are able to take pride in their own culture.

* * *

Between 1821 and 1982, almost 6.4 million immigrants came to Argentina. In 1895, immigrants made up 25 percent of the population; by 1914, this figure had risen to 30 percent, the highest proportion in the world.

No statistics record how many Matacos there once were. So we cannot know what proportion is now left.

* * *

Some 420 miles south of El Sauzalito is the city of Resistencia, the capital of the province of El Chaco.

In the central plaza of Resistencia (christened with that name because it triumphantly resisted the assaults of the savages) there is a statue. It is the copy of a statue I have seen often in art and history books and whose original I once contemplated in Rome itself. It was given to the city of Resistencia by the resident Italian-Argentine community, and it portrays the twins Romulus and Remus suckling a she-wolf.

That is how Rome saw its origins, as if there had been no previous tribes on its peninsula, no previous inhabitants. And the immigrants who came to the Argentine northeast saw themselves opening supposedly virgin territory just as the Romans did: each of them a Romulus, each a Remus, coming to establish tiny empires in a foreign land.

There is no statue in Resistencia to the ancestors of Andrés Segundo or Ernesto Reynoso. There is no statue of their ancestors anywhere.

* * *

By a strange coincidence I heard Rome mentioned the first morning I arrived in El Sauzalito. Although the reference had nothing to do with immigration, it may have had something to do with empires.

I asked Patricio Doyle why he had left Buenos Aires, what he was doing in this remote place.

"Christ was not born in Rome," Doyle answered. "He was born in Bethlehem. Who knows what will be born in this faraway land and radiate, by example, elsewhere?

* * *

Most of the Matacos I spoke with seemed unaware of their purported transcendence or of the cultural crossroads they have come to.

I hesitated before writing down that previous sentence. I really cannot be certain that it is true.

The problem is that I was barely able to communicate with the Matacos during my brief stay. We talked, of course, extensively. Yet there was, except for one occasion, no deep contact—no moment when two people come together and know they are sharing something, that there is some understanding. I lacked their language, and they used mine without eloquence, though often with great dignity. Their Spanish, moreover, besides not being their native tongue, is the language of those who dominate them, and they must have supposed that what I would write about them might be essential for future aid or grants. They were careful, therefore, of what they said. Nor did it help that I lacked an interpreter: translations at least pretend that there is some equality in the interchange. And there was the incredible reserve and intractability of the women, with whom I was never able to speak at all, and whose importance in the conservation and transmission of an oral, autochthonous culture cannot be overstated.

I was not frustrated by this lack of connection. I interpreted it as a sign that the Matacos had secret paths in their forests to which I had no access, treasures they would not yield easily. I was glad they had something hidden, and only hoped that behind their silence, or the words that are like silence, there are strengths upon which they can build as their experiment continues. As they become more self-assured, they should be able to engage in an ever more significant dialogue with the outside world.

But there was one exception, a man named Ramón Navarrete. He is the *primer consejal* (the deputy mayor) of the *municipio*, the highest political and administrative post a Mataco has ever held. I had tried to speak to him on several occasions, but he was always busy. Only on my last day in El Sauzalito—as the afternoon turned into green-hot evening—were we able to talk.

When democracy and elections returned to Argentina in 1983, Diego Soneira decided to step down as *Intendente*. The concentration of so much power in his hands allowed the community to take gigantic steps forward, but it had also created confusion and seemed a bit artificial. It was time, Soneira believed, for the people themselves to administer their own institutions, to be less sheltered from the outside world. They had to learn not to look to him for all the answers. Though the Matacos constituted a large majority of the population, they did not propose one of their own as mayor, preferring a *criollo* who was sympathetic to them and had administrative experience. They did, however, elect three consejales (aldermen), and Navarrete is one of them. He is not a natural leader, as is Ernesto Reynoso, but he is of all the Matacos the one who best understands how language and Argentine society work. He is the closest example to an "intellectual" that I found in the Mataco community.

Like intellectuals everywhere, Navarrete is anguished. He must cope with burdens he only vaguely comprehends—budgets, sick leaves, papers in triplicate, the wonders of modern-day bureaucracy—and at the same time respond to the increasing demands of Matacos who believe the *municipio* exists to provide jobs and food.

To live between two worlds, where tradition and newness constantly mingle and conflict, is after all one of the primary experiences of modernity in the Third World. It is as if, he said, he had given me a quick lesson in Mataco and then sent me into the bush to fend for myself. Would I easily survive?

Navarrete has become an explorer, the Mataco who has ventured farthest into what Mami calls "the white jungle," the jungle of civilization where people play according to different rules, where newcomers can easily get lost among swamps and traps that await and tempt them.

* * *

Navarrete learned Spanish from an Anglican missionary when he was seven years old, but it was only when he reached his first year of high school and studied grammar (many years later, as an adult) that he realized Mataco, just like Spanish, must have certain rules and categories. Since then he has been studying his own language, trying to discover its inner laws.

This is not a detached intellectual pursuit. Navarrete has seen tribes in Salta that no longer speak their original tongue. He feels that each time an old man dies, a universe of words and stories dies with him. So Navarette plans to teach the language to the Mataco children, as part of their curriculum. He has not, however, been able to teach Mataco at school, although the law specifically recommends bilingual education. The previous school director let him work, but the current administrator opposes his presence there, saying he is unqualified. (Who, though, is qualified to certify teachers of Mataco?) Navarrete is also interested in helping the promotores learn the language. He patiently explained several words I wanted to learn, but in spite of his excellent Spanish, our attempts often broke down at a loss for proper usage.

Navarrete's problem is symptomatic. If the Matacos are to become self-sufficient, the school must prepare the children for the future while the parents learn in the fields and the offices—and this must be done in a way that shows respect for their culture. Instead, the Mataco children feel unwelcome in school. The drop-out rate is outrageously high.

Navarrete's daughter, now 18, had to repeat first grade three times and finally decided to stop wasting her time. It is true that in those times, she and the rest of the family had to migrate periodically to pick cotton. Now things seem better. Several Matacos have graduated from high school, and now work in the Asociación Comunitaria. They are essential to Patricio Doyle's plan to publish the *revistita*. Navarrete's nine-year-old daughter has already completed three years of elementary school without repeating a grade and will herself enter high school in just a few years.

What would he like her to be?

"A lawyer," he says. "What we most need are lawyers who can defend our interests."

Navarrete is anguished and open and doubtful. He is trying to build bridges over rivers that keep changing course.

He is the only Mataco who did not ask me for anything.

* * *

I spent several days in El Sauzalito without meeting Diego Soneira. It turned out he was in the faraway village of El Espinillo, some 200 miles across the Impenetrable. I went there to see him on my last day in the region.

I found him trying to put a lumbermill into operation. It had been erected a couple of years before, but the contractor had done everything wrong, and the mill had never worked. In a casual conversation with regional authorities, Soneira had mentioned what a pity such economic potential was being wasted when the machinery could be repaired. He had been invited to try. What white technicians had failed to accomplish, or even propose, Soneira was going to do with Matacos. They had, after all, been operating a successful lumbermill for years.

This project serves well as a symbol of how far the Matacos have come. Instead of receiving help, Mataco operators, carpenters, and electricians were giving it to others, spreading their knowledge across the Impenetrable. And the others, in this case, were Toba Indians, rivals of the Matacos for centuries. In fact, some Matacos in El Sauzalito—whom one *promotor* playfully calls *los rezongones* (complainers)—had told me before I left that Diego should be home with them, that he did not care for them anymore.

* * *

Meanwhile, Diego would have liked nothing better than to be back in El Sauzalito. He had brought his wife and his seven children with him because the job was supposed to be over in a few days. Then several machine parts that he needed to complete the job were delayed, and the authorities also failed to give him some aid they had promised. A few days had turned into a week. The nine Soneiras, plus the five Mataco technicians, were sleeping in an abandoned brick house, cooking over an open fire in the patio. They were without running water and were assaulted each evening—at exactly five past eight—by the most venomous, stubborn, hostile mosquitoes they had ever encountered. (And these people know an awful lot about mosquitoes.) The mosquitoes were so terrible, in fact, that they forced the Soneiras to seek refuge each evening in the sweltering heat of their sleeping quarters—but managed to infiltrate their premises anyway, as painfully evidenced by the blood-stained walls.

And yet the Soneiras were all cheerful, and Diego was calm, confident, tireless. Perhaps it was better to have seen him here, as if on another adventure, starting from scratch in a relatively strange place. It may be that in this way I was able to catch a glimpse of what the man must have been like when he arrived in El Sauzalito so many years ago. There was no doubting his strength or his magnetism.

He watched me watch him and finally smiled and said: "I know what you are going to ask me. Everybody always asks me the same thing. You want to know why I came here, why I stay here?"

It was as if he had read my mind. So I asked him something different when we finally sat down. I asked him two questions. How long did he think this experiment would last? When would he know if he had been successful? He said he did not know the answer to the first question, but he may have responded to it in answering the second.

"I'll be successful when I'm not needed anymore," Diego said.

And then he went off, 150 miles of dirt road away, to search for the missing spare parts.

* * *

One day in El Sauzalito, under the burning noon sun, I ventured a little into the *monte.*

My first idea had been to be guided by a Mataco. I wanted to experience what it would be like to be submerged in a habitat where the Mataco was the master, where his sense of smell, his ears that notice the slightest twitch of a leaf, his extraordinary eyesight and foresight would make him my superior. I wanted to be in a place where all my knowledge and skill would be useless, where his culture reigned and mine was out of place. I wanted, in a way, to experience what the Matacos must feel every day as they confront white, Western civilization: to be at a loss, displaced, defenseless.

But I was not in El Sauzalito long enough to take such a trip, nor had I built up enough confidence with a Mataco so he might take me along on one of the frequent hunting expeditions.

I settled for an artificial second best. Mami called two young Matacos—eight and eleven years old—to guide me toward a still-wild area near the Rio Bermejo, where the town ends.

I was not sure if they understood just what it was that I wanted, but they moved with me toward the river, and for a while I convinced myself that I was on the verge of the desired experience. They glided barefoot through a labyrinth of undergrowth, moving through the thickets, scaring flocks of pale blue butterflies, somehow able to find their way in that tangled vegetation.

If it were not for these boys, I thought to myself, I would be lost. It was a game I was playing with myself, of course. I knew that the town was nearby and that I was in no real danger of losing my way. As if to answer me, there was suddenly a noise in the bushes and I sensed something big lurching toward us. But no wild beast emerged. It was merely a pig, one of the few remaining from a failed livestock experiment. It snorted across our path. I wondered what the two Mataco kids thought of this expedition. But they would not answer any of my questions—just a nod of their heads once in a while, a pause to look back to see if I was following.

After we reached the river, they decided to come back by another route, and they got lost. Several times we reached a wedge of canes and weeds and vines that would not let us pass. We had to backtrack. And then, again, a few more yards and the need to start over. Finally, they made their way to the river, retraced their steps to a familiar path, and managed to get me safely home.

What is the meaning of this experience?

Should I emphasize the boys' surefooted, fleeting movements at the beginning the excursion, proving how Mataco children still are acquainted with the jungle and will somehow continue in the traditions of their forefathers? Or is the second stage more significant, when they lost their sense of direction and the bushes seemed alien to them, as they would not have been to their ancestors when they were children.

Or was there no significance whatsoever in that brief exploration? Was not the boys' conduct distorted by my very presence, their need to please me, their need to interpret my rather unsophisticated and enigmatic desires?

I cannot tell. I would have to be a Mataco.

I would have to be a Mataco to know exactly where the two boys are going.

© *Ariel Dorfman*

13

Self-History and Self-Identity in Talamanca, Costa Rica

PAULA R. PALMER

In tourist brochures and school textbooks, Costa Rica is presented as a white, homogeneous country. For the most part it is; yet approximately 20,000 Indians and 50,000 blacks also live there. Few in number, geographically isolated, and poor, Costa Rica's Indians and blacks have carried on lives beyond the sight of the dominant, white society.

Until the 1950s, life had changed remarkably little for the Bribri Indians in the canton of Talamanca in southern Limón province. Some 3,000 Bribri lived in thatch and palmbark dwellings scattered through river valleys and mountain forests. At home they spoke their native tongue. They cultivated plantains, beans, cocoa, and corn. Each family was self-sufficient, except at harvest, when work was done communally, farm by farm. Although the government formally abolished the kingship of the Bribri, *sukias* (healers skilled in herbal medicine) continued to provide local leadership as well as health care. Even the United Fruit Company failed to disrupt for long the stable community life of the Bribri. When the fruit company arrived in 1910, the Bribri retreated inland. By 1930, the fruit company was gone, and the Bribri returned.

The pattern of cultural survival was similar for Talamanca's blacks. During the second half of the nineteenth century, West Indians established fishing and farming villages along the coast. A hundred years later those communities were still largely unassimilated—black, Protestant, and English-speaking. Every family cherished its Broadman Hymnal and its West Indian Reader. Community life revolved around cocoa and coconut agriculture and such Jamaican-English pastimes as cricket, baseball, calypso, and quadrille dancing.

The isolation of Talamanca diminished in the 1950s when Costa Rican citizenship was first offered to the black West Indian descendants. The government sent teachers from the inland central plateau; primary schools were built, and the younger generation began to speak Spanish.

Influence from "the outside" has increased dramatically over the past two decades. In the Bribri area of Amubri, the first residential Catholic mission was established during the 1960s. The Talamanca Indian Reserve, administered by a commission in San José, was established during the 1970s. By 1980, petroleum explorations had begun within the reserve. Since the Indians are not allowed to own private property in the reserve, mineral rights are held by the Costa Rican government. Many fear the cultural and environmental consequences of new mining projects that are planned in the area.

The black coastal communities also face growing pressure from the outside world. Cahuita National Park was established in 1970, depriving scores of black families of legal titles to their farms—all the more painful since the Parks Service, which administers the land, lacks the funds to compensate residents. In 1976, a road was completed that linked Talamanca with the Atlantic port of Limón. Government community organizers arrived and imposed their ways on people who were accustomed to taking care of themselves through their own organizations—lodges, Protestant churches, English school boards, and the Jamaican Burial Scheme society.

The most serious threat to coastal life began in 1977, with the passage of the Ley Marítimo-Terrestre (Beachfront Law), which eliminates private property rights within the first 200 meters of the seashore. Coconuts planted along the beach by the early Talamanca families became the state's "natural resources." Urban development planners from San José are currently preparing zoning blueprints for Talamanca villages that would remove all residences and farms from the 200-meter "tourist zone"—with perhaps one exception, a "typical coastal residence" to be preserved inside the national park as a tourist attraction!

How have the people of Talamanca responded? Alphaeus Buchanan, a second-generation cocoa farmer and the first manager of Coopetalamanca, the local agricultural cooperative, says:

> We're not against progress. We are a progressive people. When our grandfathers came here, there was nothing. They planted farms; built houses, schools, and churches, organized sports clubs; built roads and bridges—everything we have here, we made with our own sweat and intelligence.
>
> We want a better life for our children. We want modern

conveniences—why not? We want our children to have choices we
didn't have. Maybe they can be lawyers, mechanics, journalists,
scholars. The ones that we want to be farmers, they must be better
prepared than we are, because agriculture has to be more technical in
the future.

We can learn a lot from the teachers and technical experts that
come in, but we can't learn from them how to defend what is ours.
We have to learn that from ourselves. They will teach our children
Spanish and typewriting, and science and the history that they know,
but *we* have to teach our children our history. *We* have to defend our
property and our way of life.

The 150 members of Coopetalamanca use their cooperative as a
base to fight for the rights and the needs of their people. Economic
development is their primary goal, but to achieve that, they believe
they must attack barriers that are rooted in education and culture.
People who never see their experience reflected in the media, school
curricula, or government institutions are ill-equipped to use those
media or to negotiate with those institutions to improve standards of
living and to defend their rights.

During the late 1970s, Coopetalamanca board members identified
several needs for their education committee to consider. First, Costa
Ricans needed to be educated about Talamanca so that government
programs could be more responsive to local realities. Second, the
people of Talamanca had to be inspired to organize themselves to
defend their rights. Finally, Talamanca's youth needed a strong,
positive sense of themselves, of their cultures and their history.

* * *

I first became involved in these problems through my work on an
oral history of the Talamanca coast. Since 1974 I had been teaching in
a locally organized English school in Cahuita. I had begun tape-
recording stories from the town's oldest residents in order to create
reading material for my students. Eighty-three-year-old Mr. Johnson's
stories of turtle fishing, sailboat commerce, tapir hunting, and snake
doctoring were fascinating reading for the children of Cahuita, whereas
"Tip and Mitten" were incomprehensible. The local stories became so
popular that the board of education encouraged me to edit them
chronologically, add a description of contemporary problems and
aspirations, and publish the collection as a local history.

Something happened during the interviews for that book, '*What
Happen': A Folk-History of Costa Rica's Talamanca Coast.* The speakers,
aware that their narrations would be published, began to reappraise
the importance of their personal and collective experiences. They

began tying events together and drawing new conclusions. For example:

> When the banana company came in we cut down our cocoa and planted bananas. Then the company left. They were going to take up the tramlines, but we made them leave them there, and we built little tramcars and pulled them with mules, and for the first time we had public transportation along the coast. *We did all that ourselves!*

I, too, was changed by these conversations. A bond formed between the speakers and myself, and with it came a mutual sense of power and responsibility. I came to believe that the young people of Talamanca needed to experience this bonding to know themselves and to carry on building their communities. Young people had so much to be proud of, and they did not know it.

The idea for an oral history project at Talamanca's agricultural high school took shape during 1980. We are indebted to the high school students of Rabun Gap, Georgia, who publish *Foxfire* magazine, for their successful example of oral history as an educational process. *Foxfire* provided the model that the people of Talamanca adapted to their own situation. Our idea was to teach students oral research skills and photography, take them to interview local residents, and then use that research to tell Talamanca's story by publishing a magazine. For Coopetalamanca, the magazine project promised a way to unite people—young and old, Indian, black, and Hispanic—in search and celebration of their identity. By distributing the magazine locally and nationally, they would extend their message to larger communities.

In 1980, Coopetalamanca received a grant from the Inter-American Foundation to launch the project. Local high school staff and Ministry of Education personnel were receptive. For several years the Ministry had talked vaguely about "regionalizing" the curriculum, without specifying how. Students in Talamanca are sent instructional materials produced in the highland center of the country. Nowhere in those texts do they encounter photographs of blacks or contemporary Indians. There are no wooden houses on stilts, no mothers cooking with coconut milk, no fathers fishing with *pejibaye* spears. The oral history project offered the Ministry of Education an experimental model for bringing regional characteristics vividly into the classroom.

Thirty-seven Talamancan tenth and eleventh graders participated in the project in 1981 (forty-eight in 1982) under the supervision of two teachers, a photography instructor, and myself, the project coordinator. We began by discussing what we knew about Talamanca's history, how we had learned it, and from whom. Working groups were formed around topics of mutual interest: the old ways of the Bribri Indians, the evolution of transportation, the history of specific communities, the use of herbal medicines, the petroleum explorations, and the sea lore of coastal fishermen. Each group practiced using tape recorders and cameras and refined questions for interviews. When the students felt ready, they chose informants among their family members and neighbors—people who had lived the history and could share their experiences.

Nearly every weekend, groups of students set out in the project's orange jeep—wherever and as far as Talamanca roads go, up into the Indian Reserve, down to the Panama border at Sixaola, along the Caribbean coast. At road's end, we walked, toting camera bags, tape recorders, and lists of questions.

One of the first year's most memorable experiences was an overnight trip to Amubri in the Indian Reserve. The parents of an Indian student took a group in the family's motorized dugout up a series of rivers to the grandparents' home. Of six students and three teachers, only the Indian student, Ana Concepción, had been there before. Her parents, don Tranquilino and doña Donata, motored and poled the canoe up the tributaries of the Sixaola River, recalling their childhoods in the High Talamanca and teaching us how to greet our hosts in Bribri: *ìs a shkẹnạ* (good morning).

That afternoon and the next day, Ana's parents were our guides and translators during visits to the thatch and palmbark homes of a very old man, a very old woman, and a *sukia*. We learned about the customs and ceremonies surrounding birth and death, the training of sukias, and the scarcity of young Indians who want to learn the herbal cures. We heard of the conflict between more traditional Indians who seek out the sukia and object to petroleum explorations and the modern Indians who use the mission health post and welcome the oil company's roads.

Fascinated, students listened for hours to conversation and laughter in a language they had never heard. When the old woman, doña Apolonia, laughed from her hammock, the students, too, broke out laughing. And when she improvised a song in Bribri, dedicated to our visit, the students were spellbound.

Later, in the classroom, pupils played the tape of doña Apolonia's song over and over. A Mennonite linguist helped them translate the lyrics, and they learned what doña Apolonia was telling them:

> So sad, sad, sad, I tell you.
> The Spaniard, the white man, is here on the mountain.
> My hut is in the mountain, where he came and spoke.
> When I first came to the mountain, I sang proudly.
> Now we don't have this, don't have that.
> Now even the words have gone.
> We can't speak. . . .

How can we sing? No one understands us.
It's so sad, our silence is sad.

As a result of the Amubri experience, the students asked the high school director to let them form a class in the Bribri language. Although the course is not yet organized, because of scheduling problems, the director and the ministry have agreed that it will be offered.

The students who visited Amubri later transcribed their tapes, selected photographs, and wrote an article for the first edition of *Nuestra Talamanca, Ayer y Hoy* (*Our Talamanca, Yesterday and Today*). Students sent the photographs and complimentary copies of the magazine to all of their informants and hosts. They followed up articles with in-depth interviews with other informants on topics broached in their first talks: burial ceremonies, the controversial petroleum explorations, the history of the Catholic missions among the Bribris. After the first issue was published, they received two letters: one from an Indian man who offered to take them to ancient burial sites, and another from an Argentine writer who sought permission to use phrases from doña Apolonia's song as the epigraph to his novel-in-progress.

During the first two years of the project, other students wrote about the histories of their home towns, Indian crafts, the dangers of deforestation, snake bite cures, traditional recipes, and calypso song writers. Students who have been asked to describe what they have learned through their participation give responses like the following:

> Working on the magazine showed me that older people have a lot to share with young people. Most young people just ignore the older generation, but we have made some very good friends through our interviews.
>
> —*Maritza Rugama M.*

> At the beginning I didn't think we could really make a magazine. It wasn't easy, but we were able to do it because we learned to understand each other better and work together as a group through the trips we made and the discussions we had. We learned to especially appreciate the bilingual students; without them we couldn't have communicated with the majority of the old people who don't speak Spanish.
>
> —*Carlos Lynch A.*

> We learned to appreciate Talamanca and to make sure it will never be destroyed by people who don't appreciate our life here. Now many of us want to stay here and work for the development of our home towns. We're better prepared to do that because of our work on the magazine.
>
> —*Geronima Ramos P.*

During 1981 and 1982, Talamanca students published three 1500-copy editions of *Nuestra Talamanca, Ayer y Hoy.* Most of the magazines were sold inside Talamanca. University journalism students who helped with the final editing of the articles also sold the magazine in San José.

Small groups of students went to the capital for the publication of each issue. They gave interviews about their work to national newspapers, radio, and television, and gave talks at high schools in Limón province and in San José. The students' enthusiasm and involvement in their little-known region attracted money from several private donors for projects at the high school.

In October 1982, the Ministry of Education invited the students to give three full-day presentations about their oral history project to social studies teachers in Limón province who were discussing regionalization of the curriculum. The teachers then urged the Ministry of Education to reprint and distribute the three issues of the Talamanca magazines as text material for all schools and high schools in the country, extend the oral history project to all Limón province high schools in 1983, and publish the future oral history work of Limón students either in a magazine or in national newspapers.

The first of these projects was accomplished in 1983 when the Ministry distributed 11,000 copies of the Talamanca students' book to the nation's high schools. Whether a province-wide oral history project will be implemented depends on ministry resources and the dedication of area teachers. One Limón teacher who participated in the seminar wrote:

> The work that you have done is really quite extraordinary. It is a model for other institutions in the country. Speaking for myself, it has sparked an enormous interest to begin working with my students in a similar way.

Although grant funding expired in early 1983, Talamanca's oral history project is continuing under the supervision of local teachers trained during the initial project phase. Emphasis has shifted from publications to community interaction. The project now coordinates activities with a regional culture committee; together, students and community members plan celebrations of traditional black and Indian festivals and the national "Día del Negro" and "Día del Indígena."

The long-term impact of this kind of learning on local attitudes and national policies cannot be measured. But we who have participated know that it has enriched *our* lives. When a brawny, sixteen-year-old boy asks for a picture of doña Apolonia to put on his bedroom wall, when a child who lives in a thatch-roof house receives a thank-you letter from the minister of energy and mines for photographs, when a shy Indian girl becomes indispensable to her classmates because only

she can translate Bribri, when a seventeen-year-old who speaks
Spanish as a second language stands in front of forty teachers and
explains why a piece of national legislation is unjust to her community
. . . then something significant has happened.

CAHUITA NATIONAL PARK

Calypso by
Walter Gavitt Ferguson

National Parkers are going round,
Into my farm they love to walk,
Telling everybody all around the town,
They say, "This is National Park!"

They want to get a full detail,
How long I own this piece of land?
"No tell no lie or else you going to jail!"
That's what they made me to understand.

They want to know my mother's name,
From whence she went and whence she came,
What kind of fellow was my father?
How long since he married to my mother?

They want to know about my grandmother,
They want to know about she religion,
What kind of fellow was my grandfather?
All of this they say they must understand.

I say, "Your question is hard for me,
Give me a chance and I will see,"
Finally, I came to a conclusion,
"I find an answer to your question,"

My grandmother was an Anglican,
My grandfather was Jonathan,
They got a little boy, he was very bad, I say,
When the fellow dead, they were more than glad.

My mother was Rebecca, an Israelite,
Me daddy was Willie, an Amalekite,
When it come to me, I don't got no land,
I'm a true-born Calypsonian.

PART 6

The Question of Scale

In the rare instances in which needs, incentives, resources, luck, leadership, and hard work all match up, then small organizations tend to grow. But herein lies the dilemma. As successful efforts expand or multiply, they soon confront obstacles that are beyond their control or require resources that are outside their reach.

—Sheldon Annis

14

From Field to Factory: Vertical Integration in Bolivia

KEVIN HEALY

Night had just fallen when the string of flickering lights began to thread its way through the darkness. Hundreds of men, women, and children carrying candles inside papier-mâché cutouts were marching two abreast down the dirt street of a remote hamlet in the jungles of the Alto Beni. From the back of a pickup inching along at the rear, musicians played traditional Andean panpipes. Glistening on the roof of the cab, a miniature replica of an industrial plant, complete with smokestack, floated high above the crowd.

The celebrants riding in the truck in this Bolivian Independence Day parade were the peasant members and leaders of the Central Regional de Cooperativas Agropecuarias Industriales, El Ceibo. The newly washed truck was a reminder of all that they had accomplished. The model factory symbolized the future they were making for themselves.

Theirs is the story of an amazing organizational growth, of how the seeds planted by a few colonists joining together to rent trucks and market their cacao eventually blossomed into a nationally known federation of thirty-five cooperatives. Today, El Ceibo manages a fleet of twelve large trucks and four pickups to transport a variety of cash crops to market. It also operates an export business, a small urban industry, two urban plants to ferment and dry cacao beans, an agricultural extension division, and an education and training program to directly serve 850 members and indirectly benefit thousands of other small farm families.

El Ceibo buys and sells $1.5 million worth of cacao annually. As the federation has grown and diversified, it has had to learn how to work in two worlds, managing its farflung activities through an eighty-member staff divided between a rural office and an urban headquarters. Rural activities are coordinated from a site in Sapecho, a small town in the Alto Beni jungle. From this complex of thatch-roof dormitories, offices, processing facilities, warehouses, and a training center, El Ceibo staff members schedule pickups of cacao harvests from local farmers, monitor price changes in the national market, and make assignments for work brigades. Business managers purchase cacao from local coops, and peasant extension agents bicycle out to farm sites for demonstrations and training courses. Other workers rake cacao beans for drying in the sun or load bags of dried beans for shipment by truck to La Paz.

When the beans arrive in La Paz, they are taken to a federation warehouse for storage and marketing. The warehouse is located in a modern, three-story brick building that El Ceibo has built in Río Seco, a slum district on the outskirts of the city. The site also includes offices to coordinate marketing activities and a small plant to manufacture cocoa, baking chocolate, and candy. The entire urban labor force—including project planners, accountants, sales agents, radio operators, drivers, and industrial workers—are youths recruited from coops in the Alto Beni. They receive the same wage as the workforce in Sapecho and work for one or two years before returning home. Some of them also receive scholarships to study business management at universities during their job assignments in the capital city.

The goal of all of these activities—from leadership training to the manufacture of chocolate—is empowerment. For fourteen years, the peasants of El Ceibo have struggled to master—one by one—all of the steps that could add value to their cash crops and make their business more competitive so that the lion's share of profits could be returned to develop the communities of the Alto Beni. From the outside, it might seem that progress has been steady, but the actual journey has been as winding and treacherous as the mountain roads connecting those jungle settlements with La Paz and the outside world.

THE REGIONAL CONTEXT

El Ceibo grew up in the midst of a twenty-five-year effort to colonize the sparsely populated Alto Beni region on the eastern edge of the Department of La Paz. The prospect of rich and unlimited farmland waiting to be carved out of virgin tropical forest lured thousands of settlers from Bolivia's highlands, where Aymara and Quechua Indian families were being economically squeezed by overcrowding, land fragmentation, and low prices for cash crops. Following the abolition of serfdom through land reform during the 1950s, spontaneous peasant migrations and government-organized settlement efforts augmented the population of the Alto Beni, which currently is some seven thousand families.

The transition for settlers was not easy. Highland peasants accustomed to wide-open spaces, cool temperatures, and traditional crops suddenly had to shed their heavy woolen clothing and learn to deal with heat, insects, new diseases, and an entirely different type of agriculture. Starting over often meant starting from scratch. Land was plentiful, but it had to be cleared by machete. Most farmers were only able to clear two or three hectares of their fifteen hectare plots. Furthermore, the local *sindicatos*—uniquely Bolivian institutions that are a cross between community councils and peasant unions—required colonists to pitch in and help construct new schools, roads, and water systems. In many cases, peasants found they had simply traded one form of rural poverty for another. More than half of the would-be pioneers gave up and left.

Those who stayed found that mosquitoes, heat, and the relentless jungle vegetation were not their only problems. The best markets for crops were far off in La Paz, 165 kilometers away by a winding dirt road that was frequently blocked by landslides or axle-deep in mud. The road started in steaming jungle barely 300 feet above sea level and ended on a cool mountain plateau 13,000 feet high. The journey took two or three days (even with today's improved roads, under the best conditions, it takes ten hours).

The difficulty of the trip meant that the truck owners who were willing to make the journey had the Alto Beni colonists in an economic vise. On the one hand, farmers had to accept below market prices for their harvests or let them rot. On the other, they had to pay inflated prices for goods trucked in from La Paz or do without such staples as soap, cooking oil, matches, and kerosene.

ORGANIZATIONAL TAKE-OFF: EL CEIBO'S RISE DURING THE 1970s

In order to assist the Alto Beni's first cacao bean producers, the national government opened a modest fermentation plant in the region in the early 1970s and organized four small cooperatives to keep it supplied with cacao. The farmers, however, were soon alienated by the plant manager's authoritarian style, financial corruption, and failure to make fair and timely payments for crops. When the peasants withdrew from the government enterprise, the processing plant went bankrupt. What remained, however, were seeds: the tiny coops that would ultimately grow into the El Ceibo federation.

Those seeds were nurtured by Caritas, a Catholic Church development organization, which established a cooperative development program in 1973 with Inter-American Foundation financing. In addition to elementary courses in management and administration, Caritas also offered a loan program to support new transport and marketing activities.

As a first step, Caritas loaned $1,000 to each cooperative so that private trucks could be rented to haul cacao beans directly to markets in La Paz. When the beans were sold, the cash was used to buy consumer goods that were then shipped back in the same rented trucks for distribution among the cooperatives.

The Caritas program vividly demonstrated the power of self-help initiatives, and local groups were soon bubbling with new plans for action. This bottom-up process eventually led the coops to seize an unprecedented but potentially lucrative economic opportunity—the first direct sale by Bolivian peasants in the international cacao market.

It was a grandiose vision for loosely affiliated coops to undertake. Fortunately, leaders like Emilio Vilca were on hand to turn dream into reality. A short, stocky, tenacious peasant of Aymara descent, Vilca was the regional spokesperson for hundreds of new Alto Beni community sindicatos. Better educated than most of the colonists, he had attended high school and had taken nonformal education courses for farmers. He was also the head of cooperative development for the national peasant syndicate, and had recently traveled on a government-sponsored tour to study Israeli cooperatives firsthand.

Vilca formed a central committee to represent the cooperatives, gathered information about foreign buyers, and sent packets of sample beans to prospective customers by international mail. After receiving orders from firms in the United States, the committee arranged a special loan from Caritas to buy harvests throughout the zone from members and nonmembers alike.

One hitch remained. Export licenses for cacao beans were difficult to obtain, since the government favored exporting processed cacao. Eventually, the coops agreed to pay a fixed percentage of their profits from any foreign sales to a private Bolivian firm in exchange for the use of its export license. Officials from the Ministry of Commerce approved the deal, but only after being dragged to the makeshift coop warehouse to see that there was a large surplus beyond the needs of domestic cacao buyers.

Under this special arrangement, some 600 quintales (one quintal equals 100 pounds) of cacao beans were exported in 1976. The cooperatives grossed $25,000, part of which was used as seed capital to open a small office and a makeshift chocolate factory in the Río Seco neighborhood of La Paz. The economic benefits from the rustic facility were small, but this first experiment in adding value to members' crops had great motivational impact. In signaling a direction for the future, it bound the cooperatives more tightly together and provided a small workforce of coop members with valuable training that could be tapped when future funding made expanded industrial production possible.

Unfortunately, the economic windfall brought unanticipated problems as well. The increased income came before adequate accounting systems and investment plans were established. Despite Vilca's experience and Caritas' management courses, coop administrators lacked the skills to handle their new funds. Consequently, more urban real estate was purchased than could be productively used. The extra property tied up capital, stalling other income-generating activities and services. Other export income disappeared through lost receipts and alleged misappropriations by some of the central committee leaders. The final blow came when word was received that the U.S. buyers were dissatisfied with the uneven quality of the cacao they had received, and the Bolivian government was discouraging future export deals.

Despite this setback, the one-time sale had a lasting impact. After years of barely breaking into the La Paz markets and selling their beans short to truck-owning intermediaries, the export income provided small farmers with a new yardstick to measure the true value of their crops. It fed a growing awareness among coop members that cacao production was their best option for development, and organization was the key to harnessing that potential. The loss of the export contract underlined the importance of improving the quality of their crop if they were to take advantage of rapidly rising prices for cacao on the international market.

This led to a new strategy, yet another twist of fate in the road. The coops obtained a grant from Catholic Relief Services to buy materials for a plant to ferment and dry cacao beans and for a small pickup to collect harvests from local farmers. Coop members pooled their own labor and savings to cover construction costs.

Expectations soared. But once the plant opened, coop leaders discovered that they lacked funds to pay farmers in advance for the beans. The lack of operating capital, an obvious oversight in project design, led to production delays as the plant operated far below capacity. Coop members who handed over their crops on consignment became demoralized when nonparticipating farmers settled for lower prices from truck owners but were paid promptly in cash or consumer goods. Coop prospects began to dim again. It was becoming a familiar story: two steps forward, one or two steps back.

Nonetheless, coop members kept pushing. By organizing into a full-fledged federation, the ad hoc organization could acquire leverage—it would qualify for a bank account, loans, government help, and international assistance. And perhaps just as important, acquiring legal status would shelter the coops from some of the bureaucratic harassment that can befall informal organizations in Bolivia. At the moment of its birth in 1977, El Ceibo consisted of 14 cooperatives, each of which had 15 to 20 male members from rural communities of 50 to 60 families. All they needed now was working capital.

SHIFTING INTO HIGH GEAR

During the early 1980s, El Ceibo's transporting, processing, and marketing activities took off. A major boost came in 1981 from an IAF grant of $100,000 for operating capital, $12,000 for another fermentation and drying plant, and $30,000 for a truck to haul cacao to La Paz.

The administrative offices in Sapecho began to hum with activity as federation leaders coordinated crop pickups from small farmers along the back roads of the Alto Beni. El Ceibo purchased both wet and dry beans, drying and fermenting the wet cacao at the Sapecho plant.[1] After brief storage in an adjacent warehouse, most of the processed crop was shipped by truck to two companies in La Paz—one was Bolivia's largest chocolate manufacturer, the other produced cocoa and assorted products. By late 1981, El Ceibo was handling $1,200 worth of beans daily.

With new access to operating capital, the federation moved to control roughly two-thirds of the Alto Beni's cacao production.[2] Since the zone produced 80 percent of Bolivia's crop, more than half of the national harvest was moving through the federation's transport and marketing channels. Breaking the transport monopoly and adding value through agroprocessing had led to booming business that made the federation the chief regulator of cacao prices in the Alto Beni. By 1983, three trucks were needed to haul beans to markets in La Paz.

And when those trucks returned home, they carried basic consumer goods for distribution to 21 member cooperatives, 7 of them new affiliates. El Ceibo's rapid economic expansion during this period allowed its network of consumer stores to expand their inventories to include 18 essential staples, helping to regulate consumer prices in the Alto Beni.[3]

The federation's rapid rise was a heady experience, but maintaining its position was not easy. Competing truck owners from La Paz soon raised their prices for cacao to match El Ceibo's. That, in turn, meant higher costs for the industrial buyers who had traditionally used the truckers to obtain a steady and cheap supply of beans.

El Ceibo's processed cacao was uniformly better than previous supplies, but those benefits were offset among company executives by concern over rising prices and the prospect of a new rival. After all, if the federation could obtain adequate capital and keep growing it might someday be able to vertically integrate its operations from cacao field to chocolate factory. Consequently, the major buyers undercut this embryonic grassroots power whenever they could. One tactic was to delay payments, hoping to disrupt El Ceibo's cycle of Alto Beni buying and La Paz processing during periods when small farmers were strapped for cash. Another tactic was lobbying the public banking establishment to block potential loans that might help the federation to ride out cyclical shortages of operating capital.

Despite the economic pressure and a deteriorating national economy, El Ceibo maintained its solvency and fought back. The federation built a new warehouse in La Paz to increase its leverage during negotiations with buyers. The cool climate of the capital city retarded spoilage for up to three months—allowing El Ceibo's sales staff to wait for higher prices.

But the key factor was the growing ability of El Ceibo's leaders to manage the federation's farflung operations. These peasant leaders were becoming adept planners, bookkeepers, cost analysts, and basic accountants, thanks in part to an unexpected advisor. Bernardo Edenberger was a thirty-six-year-old economist who became disillusioned with his job at a West German multinational cosmetics corporation and left to work with poor people in Latin America. He was the first in a series of talented and committed volunteers from the German organization Servicio Técnico Alemán de Voluntarios to provide the federation with technical assistance in agronomy and accounting. His four years of guidance were an incalculable asset for El Ceibo's consolidation and economic growth.

WITCHES-BROOM, DECAPITALIZATION, AND HOT CHOCOLATE

Ironically, El Ceibo's ability to command a sizable market share was enhanced by a precipitous drop in cacao bean production in the Alto Beni from a blight known as *escoba bruja*—witches-broom. The blight, which began in the late 1970s, had a paradoxical effect. It stretched the reach of the operating capital fund, allowing El Ceibo to buy a greater percentage of a diminishing volume of beans. If witches-broom went unchecked, however, soon there would be nothing to purchase.

In 1983, El Ceibo created the Cooperative Education and Agricultural Extension Division (COPROAGRO) to help small farmers fight the blight and improve their farming methods. With financial support from Cooperación Técnica Suiza (COTESU), a foreign aid branch of the Swiss government, COPROAGRO set up an office in Sapecho and hired a staff of twenty-two peasant paraprofessionals. An IAF grant allowed some of them to travel to Ecuador and Colombia for specialized training.

The payoffs were substantial. According to a 1986 evaluation by Ecuadoran agronomists, COPROAGRO work teams serviced 2,500 hectares—about a third of the cacao farmland in the Alto Beni. Tree pruning and rehabilitation doubled average yields from 5 to 10 quintales per hectare,[4] generating an additional $750 in income per hectare. One major industrial buyer underlined these accomplishments by saying, "Without El Ceibo, cacao might have vanished from Bolivia."

But even as the federation seemed to be winning the war on the ground, the ground was slipping beneath them. Hyperinflation in the national economy was approaching 20,000 percent. By the end of 1984, the purchasing power of El Ceibo's operating funds had been slashed in half, forcing severe cutbacks. When an industrial buyer held up a large payment for three months, federation leaders helplessly watched while their customer waited for inflation to pay the major portion of his bill. Local coops likewise presented a gloomy picture, as the shelves in branch consumer stores were increasingly empty.

Fortunately, the federation found ways to blunt the impact of spiraling prices. The first major step was defensive. All accounts were converted from Bolivian pesos to U.S. dollars. Since the exchange value of the dollar rose in tandem with inflation, that helped cut further losses.

Much irreparable damage had been done, but as El Ceibo's leaders became more adept at crisis management, they cautiously decided to take the offensive. The only way to survive inflation was to outproduce it by adding further value to coop crops. After a Bolivian consulting firm agreed that it made sense, El Ceibo used a $25,000 IAF grant to build a small plant adjacent to their Río Seco offices and outfit it with used machinery to modernize their production of chocolate, which was absorbing only one percent of the federation's cacao. The new factory diversified production to include drink mixes, cocoa butter, baker's chocolate, and chocolate candy.

Some of these products became instant hits. El Ceibo's cocoa, for instance, caught on as a popular breakfast and afternoon drink, and it quickly found its way onto store shelves and vendors' stands in the low-income neighborhoods of La Paz. During 1985, cocoa sales reached $7,000 per month, not including shipments back to the Alto Beni for marketing in affiliated coop stores. At the same time, chocolate sales reached 1,800 kilos monthly, primarily to miners employed by the state-owned national mining corporation, COMIBOL.

During its second year of operation, the factory set a federation record for profits of 18 percent above costs. Some of that money was reinvested to help rent a second factory from a major client. By 1986, the expanded industrial capacity was absorbing 10 percent of the federation's cacao crop—an increase of nearly 1,000 percent in less than three years.

And some of that production had further added value. When El Ceibo began to make cacao sales to the Organisation Schweiz Dritte Welte (O.S.3.), a network for assisting cooperative enterprises in the Third World, the payments in foreign currency were inflation-proof. During 1986/87, El Ceibo exported a total of 35 tons of cocoa to O.S.3. The federation also reentered the export market for cacao beans for the first time since 1976, shipping nearly 2,000 quintales of beans to a West German buyer.

Despite the new export income, new products, and robust sales, the federation made little headway in replenishing its operating capital fund. The original $100,000 from IAF had declined in value to $50,000 and then stabilized far short of the $350,000 that would have been needed to channel all of the cacao production of the Alto Beni to La Paz. Finding the road forward temporarily blocked by hyperinflation, the federation's leaders decided to search out a detour around the avalanche.

A CARAVAN OF TRUCKS

The means to move beyond cacao and begin handling other cash crops was already on the way. In October 1982, a democratically elected civilian government took office in Bolivia after sixteen years of military rule. Peasant syndicates throughout the country were soon mobilizing to express their pent-up grievances. During this period, the Federación Especial de Colonizadores of the Alto Beni joined forces with a similar small farmers union from the Yungas area to the south, declared a strike, and closed the main road to La Paz. The farmers wanted to break the transport monopoly of the Sindicato de Volantes of Yungas, which represented some sixty truck-owning intermediaries. El Ceibo had broken this commercial monopoly with respect to cacao, but other local crops had been unaffected.

Thousands of peasant men and women manned the roadblocks, including one at Sapecho. To end the crisis, the government changed freight and passenger rates in the zone, and agreed to loan the syndicates money to buy sixty trucks. A special peasant commission subsequently lobbied to keep pressure on the government. When funds finally arrived two years later, however, there were only enough for thirty trucks, which the Empresa Nacional de Transporte (ENTA), a new public transport enterprise, imported from Brazil.

After visiting federation offices in Sapecho and Río Seco, the Minister of Transportation chose El Ceibo as a broker for the deal because of its infrastructure, its extensive administrative and management experience, and the fact that it had physical assets to offer as collateral. El Ceibo would purchase ten trucks for itself and cosign for the other twenty trucks, which would be distributed among peasant coops in the Caranavi zone of the Yungas region. The down payment was made with federation profits and fixed assessments of cacao totaling $62,000, plus a sizable government subsidy.

When the ten enormous trucks—each worth $53,000—rolled into Sapecho, federation members gathered for a huge fiesta replete with excited speeches and traditional Andean dances. Then the trucks were driven in procession to a shrine on the shores of Lake Titicaca, where a local shaman performed the traditional challa ritual—a ceremony for blessing major acquisitions such as houses and cars.

The new trucks were soon hauling bananas, grapefruit, timber, watermelons, and rice to La Paz. Other truckers operating in the Alto Beni were forced to meet the new competition by paying more for crops and cutting transport fees. The importance of this competition became quite clear whenever a coop truck broke down and was temporarily out of service. In one such instance, freight and passenger charges by other carriers shot up by 60 percent.[5]

In addition to putting more money in small farmers' pockets, the new trucks have changed social relationships in subtle ways. A coop leader offered the following observation: "Previously, drivers would make us get down off the truck to load and unload cargo, threatening to leave us behind if we disobeyed. Since the coop trucks started running, other drivers have stopped ordering us around, and show more respect."

Yet despite the rapid gains and El Ceibo's years of experience with cacao transport, the fleet ran into problems almost immediately. The trucks themselves were too big for some of the narrow jungle roads that connected widely dispersed communities. Cutting through the administrative thicket was no easier. With weak oversight and control, drivers sometimes failed to collect freight charges from passengers who were supposed to pay after selling their produce. Other times, drivers simply pocketed the money. Shortwave radio communication between Río Seco and Sapecho was also ineffective, leading to confusing schedules for truck departures and arrivals. El Ceibo responded flexibly and pragmatically. For example, it set up roadside checkpoints through local coops and used undercover investigators to prevent truck driver profiteering during the long trip to La Paz.

The federation has reorganized its transportation system several times in search of workable solutions to its problems, in some cases centralizing and in others decentralizing operations. But the debts from uncollected payments, which amounted to $40,000 in 1986, continue to climb. The two-year experiment suggests that the administrative burden of managing ten trucks may be overtaxing El Ceibo's skills and resources, and it is likely that the fleet will be reduced to ensure a more efficient operation.

El Ceibo's truck caravan also encountered difficulties in La Paz. It stirred up anxieties among local market vendors who were often linked to each other and to truck-owning intermediaries by strong family and social ties. Together, they formed a tough, tight-knit economic force. The vendors and truck owners moved quickly, persuading municipal transit authorities to issue a regulation that blocked federation trucks from several commercial zones. When trucks did enter marketplaces, porters were pressured not to unload their cargos.

The strong reaction hurt. El Ceibo lost agricultural produce, valuable time, and member morale. Having to cruise for several days with citrus rotting in the back of the truck was a discouraging beginning.

Once again, however, El Ceibo fought back. Locked out of some existing markets, the federation recently obtained an IAF grant to help purchase a two-acre lot in La Paz for its own marketplace. The site will also serve as the location for a truck garage and for future projects. A peasant-owned marketplace in the capital city is very unusual, and federation leaders recognize its symbolic importance. As El Ceibo's president Luis Cruz Mamani remarked, "We want to show the people of La Paz that we are not dirty, that peasants can own and manage a clean marketplace. And we want to show other small farmers what organization and hard work can accomplish."

BLAZING A PATH FOR DEVELOPMENT

El Ceibo's fourteen-year history clearly shows that empowerment is not merely a battle to acquire new skills and material assets. It is also an ongoing struggle—with frequent reversals—to manage these resources for sustained socio-economic development.

The federation has been unusually effective in bringing opportunities to small farmers in the Alto Beni and, at the same time galvanizing local efforts to develop the entire region. As one result, El Ceibo is receiving increasing attention from the Bolivian mass media. It is regularly visited by other coop members from throughout the country and by development professionals from home and abroad. What kinds of lessons can be learned from its history?

El Ceibo's past is full of ironic twists, not the least of which is that a seemingly hostile environment provided the freedom of social space for peasants to build a cohesive and dynamic organization. The lack of an entrenched elite allowed leaders with the grit and vision of Emilio Vilca to emerge, and the relatively egalitarian social structure that grew out of Alto Beni colonization led to broad-based cooperatives committed to participatory management of programs and delivery of services. The process of settlement itself tended to preselect people determined to improve their livelihoods, and the Aymara and Quechua pioneers who stayed proved to be dynamic organizers when given the slightest opportunity.

Cacao's comparatively favorable price and the promise of value-added profits from export and processing made it an ideal crop around which new coops could coalesce. Focusing on cacao opened new windows of opportunity that allowed El Ceibo to become a major economic player rather quickly. The Alto Beni supplied 80 percent of the national harvest, and competing commercial interests involved with the crop were relatively new and lacked the political and economic clout to throttle the new enterprise.

El Ceibo's history also shows, however, that self-sustaining development may require prolonged outside investment. Indeed, that history underlines the vital role of being able to broker and capture external resources on a continuing basis in order to complement and galvanize local resources such as land, labor, crops, and even cash. Recognizing this, the federation has recently established a development projects office. The tendency of its leadership to seek loan funds instead of grants to maintain and expand program activities is a promising sign of progress toward eventual self-financing.

In an economy as volatile as Bolivia's, of course, even earnings may be a deceptive indicator of future success. For example, El Ceibo has been earning enough money to pay off on time its debt to ENTA for the fleet of ten trucks, but because of depressed farm prices and inadequate administration, the federation has been unable to save enough money each month to counteract depreciation. At the present rate of savings, it will be able to replace only seven of the trucks when they wear out.

Other problems such as the growing intrusion of coca production in some of the newest colonies in the Alto Beni for processing into cocaine loom on the horizon. Nonetheless, El Ceibo has shown a deft capacity for responding to each crisis by pushing ahead on a new front. Its organizational history even suggests that grassroots development on this scale has to be multidimensional, that the whole is greater than the sum of the parts. Diversified activities may create management problems, but they may also usher in unexpected opportunities. One reason for El Ceibo's ability to weather the unrelenting storm in the Bolivian economy, the nation's worst in this century, may be the federation's willingness to explore new income-earning opportunities. Building on soft ground teaches you to rely on multiple supports. Although the federation has had to count on external financing from a variety of sources, one wonders what could have been accomplished if the state had been more effective in clearing the way. Indeed, El Ceibo itself has led the way in pushing the production and development of a potentially important industrial and export crop.

This returns us to the point where the story began—the candlelit model factory. Survival means pushing ahead with plans for industrialization. The market is there, as the order for 1988 from O.S.3. for 40 tons of cocoa powder demonstrates. The federation has already opened communications with the government of West Germany for the possible multi-million dollar financing of a large industry and has acquired urban property as its future site. This is El Ceibo's dream—to absorb all the Alto Beni cacao into industrial production under peasant control and ownership.

The federation is ready to take the next logical step and become a *chocolatier par excellence*. Considering the long odds against what they have already accomplished, who is to say they cannot? El Ceibo has broken into the world of export markets, which includes the Swiss, who are among the world's most quality-conscious consumers of chocolate. The Nestlés, Hersheys, and other giants of world production may someday have to take heed—these peasant upstarts are finding a way.

NOTES

1. See Chapter 8, "What to Think about Cooperatives: A Guide from Bolivia," for a longer discussion of this process.

2. Again, see Chapter 8 for a fuller description.

3. The benefits were not restricted to El Ceibo members. As Tendler pointed out, the economic benefits from El Ceibo's central transport and commercial role extended to nonmembers as well. Tendler labeled these nonmember participants "free riders," since they enjoyed the best of both worlds—the services coop members received, but none of the dues payments. However, it was to some extent a two-way street. El Ceibo's access to the crops of nonmembers meant greater sales volume and greater economic leverage for the federation.

4. These yields are still unimpressive by the standards of cacao-exporting countries. Average yields in Brazil, for example, are 15 quintales per hectare.

5. Again, see Tendler for similar effects on the cacao market after introduction of peasant-controlled trucks.

15

Can Small-Scale Development Be Large-Scale Policy?

SHELDON ANNIS

HOW LARGE CAN SMALL-SCALE BECOME?

Nongovernmental grassroots organizations are so frequently lost in self-admiration that they fail to see that the strengths for which they are acclaimed can also be serious weaknesses.[1]

- In the face of pervasive poverty, for example, "small-scale" can mean merely "insignificant."
- "Politically independent" can mean "powerless" or "disconnected."
- "Low-cost" can mean "underfinanced" or "poor quality."
- "Innovative" can mean simply "temporary" or "unsustainable."

Indeed, it is not so surprising that well-organized, externally financed, private organizations should be able to launch local projects that are small in scale, politically independent, low cost, and innovative. But stepping back and considering the magnitude of need, the much harder question is: Ultimately, how large can small become? Can that which is local build upon itself so that small is institutionalized and widely replicated?

Is large-scale small-scale development self-contradicting? Can a species of development flourish that maintains the virtues of smallness—but at the same time reaches large numbers of people, transfers genuine political power to the poor, and provides high quality social services that are delivered by permanent, adequately financed institutions?

In Latin America, I believe, such a process is already taking place.

Every Latin American country is now interlaced with a thickening web of grassroots organizations. These organizations are increasingly intertwined not only with each other but with the state. As a result, a policy built upon the idea of large-scale, small-scale development—something that might have appeared naive or whimsical just a few years ago—is emerging as a serious choice for Latin America in the 1990s.

This assertion is based on three propositions about the characteristics of grassroots organizations and their relationship to the state.

1. When grassroots organizations proliferate, they form self-organizing systems. That is, despite (or because of) their diversity, organizations tend to sort themselves out by function and by turf. They specialize, differentiate, and arrange themselves hierarchically.

2. Although foreign private voluntary organizations can serve critical roles as catalysts, they seldom provide a larger framework that sustains grassroots growth over the long run. The more important incentives that foster grassroots growth come from the state, even though grassroots organizations and the state may be in an adversarial relationship.

3. Webs of organizations are interlocked not only with each other and the public sector, but they are also highly responsive to "macro" policies that affect external debt, international terms of trade, currency valuation, and import/export conditions. Local organizations are also highly sensitive to domestic policies that are not ostensibly grassroots-oriented, i.e., tax structures; broad health, education, housing, and environmental policies; social security coverage; agricultural pricing and credit subsidies; placement of infrastructure; utility rates, and so forth.

If so, the answer to the initial question—How large can small become?—depends not only on the internal characteristics of small organizations (who are their leaders, how are they managed, and so on); but equally important, on the larger institutional and policy environments that bring such organizations to life and sustain their growth.

GRASSROOTS ORGANIZATIONS AND THE IDEA OF SCALING UP

If anything is certain about the nature of grassroots organizations, it is that—whatever they are—they are not homogeneous units. Church groups, labor organizations, Boy Scouts, political action committees, self-help organizations, village potable water associations, communal labor arrangements, squatter associations, worker-owned businesses, ethnic burial societies, transportation collectives, peasant leagues, Catholic "reflection" groups, tribal federations, microentrepreneur credit associations . . . all differ from each other and from their equivalents in different countries.

Yet, setting aside the diverse social underpinnings, purpose, political ideology, transience, or relative impact of particular organizations, the important point is this: even though organizations appear and disappear with sometimes astonishing rapidity, organization has become relatively constant in Latin America over the past twenty or so years. Even though the poor today are organized very differently from country to country, they are all—in one form or another—organized.

In a cultural sense, it can be said that organization among the poor has always been constant. After all, no group survives if it is disorganized. What is new is the richness of organizations that are not simply outgrowths from the traditional templates of kinship, tribe, ethnicity, language, village, and neighborhood.

This newer generation of organizations has several sources of dynamism. First, it thrives on the spread of ideas that has washed over Latin America in recent years—liberation theology, feminism, cooperativism, black power, Indian rights, unionism, worker self-management, and revolutionary politics. Second, it reflects the changing social characteristics of the poor—today they are better educated, healthier, with greater access to electronic media, roads, and technology. And finally, it is supported by the presence and financing of outsiders and by the gradual deepening of democratic processes throughout the region.

Today, there is an intricate coral reef-like maze of organizations among the poor. With seemingly limitless social energy,[2] they die, are resurrected, and spawn new hyrids of old ideas.

Yet for all this late-1980s diversity, when one goes from country to country visiting these organizations, what is perhaps most striking is that—despite the dramatic differences in history, politics, environment, economic system, culture, and so forth—the concerns, objectives, and patterns of organizational growth tend to be remarkably predictable from place to place. Everywhere, farmers want credit for production, roads to enable marketing, medical and educational services for their families. Underemployed workers want jobs, recognition, and new skills. Urban squatters want legal title to the land they live on; they want water, roads, buses, and parks for the communities they create. Indigenous minorities want collective legal rights, assurances of land rights, and recognition of pluralism within educational systems.

In response to these familiar needs, people tend to organize and reach out in similar ways. For example:

- If landless rural laborers see empty tracts, they will begin to talk among themselves about how to get land. They will form committees, put forward leaders, and weigh the collective versus individual risks of land invasion.
- If someone in an isolated hamlet knows a powerful politician or an official in the Ministry of Public Works, the hamlet will be encouraged to organize a self-help association to figure out what that connection might help them obtain. Their decision to build a road will not be based simply on the need for a road, but on the perception that they might briefly obtain a bulldozer.
- If landless, assetless farmers know that group membership can help them secure low-interest bank loans, they will form cooperatives or other organizations that give them access to the banking system.
- If Catholic homemakers can receive mated rabbits from a diocese nutrition program, then Catholic homemakers will very likely form the Catholic Homemakers Rabbit Growers Association.

The point here is that poor people organize not only in response to their needs, but in response to incentives. The growth of organizations is driven from within, and from without.

In the rare instances in which needs, incentives, resources, luck, leadership, and hard work all match up, then small organizations tend to grow. But herein lies a dilemma. As successful efforts expand or multiply, they soon confront obstacles that are beyond their control or require resources that are outside their reach. The farmers who found that they could successfully grow vegetables together in their village find they can not get their vegetables to market without a truck, without bribes, without a road, or without access to markets in the capital. A group of squatters who have gained physical control over a piece of land find that they cannot get municipal services and build substantial homes until they also have title to the land. A rural community that has just built a new schoolroom with raffle ticket financing and volunteer labor finds that it cannot get a second teacher, textbooks from the Ministry of Education, or force the primary teacher not to take four-day weekends in the capital.

These second-phase problems often make the first-phase problems look easy by comparison. So small organizations acquire specialists (bookkeepers, university-trained managers, Peace Corps volunteers).

Or more commonly, they link forces with kindred organizations that have greater lobbying and technical power. These higher-order, intermediary groups prod externally for sources of funding; they form ephemeral political alliances of convenience; they technify and professionalize; and they spin off lower-order groups.

GRASSROOTS ORGANIZATIONS AND THE STATE

As grassroots groups attempt to scale up, they invariably become interested in providing services that states cannot provide, will not provide, or provide in a manner that local groups do not like. When this happens, the private groups weigh four choices:

- They can provide parallel services with their own internal resources (e.g., Catholic groups creating their own internally financed and managed school systems).
- They can create parallel service-delivery systems by seeking support from private voluntary agencies, development institutions, foundations, or even the state itself.
- They can pressure the state to provide new or better services, generally by bartering in political loyalty.
- They can "co-produce" the services with the state through a division of labor based on comparative advantage (e.g., grassroots groups mobilize local producers to borrow from the state-run banking system).

Grassroots groups in Latin America usually perceive themselves to be in adversarial relation with the state. Inevitably, they emphasize their separateness, their political independence, and their nongovernmental character. Yet in practice, nongovernmental organizations tend to be most numerous and most important where the state is strong; and generally, the larger, more democratic, better organized, and more prosperous the public sector, the greater are the incentives for the poor to barter for concessions or to co-produce with the state. In states like Mexico or Costa Rica, it is virtually impossible to draw fast lines that define where grassroots organizations end and the government begins.

In small, poor countries, like Benin, or politically repressed countries, like Paraguay, citizens have a severely limited range of incentives to encourage organization. Local organizations exist, certainly, but the web is far less textured and intricate than one would find in a more developed country, like Ireland, or in a freer country, like Argentina. A rich and democratic country, like the United States, has enormous organizational density in even its "poorest" neighborhoods: block clubs, crime watch committees, labor unions, political action groups, Boy Scouts, ward committees, NAACP, Urban League, professional associations, small business associations, church homemaker clubs, PTA, credit unions, health maintenance organizations, community center members, better housing coalitions, renters associations, veterans rights associations, ethnic associations, retiree lobby groups, church youth groups, Gray Panthers, and so forth.

All of these organizations develop complex linkages with the public sector. Invariably, these linkages strengthen over time. In Latin America:

- The landless farmers who got land will then form an agrarian reform beneficiaries association to get subsidized credit and state-built infrastructure.
- The civic action road-building committee, if it gets its feeder road, will then turn its attention to a school addition or potable water system; or perhaps, join with neighboring committees to lobby for a bridge, a major access road, or a secondary school.
- The tribal people's association that establishes that they own land in principle, will then go to courts, ministries, and external agencies over issues of mineral exploitation, schooling, or placement of dams.
- If members of small-farmer cooperatives obtain subsidized credit for their members, they then begin to think about public grain elevators, price supports, agricultural extension, crop insurance.
- If a group of squatters obtains title for their land, they will proceed to target one municipal agency after another to get water, electricity, credit, schools, buses, daycare, and parks.

It is important to recognize that the process is not one-way. Just as the poor are deeply interested in the resources of their governments, so too, their governments are deeply interested in them—even if for all the wrong reasons.

First, extending services implies political obligation. Particularly in Latin American cities, the exchange of public resources for political obligation is a cornerstone of state control.

Second, local organizations are often viewed by the state as appropriate instruments for carrying out high profile, state-sponsored service campaigns, i.e., vaccination and family planning crusades, literacy brigades, rural reforestation projects.

Third, states (which are increasingly strapped by the burden of external debt) are readily able to see potential benefits of "cost sharing" and "cost recovery." Indeed, when grassroots development is understood to mean "letting the poor pay for services themselves," it almost always sounds like an excellent solution to the problem of poverty.

Fourth, even the most unenlightened and bureaucratic state agencies recognize that services are likely to be delivered more efficiently if there is input from those who are supposed to receive the services. If only rhetorically, community participation is now preached virtually everywhere in Latin America.

In other words, at the same time that grassroots organizations are trying to wrest services and concessions from the state, the state is generally trying to break itself into finer and finer units of political and bureaucratic control. What happens in practice is a kind of interpenetration—a blending in which the so-called governmental and nongovernmental meld together. The term nongovernmental organization—though it may have meaning at conferences, in external fundraising, and in the academic literature—tends to lose its focus when applied to the tens of thousands of real-world organizations that actually do organize the poor in Latin America.

GRASSROOTS ORGANIZATIONS AND PUBLIC POLICY

If grassroots organizations and the state inevitably interpenetrate, the real question is: how to make this interpenetration good for the poor?

That, in turn, depends on the character of public policy.

To illustrate how and why this is so, I have formulated a set of questions about state-grassroots relations that are derived from several years of evaluative research at the Inter-American Foundation. What is suggested is not a checklist of right and wrong policies—rather, a guide that points where to look when thinking about what makes and unmakes healthy grassroots organizations in particular countries.

1. *What kinds of juridical frameworks govern the formation and operation of grassroots organizations?* What kinds of laws define an organization's right to enter into contract, borrow money, legally represent a group's interest to national authorities? Is there, for example, a "law of cooperatives?" If so, what are its provisions and fine points? Are cooperatives treated as businesses when holidays are granted from certain taxes or when tariffs are waived on imported machinery? Are there mechanisms by which legally constituted groups of the poor can receive export credits? Under what legal conditions can land be owned collectively—and then sold or passed on by inheritance? (The complexities of this problem can be appreciated by

studying the *ejido* system of Mexico.) And then, does the legal recognition of certain grassroots groups (generally called *personería jurídica* in Latin America) constitute a barrier which discriminates against non-recognized organizations? Or against church-related groups, where separation of church and state is an issue?

2. *What is the structure of opportunity within the banking system for the organized poor?* Generally, how is credit allocated within the economy? Are there mechanisms whereby informal sector entrepreneurs can qualify for credit within the banking system? Do special "windows" for the poor—generally set up by international development agencies—sustain themselves within the banking system, or are they simply concessions to international lending programs? Are there fiscal or tax incentives that feed back into local organizations—for example, earmarked taxes that recapitalize microentrepreneur credit or small-farmer loan funds?

3. *What is the structure of educational opportunity?* Within the total national expenditure on public education, what is the relative allocation of resources to primary education (which generally favors the organization of the poor), versus higher education (which generally favors the organization of the middle and upper class)? Is state educational decisionmaking highly centralized, or are there mechanisms for local inputs into curriculum design and choice of culturally appropriate educational materials? Can the needs of religious and ethnic minorities be fairly met? Are parent-teacher associations able to exert pressure? Are non-school job training opportunities and adult literacy programs widely available to the poor?

4. *What is the state attitude toward labor-intensive construction and how does the state make its decisions about infrastructure?* In general, does the state respond to labor or capital-intensive construction technologies; and if labor-intensive, what is the social basis for actually carrying out construction and public works programs? How do Food-for-Work programs operate? Do they strengthen or undercut existing community organization? Similarly, is there citizen participation in decisions about where infrastructure is placed? Do those affected by infrastructure decisions have organizational mechanisms to legally and effectively dispute them?

5. *What is the social character of social security programs?* Is there group coverage for informal sector workers? How do subsidies run within the larger social security system, i.e., are non-organized poor workers excluded while the state transfers subsidies to its own well-organized employees or to middle-class workers? Are campesinos covered? If so, on what organizational criteria? Is there community participation in group medical coverage? In social security health services?

6. *How is labor formally organized?* What kinds of labor organizations are legal and independent? Are they dominated by political parties, and if so, what are the trade-offs? Does minimum wage legislation, collective bargaining legislation, and the right to strike include the poorest and less organized groups—or do laws simply reinforce the privilege of organized labor elites? Are domestic workers—especially maids—extended protection by the state—for example, severance pay from their employers, retirement benefits, protection against sexual harassment?

7. *Does urban housing policy encourage self-help construction?* How does the government recognize urban squatters? What are the rights of organized renters? Do building codes militate against self-help construction? Can marginal urban squatters obtain group credit for building? Can they get technical assistance as organized groups? Can decisions on where to put highways, sewers, and telephone, electricity, water, and transportation lines be affected by the urban poor as well as the middle class?

8. *What agricultural technologies does the state endorse?* Does state policy have a commodity export orientation that is biased against small farmers? Are agricultural price supports in force; and if so, who benefits from them? How do agricultural extension services reach the small farmers? How is new agricultural technology diffused? How aggressive is the state in land redistribution? Whose interests are served by feeder roads, irrigation projects, and marketing boards?

CONCLUSION

The central point here is that state policy is crucially important in determining the character and capacities of grassroots growth—and ultimately, in providing the answer to the question that was posed at the outset: How large can small-scale become?

Those of us who, by instinct and experience, do not like governments or central authority may wish for a purer (that is, a stateless) development scenario. In our mind's eye, we can imagine tens of thousands of diverse, independent, autonomous nongovernmental organizations that challenge or replace the functions of the state. We see a vast, decentralized profusion of independent organizations—as if development were a rich spread of wildflowers rather than a cultivated field.

It may well be that wildflowers do grow by themselves. But grassroots organizations do not. The are cultivated, in large measure, by just policies and competent government agencies that do their job.

The implication is not that grassroots groups should necessarily view states with friendlier eyes than they have in the past, and certainly not that grassroots groups should allow themselves to be absorbed into the state's political apparatus. To the contrary, groups that think of themselves as nongovernmental generally have every reason to view states with suspicion and mistrust.

The poor are still poor, and the oppressed are still oppressed. Yet that is not to say that nothing has changed on the social and political landscape of Latin America. Today, the poor are connected to each other and to their governments in ways unprecedented in the past. And it is precisely that new and evolving relationship that gives hope that the notion of large-scale small-scale development is not really a contradiction in terms.

NOTES

1. A slightly modified version of this article appeared in *World Development*, 15, Autumn, 1987 (Pergamon Press).

2. For a discussion of the notion of "social energy," see Albert Hirschman's essay in Chapter 1 of this volume.

Selected Readings on Grassroots Development

Aliband, Terry. *Catalysts of Development: Voluntary Agencies in India* (West Hartford, CT: Kumarian Press, 1983).

Barclay, A. H., Jr., et al. *The Development Impact of Private Voluntary Organizations: Kenya and Niger* (Washington, DC: Development Alternatives, Inc., 1979).

Bolling, Landrum R., with Craig Smith. *Private Foreign Aid: U.S. Philanthropy for Relief and Development* (Boulder, CO: Westview Press, 1982).

Breslin, Patrick. *Development and Dignity* (Rosslyn, VA: Inter-American Foundation, 1988).

Brokensha, David, D. M. Warren, and Oswald Warner (Eds.) *Indigenous Knowledge Systems and Development* (Lanham, MD: University Press of America, 1980).

Castells, Manuel. *The City and the Grassroots: A Cross-Cultural Theory of Urban Social Movements* (Berkeley: University of California Press, 1983).

Cernea, Michael (Ed.) *Putting People First: Sociological Variables in Rural Development* (London and New York: Oxford University Press, 1985).

Chambers, Robert. *Rural Development: Putting the Last First* (New York: Longman, 1983).

———. "Normal Professionalism, New Paradigms and Development," *Discussion Paper 227* (Sussex: Institute of Development Studies, 1986).

Cohen, John, and Norman Uphoff. "Participation's Place in Rural Development: Seeking Clarity through Specificity," *World Development,* Vol. 8, No. 3: pp. 213-236 (March 1980).

Dichter, Thomas W. "The Neglected Middle-Scale: Implications of Size," *Findings '86* (Norwalk, CT: Technoserve, 1986).

Diskin, Martin, Steven E. Sanderson and Willicam C. Thiesenhusen. "Business in Development: A Workable Partnership," Inter-American Foundation Monograph and Working Paper Series, No. 2 (Rosslyn, VA: Inter-American Foundation, 1987).

Drabek, Anne (Ed.) "Development Alternatives: The Challenge for NGOs," *World Development,* Vol. 15, Fall Supplement (1987).

Esman, Milton J., and Norman T. Uphoff. *Local Organizations: Intermediaries in Rural Development* (Ithaca: Cornell University Press, 1984).

Esteva, Gustavo. "Development: Metaphor, Myth, Threat," *Development: Seeds of Change*, Vol. 3 (Rome: Society for International Development, 1985).

Fisher, Julie. "Development from Below: Neighborhood Improvement Associations in Latin American Squatter Settlements," *Studies in Comparative International Development*, Vol. 19, No. 1: pp. 61–85 (1984).

Freire, Paolo. *The Pedagogy of the Oppressed* (New York: The Seabury Press, 1986).

Fugelsand, Andreas, and Dale Chandler. *Participation as Process—What We Can Learn from the Grameen Bank, Bangladesh* (Oslo, Norway: North American Air Defense Command, 1986).

Galjart, Benno, and Dieke Buijs (Eds.) *Participation of the Poor in Development: Contributions to a Seminar* (Leiden, Netherlands: University of Leiden, Institute of Cultural and Social Studies, 1982).

Gorman, Robert F. (Ed.) *Private Voluntary Organizations as Agents of Development* (Boulder, CO: Westview Press, 1984).

Gran, Guy. *Development By People* (New York: Praeger, 1983).

―――. *An Annotated Guide to Global Development: Capacity Building for Effective Social Change* (Olney, MD: Resources for Development and Democracy, 1987).

Hakim, Peter. "The Inter-American Foundation: Lessons from Its Grassroots Development Experience" (Rosslyn, VA: Inter-American Foundation, 1982).

Healy, Kevin. *Caciques y Patrones, Experiencia de Desarrollo Rural en el Sur de Bolivia* (Cochabamba, Bolivia: Centro de Estudios de la Realidad Económica y Social, 1983).

Hellinger, Steve, Doug Hellinger, and Fred O'Regan. *Aid for Just Development: Report on the Future of Foreign Assistance* (Boulder, CO: Lynne Rienner Publishers, 1988).

Hirschman, Albert O. *Getting Ahead Collectively: Grassroots Experiences in Latin America* (New York: Pergamon Press, 1984).

Hollnsteiner, Mary Racelis. "Mobilizing the Rural Poor Through Community Organization," *Philippine Studies*, Vol. 27, No. 3: pp. 387-411 (1979).

Hyden, Goran. *No Shortcuts to Progress: African Development Management in Perspective* (Berkeley: University of California Press, 1983).

Inter-American Foundation. *They Know How* . . . (Rosslyn, VA: Inter-American Foundation, 1976).

Johnston, Bruce, and William Clark. *Redesigning Rural Development: A Strategic Perspective* (Baltimore, MD: Johns Hopkins University Press, 1982).

Korten, David C. (Ed.) *Community Management: Asian Experience and Perspectives* (West Hartford, CT: Kumarian Press, 1987).

―――. *Development as Empowerment: Search for a New Development Management* (Boulder, CO: Lynne Rienner Publishers, 1987).

Korten, David C., and Felipe B. Alfonso (Eds.) *Bureaucracy and the Poor: Closing the Gap* (West Hartford, CT: Kumarian Press, 1985).

Korten, David C., and Rudi Klauss. *People-Centered Development:*

Contributions Toward Theory and Planning Frameworks (West Hartford, CT: Kumarian Press, 1984).

Leonard David, and D. R. Marshall (Eds.) *Institutions for Rural Development for the Poor: Decentralization and Organizational Linkages* (Berkeley: Institute for International Studies, University of California, 1982).

Linden, Eugene. *The Alms Race: The Impact of American Voluntary Aid Abroad* (New York: Random House, 1976).

Lissner, Jorgen. *The Politics of Altruism: A Study of Political Behavior of Voluntary Development Agencies* (Geneva: Lutheran World Federation, 1977).

Maguire, Robert. *Bottom-up Development in Haiti* (Rosslyn, VA: Inter-American Foundation, 1981).

Marwell, Gerald, and Pamela Oliver. "Collective Action Theory and Social Movements Research," *Research in Social Movements, Conflict and Change*, Vol. 7, pp. 1–27 (1984).

Mashek, Robert W., and Stephen G. Vetter. *The Inter-American Foundation in the Dominican Republic: A Decade of Support for Local Development Organizations* (Rosslyn, VA: Inter-American Foundation, 1983).

Masoni, Vittorio. "Non-Governmental Organizations and Development," *Finance and Development*, Vol. 22, No. 3: pp. 38–41 (September 1985).

Meehan, Eugene J. *In Partnership with People: An Alternative Development Strategy* (Rosslyn, VA: Inter-American Foundation, 1978).

Milofsky, Carl. "Structure and Process in Self-Help Behavior," *Program on Non-Profit Organizations Working Paper No. 17* (New Haven: Institution for Social and Policy Studies, Yale University, 1980).

Montgomery, John. "The Populist Front in Rural Development: Or Shall We Eliminate the Bureaucrats and Get on with the Job," *Public Administration Review*, Vol. 39, pp. 59-64 (January/February 1979).

Nelson, Joan. *Access to Power: Politics and the Urban Poor in Developing Nations* (Princeton: Princeton University Press, 1979).

Oakley, Peter, and David Marsden. "Approaches to Participation in Rural Development" (Geneva: International Labour Organization, 1984).

Oliver, Pamela, Gerald Marwell, and Ruy Teixeira. "A Theory of Critical Mass: Interdependence, Group Heterogeneity, and the Production of Collective Action," *American Journal of Sociology*, Vol. 91, No. 3: pp. 522–56 (1985).

Olson, Mancur. *The Logic of Collective Action* (Cambridge, MA: Harvard University Press, 1965).

Otero, Maria. *The Solidarity Group Concept: Its Characteristics and Significance for Urban Informal Sector Activities* (New York: Private Agencies Collaborating Together, 1986).

Paddock, William and Elizabeth. *We Don't Know How: Audit of What They Call Success in Foreign Assistance* (Ames, Iowa: Iowa State University, 1973).

Padron, Mario C. "NGOs and Grassroots Development; Limits and Possibilities" (The Hague: Institute of Social Studies, 1982).

Piven, Frances, and Richard Cloward. *Poor People's Movements: Why They Succeed, How They Fail* (New York: Random House, 1977).

Rahman, Anisur (Ed.) *Grass-Roots Participation and Self- Reliance: Experiences In South and South East Asia* (New Delhi: Oxford & IBH Publishers, 1984).

Riddell, Roger. *Foreign Aid Reconsidered* (Baltimore, MD: Johns Hopkins University Press, 1987).

Salmen, Lawrence F. *Listen to the People: Participant-Observer Evaluation of Development Projects* (Oxford: Oxford University Press for the World Bank, 1987).

Smith, Brian. *The Politics of International Charities* (Princeton: Princeton University Press, forthcoming).

Sommer, John G. *Beyond Charity: U.S. Voluntary Aid for a Changing Third World* (Washington, DC: Overseas Development Council, 1977).

Tendler, Judith. "Turning Private Voluntary Organizations into Development Agencies: Questions for Evaluation," *Program Evaluation Discussion Paper No. 12* (Washington, DC: United States Agency for Internal Development, 1982).

————. "Fitting the Foundation Style: The Case of Rural Credit" (Rosslyn, VA: The Inter-American Foundation, 1981).

Tendler, Judith with Kevin Healy, and Carol Michaels O'Laughlin. "What to Think about Cooperatives: A Guide from Bolivia" (Rosslyn, VA: Inter-American Foundation, 1983).

Uphoff, Norman. *Local Institutional Development: An Analytical Sourcebook with Cases* (West Hartford, CT: Kumarian Press, 1986).

van der Heijden, Hendrik. "Development Impact and Effectiveness of Non-Governmental Organizations: The Record of Rural Development Cooperation" (Paris: Organization for Economic Cooperation and Development Development Center, 1985).

Ward, Peter (Ed.) *Self-Help Housing: A Critique* (London: Mansell Publishing, Ltd., 1982).

Wasserstrom, Robert. *Grassroots Development in Latin America and the Caribbean: Oral Histories of Social Change* (New York: Praeger, 1985).

White, Karen, Maria Otero, Margaret Lycette, and Mayra Buvinic. "Integrating Women into Development Programs: A Guide for Implementation for Latin America and the Caribbean" (Washington, DC: International Center for Research on Women, 1986).

Yudelman, Sally. *Hopeful Openings: A Study of Five Women's Development Organizations in Latin America and the Caribbean* (West Hartford, CT: Kumarian Press, 1987).

Contributors

SHELDON ANNIS is a fellow at the Overseas Development Council in Washington and a visiting lecturer at Princeton University's Woodrow Wilson School. Formerly, he was senior research officer at the Inter-American Foundation, where he edited the journal, *Grassroots Development*. His recent books include *God and Production in a Guatemalan Town* (University of Texas Press, 1987) and *Costa Rica's Dual Debt* (forthcoming). He holds masters and doctoral degrees from the University of Chicago.

WILLIAM BARBIERI wrote the epilogue to "Indian Colonization in Paraguay." Having lived and worked in Latin America for twelve years, he is now IAF senior representative for Central America; he was representative for Paraguay and Argentina. He holds masters degrees in history and in theology.

PATRICK BRESLIN is a research officer at the Inter-American Foundation. He has lectured and published extensively on Latin American literature and folk music. He holds a doctorate in political science from the University of California at Los Angeles and has published a novel, *Interventions* (Doubleday, 1980), and *Development and Dignity* (Inter-American Foundation, 1988).

MAC CHAPIN is an anthropologist who was formerly IAF representative for Panama.

STEPHEN COX is Ford Foundation representative for Mexico and Central America. Formerly he was IAF representative for Peru and Bolivia and was a staff member of Agua del Pueblo in Guatemala. He holds a masters degree in public policy from Harvard.

ARIEL DORFMAN is a Chilean novelist, journalist, and poet who has published seventeen books translated into twenty languages. He is a visiting professor at Duke University. His recent books are *Last Waltz in Santiago* (Viking, forthcoming), *Last Song of Manuel Sendero* (Viking, 1987), *Widows* (Vintage, 1983), and *The Empire's Old Clothes* (Pantheon, 1983). His work appears regularly in the *New York Times, The Village Voice,* the *Los Angeles Times,* the *Washington Post, The Nation, Le Monde,* and *El País.*

CORNELIA BUTLER FLORA is a professor in the Department of Sociology, Anthropology, and Social Work at Kansas State University. She has worked and published extensively in the areas of farming systems research, women in development, and popular culture. She is the author of numerous books and articles, including *Pentecostalism in Colombia: Baptism by Fire and Spirit* (Associated University Presses, 1976).

JAN L. FLORA is a professor in the Department of Sociology, Anthropology, and Social Work at Kansas State University. He has done research on agrarian structure in Cuba, Colombia, China, and Nicaragua. He is the author of *Change in Rural America* (Mosby, 1978) and *Sociology of "Developing Societies" in Central America* (MacMillan, forthcoming).

PETER HAKIM is staff director of the Inter-American Dialogue. He was previously the vice president for research and evaluation at the Inter-American Foundation and served as a program officer in Latin America for the Ford Foundation. He writes frequently on U.S.-Latin American relations and is the principal author of *Development, Reform, and Malnutrition in Chile* (MIT Press, 1978). He holds masters degrees from Princeton and Cornell Universities.

KEVIN HEALY has been traveling to Taquile for nearly twenty years—first as a Peace Corps volunteer and later as an IAF representative. He has been the Foundation representative to Bolivia since 1978. He holds a doctorate in development sociology from Cornell University and is the author of *Caciques y patrones, una experiencia de desarrollo rural en Bolivia* (Centro de Estudios de la Realidad

Económica y Social, 1983) and articles on the impact of cocaine on development in Bolivia.

ALBERT O. HIRSCHMAN is professor emeritus of social science at the Institute for Advanced Study in Princeton and former professor at Harvard, Yale, and Columbia. Among his many books are: *The Strategy of Economic Development* (Yale University Press, 1958); *National Power and the Structure of Foreign Trade* (University of California Press, 1945); *Development Projects Observed* (Brookings Inst., 1967); *Exit, Voice, and Loyalty* (Harvard University Press, 1970); *The Passions and the Interests* (Princeton University Press, 1977); and *Essays in Trespassing* (Cambridge University Press, 1981). His chapter in this book was taken from *Getting Ahead Collectively: Grassroots Experiences in Latin America* (Pergamon Press, 1984), which is based on his observations in the field of nearly fifty projects assisted by the Inter-American Foundation.

PAULA R. PALMER has been encouraging and teaching oral history in Talamanca, Costa Rica, for thirteen years. She is the author of two books on Costa Rica's rural Afro-Caribbean population: *What Happen: A Folk-History of Costa Rica's Talamanca Coast* (San José, Ecodesarrollos, 1977) and *Wa'apin man: La Historia de la costa talamanqueña de Costa Rica, según sus protagonistas* (San José: Ministerio de Cultura, Juventud y Deportes, Instituto del Libro, 1986), and co-author, with Bribri Indians Gloria Mayorga and Juanita Sánchez, of *Cuidando los Regalos de Dios: Testimonios de la Reserva Indígena de Cocles/Kéköldi* (University of Costa Rica, 1988). She is currently participating in the African Diaspora Research Project at Michigan State University.

BRUNO PODESTA is executive director of the Grupo de Estudio para el Desarrollo (GREDES) and professor at the Universidad del Pacífico in Lima, Peru. He is now completing a book entitled *Monitoring Grassroot Development Projects.*

MARIA REHNFELDT was director of Paraguay's Asociación de Parcialidades Indígenas from 1977 to 1978. Currently, she is a graduate student in anthropology at the University of Kansas and is doing fieldwork with the Mbya Indians in Paraguay.

MARTIN J. SCURRAH, an Australian citizen residing in Peru, was until recently professor of organizational behavior in Lima's Escuela de Administración de Negocios para Graduados (ESAN), a graduate school of business administration. He is currently associate director of the

Grupo de Estudios para el Desarrollo (GREDES) and author or co-author of a number of books and articles, including *Agriculture, Bureaucracy and Military Government in Peru* (Cornell University Press, 1980); *Personalidad, Poder y Participación*; *Experiencias Autogestionarias en América Latina* and *Comunidad y Empresas en Peru.*

ROBERT SMITH is a professor of anthropology and curator of ethnology at the University of Kansas.

JUDITH TENDLER is a professor of urban planning at the Massachusetts Institute of Technology. Formerly, she taught at the University of California at Berkeley. She has been a consultant to the Ford Foundation, the World Bank, the Inter-American Development Bank, the United States Agency for International Development, and the IAF. Her books include *Inside Foreign Aid* (Johns Hopkins University Press, 1977) and *Electric Power in Brazil: Entrepreneurship in the Public Sector* (Harvard University Press, 1968).

STEPHEN VETTER is vice president of programs at the Inter-American Foundation. Previously, he served as the IAF representative to the Dominican Republic, Jamaica, Mexico, and Brazil. He holds a masters degree in foreign affairs from Ohio University. With Robert Mashek, he is co-author of *The Inter-American Foundation in the Dominican Republic: A Decade of Support for Local Development Organizations, 1971-1981* (Inter-American Foundation, 1983).

RON WEBER edited many chapters in this book and contributed to writing "The Experience of Worker Self-Management in Peru and Chile." He has published more than sixty poems in literary journals and small press anthologies. He holds a bachelors degree in political science from the University of Florida.

ELAYNE ZORN is a Ph.D. candidate in anthropology at Cornell University and currently an Inter-American Foundation fellow. She is the author of various publications on Andean weaving and ethnography. She also is a weaver and holds a degree from the California College of Arts and Crafts.